How We Act

How We Act

Causes, Reasons,
and Intentions

BERENT ENÇ

CLARENDON PRESS · OXFORD

OXFORD
UNIVERSITY PRESS

Great Clarendon Street, Oxford OX2 6DP

Oxford University Press is a department of the University of Oxford.
It furthers the University's objective of excellence in research, scholarship,
and education by publishing worldwide in

Oxford New York

Auckland Bangkok Buenos Aires Cape Town Chennai
Dar es Salaam Delhi Hong Kong Istanbul Karachi Kolkata
Kuala Lumpur Madrid Melbourne Mexico City Mumbai Nairobi
São Paulo Shanghai Taipei Tokyo Toronto

Oxford is a registered trade mark of Oxford University Press
in the UK and in certain other countries

Published in the United States
by Oxford University Press Inc., New York

© Berent Enç 2003

The moral rights of the author have been asserted

Database right Oxford University Press (maker)

First published 2003

British Library Cataloguing in Publication Data

Data available

Library of Congress Cataloging in Publication Data

Data available

ISBN 0–19–925602–0

10 9 8 7 6 5 4 3 2 1

Typeset by Kolam Information Services Pvt. Ltd., Pondicherry, India
Printed in Great Britain
on acid-free paper by
T. J. International Ltd.,
Padstow, Cornwall

To the memory of my father

ACKNOWLEDGEMENTS

The idea for this book was inspired by the enthusiasm of my students in a seminar I taught at the University of Wisconsin–Madison in 1998. Since then I have benefited from the critical input I received from my students in other courses on related topics, and from colleagues who have read different chapters at various stages of incompletion and have helped me with their generous feedback.

The list of the students who have corrected my mistakes and given me new ideas is too long to produce here. But I would like to express my special appreciation to the help given to me by Joey Baltimore, Martin Barrett, Tom Bontly, Sara Chant, Zachary Ernst, Noel Hendrickson, Greg Mougin, Sara Gavrel Ortiz, and Richard Teng.

Among colleagues, I would especially like to express my gratitude to Fred Dretske, who read an earlier version of all of the chapters, and to two anonymous referees of OUP, whose critical input and helpful suggestions helped improve the penultimate draft. In addition, I am deeply indebted to the supererogatory efforts of many of my colleagues who read several of the chapters and provided invaluable critical appraisal. In this connection, I especially thank Ellery Eells, Brie Gertler, Daniel Hausman, Terry Penner, Larry Shapiro, Alan Sidelle, Elliott Sober, and Dennis Stampe.

In addition, papers that form the nucleus of some of the chapters were read at colloquia, and I benefited from the comments I received from the members of the audience at University of Calgary, University of Alberta, King's College London, University of Warwick, and Duke. Special thanks are due to Güven Güzeldere, Mohan Matthen, David Papineau, Michael Luntley, and David Sanford.

Finally, I would like to thank my long-time friend, James A. Jung, for suggesting the title of this book to me, and urging me to pay more attention to John Dewey, and to his views on habit. (I fear his advocacy for Dewey has gone unheeded.)

Throughout the four years from its conception to its conclusion of this project my wife Jennifer Vaughan Jones has been so unconditionally encouraging and supportive that I doubt, without her, I would have started it; and I am sure, without her, I would not have completed it.

Parts of Chapter 4 were taken from my 'Causal Theories and Unusual Causal Pathways', published in 1989 in *Philosophical Studies*, 55: 231–61. This has been made possible with kind permission from Kluwer Academic Publishers.

Parts of Chapter 2 were taken from my 'Units of Behavior' published in 1995 in *Philosophy of Science*, 62: 523–42. The copyright is © 1995 by the Philosophy of Science Association. Permission to use this material has been granted by the University of Chicago Press.

The Publisher very much regrets Berent Enç's untimely death after submission of his typescript, and would like to thank Fred Dretske for his help in overseeing the book through to publication.

CONTENTS

LIST OF FIGURES

Introduction

What happens when we act? How do we form an intention to do something? How does the fact that we intended to do something explain some of the things we do? What needs to be true about us for us to have done something voluntarily?

These are questions we normally do not ask when we speak of others' actions, ascribe intentions to them, or wonder if they are doing this or that voluntarily. These concepts come easily to us, and we typically assume that if we were to reflect briefly on such questions, we probably could come up with perfectly reasonable answers. I tend to think that this kind of assumption has been the seed for continued interest in the philosophy of action. The rich literature and the vast spectrum of divergent views are a testament to the difficulty of coming up with 'perfectly reasonable answers'.

You wake up in the middle of the night. You wonder whether you should stay in bed and try to fall asleep or go to the basement and read. You realize that tossing and turning will probably wake up your companion sound asleep next to you; you decide to get up, leave the cosy warmth of the bed and go down, in the full knowledge that your reading for an hour or so will probably make you less alert the next day.

Now your waking up was not an action, but your going down to the basement was. Obvious! What exactly is the difference? According to one school of thought, your going down to the basement was an action because there was a prior mental action: you *made a decision, performed an act of will*. It was thanks to those mental acts that your getting out of bed, grabbing your book, and going downstairs were all voluntary acts, whereas no comparable act of will of yours was involved in your waking up. Similarly, if you can 'will yourself to sleep', then you will have performed an act, whereas if you just fall asleep, then you will not have *acted*.

In this book I reject this school of thought. Chapter 1 is devoted to a series of considerations developed through analogies drawn from theories of knowledge and of perception. These considerations are designed to show that it is a mistake to think of these occurrences in our minds as *original* actions—actions that we take in our capacity as full agents and that are irreducible to event causation. What I offer, instead, in subsequent chapters, is a sustained treatment of action that confines itself just to events of the natural order of things, and to the causal relations among them. My thesis is that, by assuming nothing more than a world of material things, we can understand the nature of decisions, of intentions, of voluntary action, and the difference between actions and things that we do when we are merely passive recipients of courses of events. (In saying this, I do not mean to imply that I will here offer a solution to the so-called mind–body problem. In what follows, I just help myself to the assumption that mental attributes like beliefs, desires, hopes, value judgements, and so forth, are manifestations of the physical world, and that what is generally referred to as naturalism is the correct view about such mental events and states.)

Chapters 2 and 3 present a rigorous development of a causal theory of action, which has as its central thesis the proposition that an act consists of a behavioural output that is caused by the reasons the agent has for producing that behaviour—reasons that consist of the beliefs and desires of the agent. More specifically, reasons feed into a computational process of deliberation, the causal consequence of which is the formation of an intention. The intention causes the behavioural output. On this thesis, actions are defined as changes in the world that are caused by mental events.

This much is not very original. It follows a tradition that became what used to be called 'the standard view' thanks to a seminal essay by Donald Davidson ('Actions, Reasons, and Causes' (1963: reprinted in Davidson 1980)). What I hope is original in these two chapters is a careful formulation of a foundationalist conception of action, in which actions are divided into two subcategories: basic acts and non-basic acts. Drawing on studies of animal behaviour, basic actions are defined as complex units of behaviour, packaged wholes, caused by the internal mental states of the agent. So the basic act of one's opening a beer bottle is shown to consist of a series of co-ordinated arm–wrist–hand motions (a complex event) caused by one's intention to open the bottle (the onset of which is also assumed to be an event).

The category of non-basic acts is then conceived as one's bringing about events the cause of which can be traced back to the complex event that constitutes one's basic act. The details of this view, as well as a defence of a principle of individuation for actions, are developed in Chapter 3.

It is easy to declare that action can be defined in the framework of a causal theory and to point out that such a definition of action and psychological naturalism make a happy union. What is much harder is to show that the definition can be defended against some powerful objections, which have become especially forceful in the last decade or so.

One such objection derives from a somewhat technical problem that plagues all causal theories. (It is one of the many virtues of John Bishop's defence of a causal theory of action in his *Natural Agency* (1989) that it confronts this problem squarely.) When an action is defined as a behavioural output that is caused by an intention, it is possible to show that the definition does not give a sufficient condition for action: intentions can cause behavioural outputs through unusual (deviant) pathways; and when they do, these behaviours do not constitute rationalizable actions. A favourite example is the case of a person who intends to do a vile deed (such as swerve his car to kill a pedestrian). The realization of what he intends to do fills him with revulsion, which, in turn, causes an involuntary jerk, and the jerk results in the intended act. Now if a causal theorist cannot show what, in general, distinguishes between 'deviant' and 'normal' causal pathways, and above all, cannot manage to do this in purely causal terms, then the causal theory becomes vulnerable to the following objection. There are clear intuitions that guide us in judging whether a behavioural output is an action or not. Since these intuitions cannot be explained in causal terms, they must be based on some non-causal conception of action. Hence even if a causal account of action were true, it clearly needs to be supplemented by something else. That proves that a purely causal definition of action is bound to be unsuccessful. This objection is addressed in Chapter 4. There I review the vast literature that houses the attempts and failures of the history of 'deviance', and I offer what I hope is a general and original solution to the problem.

A second, and much more influential, objection consists in pointing out that conceiving of action as the result of a chain of events that are causally connected removes the *agent* from the picture altogether. Being the conduit for a causal chain is a *passive* affair; being an agent is being *active*. The former cannot possibly exhaust what is involved in the latter.

Chapter 5 is devoted to a defence against this objection. The defence consists in developing a model of deliberation, which, it is argued, distinguishes rational action from behaviour that is reflexive, impulsive, or compulsive. The thesis I defend in the rest of the book is that all commonplace notions that we associate with agency, like forming intentions, acting intentionally, being free to choose from among options, acting voluntarily, and so forth, can be derived from the causal (computational) model of deliberation.

Chapter 6 is an essay on intentions and intentional action. The focus is on the relation between the rational explanations of action that cite the agent's intentions and the psychological state of intending.

Finally, in Chapter 7, I take up notions of acting voluntarily, and of being free, and show that these notions are not beyond the reach of the causal theory of action.

If the objectives I pursue are adequately met, the causal theory developed in this book will, I hope, complement nicely the programme of naturalism in the philosophy of mind.

1

Volitions

INTRODUCTION

The natural place to begin is to ask a general question with which most treatises on action begin: 'what distinguishes *actions*, things agents do voluntarily (or intentionally), from their non-voluntary behaviour?'[1] It seems that we have no difficulty in identifying specific things we do as belonging to one or the other group. Barring a few esoteric cases, this bipartate classification of behaviour appears to be done without much dissent or controversy.[2] For example, raising one's arm, winking conspiratorially, whisking egg whites, hitting the bull's eye in a game of darts are normally accepted as *actions* that agents perform. The other side of the divide, that of non-voluntary behaviour, covers a diverse group of things one may be said to have done, such as thrashing about in one's sleep, wincing, sneezing, blinking.[3] (For the present purposes I will ignore non-voluntary or unintentional actions that are related to voluntary actions, like inadvertently knocking a cup in the process of reaching over for a magazine—these will be discussed at length in a later chapter.)

Given the ease with which this division is made by all of us in practice, it strikes people who are not familiar with philosophical action theory as odd that there could be so much written, so many opposing

---

[1] I plan to attend to the distinction between 'voluntary' and 'intentional' in later chapters. For our present purposes I will pretend that they are variants of the same contrast to 'mere behaviour'.

[2] Brand (1984) proposes a tripartite division: happening, mere doing, acting. In my opinion, a twofold distinction is sufficient to discuss the problems that are of interest to action theory. So I will ignore those happenings constituted by limb movements that have no internal causes, as in my arm's rising because someone pulls my arm up.

[3] Some will want to include in this second category not just things (like sneezing) one may properly be said to have done, but also things that occur in one's body (such as nail growth, peristalsis, stomach growl). The defence for this more liberal approach depends on observing that there is no principled difference between a sneeze and a stomach growl, and on the thesis that behaviour is nothing other than an output of an organism in response to some inner causes. On this thesis, tree leaves turning colour in the autumn is regarded as tree behaviour. Nothing that I plan to say in this chapter requires taking a position on this issue.

views argued for, in the attempt to answer the general question. True to philosophical form, I propose to add to this literature, take sides in controversies, and defend one specific way of answering the question.

Before I begin defending the positive view, which will be developed in the subsequent chapters, I propose to devote this chapter to a bird's-eye view of the general terrain, and eliminate a large portion of the terrain from consideration. From this point of view, we can see that the predominant way of distinguishing voluntary action from non-voluntary ('mere') behaviour consists in identifying some special class of causes located within the agent, and stipulating that voluntary action is marked by the effective role played by such causes. The problem is thus reduced to specifying what will count as the proper class of internal causes. This way of approaching the problem forces an immediate choice between two options on the theorist. One option is to designate some mental *action* as the cause.[4] The second option, in a more reductionistic spirit, is to analyse actions into behaviour caused by some special class of *mental events* that are not themselves actions. In this chapter I propose to examine the first option. In other words, I will evaluate the thesis that a behaviour is voluntary just in case it is caused by (or is constituted by) a mental act that does not yield itself to an analysis in terms of event causation. The favourite mental act in this context is an act of the will, or a volition—acts that are thought to be essential to agency in that agents always initiate their actions 'through' them. Other candidates for such irreducible actions, like the act of deciding or of forming an intention, may be considered, but I will concentrate on volitions.[5] The conclusion I intend to argue for is that we have good reasons to reject this thesis because we have good reasons to think that such acts of volition do not exist.

I should emphasize the special nature of the thesis I propose to reject so that the reader does not assume that I want to deny a faculty that may properly be called 'the will', or that I want to denounce all mental acts.

---

[4] As it will be clear as we proceed, there will be choices to be made within this option concerning the relation between the designated mental act and overt bodily action.

[5] As Ryle observes, the issues that surround the proposal that the privileged mental act be taken to be a volition also arise when any one of these other mental acts is substituted for volitions. I will not extend the discussion of this chapter to include them: '[The same objections apply] to resolving or making up our minds to do something, and…nerving or bracing ourselves to do something' (Ryle 1949: 67).

The thesis or perhaps the cluster of theses I shall be arguing against in this chapter share the following features: (i) an essential aspect of agency is that agents have the capacity to perform mental acts (acts of volition) that are not reducible to causal relations between events; (ii) overt voluntary actions are caused by or constituted by such acts of volition; and (iii) these acts of volition stand apart from the agent's other acts in that they are what render the other acts voluntary. Other conceptions of the will and of mental acts will be discussed and endorsed in later chapters.

REGRESS ARGUMENTS

Ryle's Regress

Infinite regress arguments seem to find an especially hospitable environment in action theory. I shall begin with Ryle's, which is possibly the best-known of them.

Ryle (1949) notes that, when one postulates volition to be the element that makes actions voluntary, part of the motivation is to bring such actions into a framework where evaluations of these actions, as resolute, meritorious, or wicked, and the like, is made possible. Ryle also observes that mental actions themselves sometimes permit such evaluations: 'A thinker may ratiocinate resolutely, or imagine wickedly; he may try to compose a limerick, and he may meritoriously concentrate on his algebra. Some mental processes then can, according to the theory, issue from volitions. So what of volitions themselves? Are they voluntary or involuntary acts of mind? Clearly either answer leads to absurdities' (p. 65). If an act of volition is not voluntary, how could the bodily act that issued from it be voluntary? If, on the other hand, the act of volition *is* voluntary, then it must issue from a prior act of volition, *ad infinitum*.[6] So the only recourse seems to be that of stipulating that the voluntary/involuntary dichotomy simply does not

---

[6] This regress argument has venerable antecedents. Hobbes was using basically a form of this regress when he argued against free will. His reasoning was simply that, since to act freely one must have the capacity to act as one wills, in order to have free will (i.e. to will freely), one must have a capacity to will as one wills, which he dismissed as 'an absurd speech' (Hobbes 1840: iv. 240). Pink, who has a very detailed discussion of Hobbes's regress argument (Pink 1996: 26–45, 187–227), maintains that this type of reasoning, which leads to the rejection of the power to have control over what one wills, has been endorsed by much of Anglo-Saxon theory, from Hume through Ramsey and Ryle.

apply to these acts of volition, and that of taking it to be a self-evident axiom that these acts of volition are special kinds of acts over which the agent has ultimate and full control.[7]

In other words, arguments like Ryle's regress have a key result: they force the proponents of volitions into protecting these acts from the embarrassment threatened by certain types of questions—questions that it is legitimate to ask about ordinary acts. The volitionists want to block these questions by declaring that volitions are privileged acts that are *essentially* voluntary; they are the simple irreducible brute facts about agency. I, on the other hand, am of the opinion that it is a mistake to allow such *sui generis* acts of agency into our ontology. This chapter is devoted to a sustained argument for this opinion.

Danto's Regress

We can arrive at Ryle's conclusion through a more circuitous route that involves two infinite regress arguments. To describe the first, which I will call Danto's regress, let me suppose something for which I will argue in Chapter 2. Let me suppose that some actions consist in causing something to happen. For example, Pat's killing his uncle consists in Pat's doing something that causes the death of the uncle, or my beating egg whites consists in my doing something that causes the egg whites to reach a certain state. The effect here, the death of the uncle, is an *event* and the cause, and the agent's bringing about this event, is the *action*. The sentence that attributes an act to the agent, 'He killed his uncle', entails that an event took place—that is, it entails, 'The uncle died'. But the sentence 'The uncle died' does not entail 'Someone killed the uncle'. I will adopt here a terminological convention common to action literature, and refer to the event the description of which is entailed by the description of the action, but not conversely, as the *result* of the action. Since the word 'result' has a much wider use, I will flag this highly technical meaning of this word by spelling it as *result*. More specifically, if ascribing a particular action type A to an agent S semantically entails that some mere event type, R, took place, or some state of affairs, R, obtained, whereas the

---

[7] Ryle himself considers this move and argues that having to posit 'such occult thrusts of action' is the result of misunderstanding the question, 'what makes a bodily movement voluntary?' as a question about the causal antecedents of the movement. I, on the other hand, belong to a large group of philosophers who are committed to the thesis that the question is indeed a question about the causal antecedents of the movement.

statement that R obtained does not entail that some action was performed, then R will be said to be the *result* of A.[8] So the *result* of my beating the egg whites to the stiff-peak stage is the whipped state of the egg whites. The *result* of my moving my wrist in that specific way is that specific motion of my wrist.

Strictly speaking, the definition just offered falls short of capturing the intended notion of a *result*. For 'Sally danced a *pas de deux* at t' entails, but is not entailed by 'Sally was alive at t'. But Sally's being alive at t is not what is intended to count as the *result* of Sally's dancing at t—the *pas de deux* (or Sally's portion of it).[9] So the definition needs to capture the relation that can be syntactically described in some cases. The cases in question are those when the action description employs a transitive verb that has an intransitive counterpart, as in 'raise' and 'rise' for example, my raising the box to the second floor (using a pulley) has as its *result* the box's rising to the second floor. This relation can also be captured by using a transitive verb and its passive voice, for example, my *shovelling* the snow has as its *result* snow's *being shovelled*. But the syntactic criterion is not generalizable, for example, my bargaining for the rug has as its *result* the event in which the bargaining for the rug took place. Although the notion of *result* that is intended may be intuitively transparent, an official definition is in order because the notion will be used extensively throughout the book.

*Definition of *Result**

The event R is the *result* of an action A of agent S if and only if:

(1) 'S did A' entails but is not entailed by 'R occurred', and
(2) 'R occurred' carries all the information that is contained in 'S did A' *except* for the fact that some action of S's was involved in the production of the event R.[10]

To return to the supposition that actions consist in causing something to happen, we can state it more generally as follows: sometimes S's doing A consists in doing something, A', which causes the *result*, R, of A. Accordingly, the token act of my moving my wrist in that way

---

[8] This characterization of a 'result' follows McCann's (1974: 452) notion of a *result*: 'Results, then, are events which are necessary for those actions whose results they are. But...they are never sufficient for those actions.' McCann credits von Wright (1963) and Stoutland (1968) for introducing and using this terminology. Bishop uses the expression, 'an event *intrinsic* to an action'. I prefer Bishop's expression to the clumsy *result*, but I shall stick to the latter, for it is the more widely used term.

[9] I am indebted to David Sanford for pointing out this to me.

[10] The second clause is inspired by a suggestion from Fred Dretske.

(A') when I beat the egg whites (A), gets cashed out as my doing something which causes the event, R, of the motion of my wrist.[11]

Given this causal analysis of action in terms of the notion of a *result*, we can recast an argument of Danto's which he uses in support of the need for positing *basic acts*.

If, in each case in which I do something, I must do something else through which the first thing is done, then nothing could be done at all. (Danto 1973: 28)

It may be argued upon penalty of infinite regression that if, in order to perform an action, we must always perform some other action as *part of* performing it, then we could perform no action whatever. [The context makes clear that for Danto, S's action A is *part of* S's action A' if the result of A' is caused by A.] So if we perform any actions at all, we must perform some which do not have further actions amongst their component parts. These I designate as *basic actions*. (Danto 1970: 109)

Danto's point is simply that, every time we act, there must be some action of ours (that is, the basic action) the *result* of which is not caused by some action of ours; otherwise actions could never begin. There are several problems with this vision of basic acts, some of which will be discussed in Chapter 2. There I will be defending a different notion of basic action, which, I tend to think, gets closer to what Danto may have intended. But the one problem that is relevant to our purposes here is that, on Danto's view, it is very hard to maintain, as Danto wants to, that one's moving one's bodily limbs are the paradigm basic acts.

McCann's Regress

Consider the example of my beating the egg whites. There Danto will have it that my wrist motion is the basic act. That means that the following propositions are true:

(1) There is nothing, in addition to my wrist motion, I need to *do*, through which I move my wrist.

(2) In order to move my wrist in that way, there is nothing I must *do* which will cause that motion of my wrist.

---

[11] It is important to keep in mind here that the notion of a *result* is derived from a semantic relation between an act description and an event description. Even if we assume that my opening the door is one and the same act token as my letting the cat in, the door's opening is the *result* of my opening the door, but not the *result* of my letting the cat in.

However, on one reading of these two propositions, they are clearly false. On that reading, my flexing and relaxing certain muscles in my arm is something that I do that causes the wrist motion—it is through making those muscle movements that I move my wrist. Similarly for my flexing and relaxing those muscles: I must send signals through my efferent nerves to those muscles in order to move them. Clearly, this is not the reading intended by Danto. My sending nerve signals or my flexing and relaxing certain muscles are not (typically) *actions* of mine. (The expression 'in order to' in proposition (2) is obviously designed to disqualify such physiological events from being candidates for actions.) As Danto might say, they are not *bona fide* actions of mine: the *first thing* that I intentionally do is to move my wrist in that way. But this is itself problematic, if as Danto implies, basic actions are to be used as the base clause in a recursive definition of action, such as the following.

> *Foundationalist Definition of Action (FDA)*
> S's behaviour B is an *action* if and only if:
>   (1) B is a basic act of S's *or*
>   (2) The *result* of B is caused by an action of S's.[12]

Suppose that we want to avoid stipulating *by fiat* a class of basic acts. In that case, how do we show that my flexing and relaxing my muscles is *not* an action? Since we cannot *stipulate* that it is not a basic action, the first clause will not help us. What we need is to appeal to the second clause and try to show that the behaviour that causes the relevant events occurring in my muscles (for example, the behaviour that consists in my sending the nerve signals to those muscles) is itself *not* an action. But that, in turn, would require showing that my bringing about the event in my motor cortex that causes these signals to be sent is *not* an action, and so on. In other words, if we cannot give reasons for the stipulation that appoints bodily movements to the status of basic acts, we will be prey to a new infinite regress argument. Let us call this McCann's regress. The search will inevitably lead us to a mental action, for example, an act of volition. What, then, does an agent's performing an action, like an act of volition, consist in? Again, we have to realize that the threat of infinite regress can be thwarted only if we stipulate, as we did with Ryle's regress, that such mental acts

---

[12] As I shall discuss in Ch. 2, causal relation is only one of the many 'generative' relations that need to be included in a more careful formulation of this definition.

are of a special kind. But now we can give a reason for the stipulation: these acts of volition are special because they do not have neutral non-actional events or states that can be designated as their *results*.

The reasoning involved in this stipulation can be spelt out in terms of the following set of questions and answers. In virtue of what fact does 'my opening the door at t_0' correctly describe a specific action of mine? It describes an action of mine because the event of the door's opening is brought about by an *action* of mine, namely, my moving my arm, instead of, say, by the wind. But in virtue of what fact does 'my moving my hand at t_{-1}' correctly describe what happens as an action of mine, as opposed to, say, its *misdescribing* the motion of my arm, which was actually the effect of some surgical stimulation of my motor cortex? The motion of my arm is the *result* of an *action* of mine because it was caused by my action of willing. In virtue of what fact does 'my willing at t_{-2} my arm to move' correctly describe an action of mine? Here the questioning stops because the event of a *willing* taking place in my mind, it is presumed, cannot occur without my performing the act of willing. The sentence that describes the event in which a willing takes place *entails* the sentence that attributes to the agent an act of willing. In this sense, we can say that the act of willing has no *result*.

VOLITIONS AS BASIC ACTS

McCann

This is indeed the line of thinking pursued by McCann. McCann introduces what he calls 'the action–result problem' as 'the problem of providing an account of how it is, when events and processes qualify as results of human actions, that they do so qualify' (1974: 453). McCann initiates his infinite regress by pointing out, 'The result of A qualifies as a result because it is brought about by performing the more basic action B' (456). The chain of some event's being caused by a more basic action can stop only if we can find an action that has no *result* so that we do not have to posit the existence of a prior act as the cause of that *result*. McCann observes that we cannot stop at Danto's basic acts, for these acts, like moving one's arm, have *results* which on some other occasion may or may not be associated with the *act* of moving one's arm. If basic acts are to provide the base clause in some foundationalist definition of *action*, such basic acts would have to be acts that have *no *results**. On this criterion, Danto's basic acts fail to be basic; they fail to solve McCann's 'action–result problem'. McCann goes on to point out quite rightly that 'the situation is not essentially different if…we admit still more basic actions of physical exertion, these being understood to serve as causal means to acts like arm raising. For here, too, we are dealing with actions that have results —namely, the tensing of muscles—and here, too, the gap between action and result needs to be bridged' (456–7).

It is important to notice that the search for an action that has no *result* is nothing other than a search for a *basic* action. It would be a mistake to ignore this and to cast one's net wide enough with the hope of catching any act that lacks a *result* if the aim is to solve McCann's action–result problem. Moya (1990) falls victim to this mistake when he offers his 'meaningful acts', such as voting for a motion, making an offer, or greeting someone, the descriptions of which do not imply *results*, as a solution to 'the result problem'.[13] For these are actions which require causally more basic acts like raising one's arm, or tilting one's hat, which in turn have *results*. A non-foundationalist conception of *resultless* acts, like Moya's, will not stop McCann's regress.

This reasoning leads McCann to declare that the most basic action, the act that stops the infinite regress, is to be found in the mental act of volition. He sees volitions as being essential to actions, as 'being the key element in the process necessary for the results of those actions to count at all as changes brought about by the agent' (467). The fact that volitions lack *results* gives them a privileged status. Since they involve an agent, they can be shown to be essentially under the agent's control. If we wonder whether this last proviso opens the gates to Ryle's regress, we need to highlight the fact that volitions are a *special kind* of action: 'To suppose that if volition provides the element of control in actions like raising one's arm, volitions can exhibit control only through something like a further volition, is rather like supposing that if we explain the wetness of a wet street by saying there is water on

---

[13] Moya argues that these actions are necessarily intentional; their performance requires that the agent has mastered certain concepts; they can be evaluated as right and wrong, or as having been performed correctly or incorrectly; they commit the agents to further actions or to not doing certain things. But it is not at all clear how these features (apart from the fact that they are necessarily intentional) are linked to the defining feature of these meaningful acts, namely, their lacking *results*.

it, we must explain the wetness of water by postulating further water' (McCann 1974: 472). The analogy is apt in more ways than McCann may have intended. Even if we grant that in explaining something by pointing to a second thing we need not explain why this second thing has the features in virtue of which it provides an explanation for the first, it may be legitimate independently to ask why the second has those features. In this spirit, even though mentioning water does fully explain the wetness of the street, it seems fully proper to ask what makes water a 'wetting agent'. Indeed if clause (1) of the Foundationalist Definition of Action is to be satisfied only by volitions, it would behove the theorist to say in virtue of what volitions are actions— actions that can cause the *results* of other actions.[14]

Ginet

Ginet (1990), using a different line of reasoning, arrives at a view about volitions quite similar to McCann's. Recognizing the difficulties that face a theory of agent causation, the theory that postulates a causal relation between an agent and an act, like the act of willing, Ginet proposes to understand volitions as *simple* mental actions—simple in the sense of not having an internal causal structure.

It [the volitional act] does not contain within itself the structure of one mental event causing another...The part of the experience of voluntary exertion that I call volition does *not* include the perceptual part, the seeming to feel the exertion. It is simply the willing or trying to make the exertion. (15)

Volition is the initial part or stage of voluntary exertion (and thereby of any action that involves voluntary exertion, such as opening a door or waving goodbye or saying 'hello'). It is the means by which I cause my body's exertion when I voluntarily exert it. So when I succeed, it is by this trying, by this volition, that I cause it. (30–1)

The occurrence of this volition makes itself known to the agent, according to Ginet, by an intrinsic 'actish phenomenal quality' that accompanies it (13). (Ginet asks us to recognize this quality by asking us to pronounce the French word 'peu' silently in our minds. What we experience is different from the unbidden occurrence of the word in our mind. And the difference consists in the actish phenomenal quality

---

[14] It is to McCann's credit that he recognizes that his theory of volitions does not enable us to analyse action in general (1974: 471).

that occupies the first mental occurrence.) So Ginet's foundationalist theory of action has his simple acts of volition as its basic acts. Like McCann's basic acts, these acts are not causally related to any antecedent acts, and they are, by their nature, voluntary. The differences between McCann and Ginet arise from the relation they conceive as holding on the one hand between the agent and the basic acts, and on the other, between these basic acts and the agent's overt (bodily) acts, and as such do not matter for the present purposes.[15]

Pink

Unlike Ginet and McCann, Pink (1996) argues for the necessity of a second order action of the mind. The act introduced for this purpose is *deciding*. For Pink, deciding to do A is a kind of psychological action with a 'content which specifies a further action, doing A, which the decision serves to cause and explain' (17). The fact that desires are passive and decisions and intentions are active is said to rest on a fundamental difference between desire rationality and intention–action rationality. The latter is the kind of rationality that must govern any exercise of *control* (1996: 49). After performing practical reasoning, the agent takes a decision to perform an action. The taking of such a decision (i) is a second order action in that it is an action that directs the agent to perform an overt, first order action, and (ii) is fully under the agent's control in that it is a product of practical rationality. In spite of the differences between Pink's second order agency and the volitions introduced by Ginet and McCann, the common thread among them all is the fact that these mental acts are conceived by the authors as the *first*, the *basic*, action an agent takes in all voluntary actions. All actions originate from these first acts. I will label any foundationalist theory that requires such special mental acts as the basic elements *volitional theories* of action.

FOUNDATIONALISM IN ACTION THEORY

The picture of an act of will that emerges in response to Ryle regress or to the McCann regress, or to the difficulties Ginet finds in causal

---

[15] A thoughtful and convincing critique of Ginet's theory of simple acts can be found in O'Connor (1993).

accounts, is one where the volition is an act an agent performs without having to perform some other act in order to perform it, or without having to perform some other act that causes the event of a willing to take place in the mind. It is something an agent can 'do forthwith'. It is the first, the most immediate kind of an act that forms the nucleus of all voluntary actions.

The picture here is a familiar one: it is what we find in all foundationalist theories. Consider a foundationalist account of knowledge:

> *Foundationalist Definition of Knowledge (FDK)*
> S knows that p if and only if:
> > (A) S knows that p directly (without there being any other proposition from which this knowledge of p is derived), *or*
> > (B) There is a proposition q such that
> > > (i) S knows that q, and
> > > (ii) q stands in some specific justificatory relation to p, and
> > > (iii) S infers from q that p, and as a result, comes to believe that p based on her belief that q, and
> > > (iv) p is true.

The infinite regress threatened by clause (B) of FDK is similar in structure to that threatened by clause (2) of the Foundationalist Definition of Action, FDA. And the threat is blocked by adding the base clause (A) to FDK in disjunction with (B). Clearly (A) parallels clause (1) of FDA.

Leaving aside any objections one may have in general to foundationalist theories, or specifically foundationalism in epistemology, we need to examine how the respective base clauses are to be satisfied in these two theories in order to decide how much of an analogy basic knowledge provides for volitions as basic actions.

In the case of knowledge, clauses (i) to (iii) of (B) appeal to a relation in which one proposition counts as *evidence* for a second. This *evidential* relation is then coupled to a *basing* relation, so that believing the second on the *basis* of the first, provided that p is true, constitutes knowledge. Now for the base clause (clause A) to complete the analysis, we expect that it is possible to know a proposition without that proposition being related to any other proposition through the basing relation. What criteria, then, should a belief satisfy in order for it to constitute this 'basic' knowledge? A condition of adequacy for a foundationalist analysis of knowledge must be that what counts as knowledge in the base clause has something in common with what is defined as knowledge in the recursive clauses. Since the structure of the foundationalist account rules out the basing relation as this common element, the common feature will clearly be located in the notion of evidence.

As a matter of fact, some favourite candidates for the sort of propositions that can satisfy (A) are *self-evident* propositions. The Cartesian appeal to 'indubitable truths' or the empiricist one to 'incorrigible truths' that are expressed by propositions that report one's own psychological (or perceptual) states are two examples. Whatever the candidates for the base clause of FDK might be, the onus is on the theorist to say why one's acceptance of these privileged propositions constitutes knowledge—that is, why it guarantees their truth in the absence of the sort of justification envisaged by clauses (i)–(iv) of (B). In the case of knowledge, one can find some plausible answers to such questions.[16] But the model does not carry over to a foundationalist account of action very gracefully. Analogous to the question we were contemplating about basic knowledge, we need to ask, 'in virtue of what do these basic elements (e.g. volitions) count as *actions*?' What is it about the mental episodes of a person such as willings that allows them to constitute actions—actions that are capable of causing overt behaviour? There seem to be two, and only two, possible routes one can take in search for answers here. My objective in this chapter is to argue that one of these routes should be avoided.

One route is to search for an event causation analysis of actions in general. This will have that consequence that acts of volition are acts simply because an agent's willing something is reduced to a causal relation between two events. For example, the act of willing the arm to move may be analysed into some event in the agent causing the event of the motion of the arm. Or in the same spirit, a Lockean picture of the will may be adopted. In this picture, the will is conceived as a power one has to do something (or forbear from doing something) on the model of the 'power' an acid has to dissolve a metal.[17] Such powers or dispositions are best understood in terms of the structural features of

---

[16] In fact, the main problem with foundationalism in epistemology does not lie in showing why belief in such self-evident propositions constitutes knowledge. It rather lies in showing how propositions whose direct knowability is indisputable can act as the *basis* for indirect knowledge.

[17] Locke 1689: II. xxi. 3–4.

a substance (or of a system) that enable it to produce certain types of outputs in response to specific types of inputs. On this view, 'acts' of will are conceived as events that occur in the agent, and the faculty that produces these events is the decision-making mechanism of the agent.

This is the view I propose to develop in the following chapters. I shall argue that it is possible to offer a purely causal model for the deliberative process that underlies practical reasoning. The end-result of this deliberation is the formation of a decision to act a certain way. I shall also suggest that the faculty of the will may be conceived as the system that is capable of carrying out the deliberation. On this conception, 'acts of will' are constituted by the overt outputs of such a system.[18]

What I am criticizing in this chapter is a conception of the acts of volition in which such acts, by their intrinsic nature, defy analysis in terms of event causation. They are either caused by the agent or are simple manifestations of agency. This is what I had in mind as the second route—the route to be avoided.

On this second route to an answer to the question of why these basic elements (i.e. volitions) are *actions*, it is declared, by what seems to me to be nothing other than brute force, that these are *sui generis* acts of agency. Agents are supposed to be capable of performing such acts (and here words start failing us—'at will'? surely not! 'forthwith'? 'directly'?) without any other episode or event being their sufficient causes. When we look for evidence for the existence of such a power that we are supposed to possess—the capacity to will, the power to cause changes in our bodies or in the world, that is, the power to *initiate* causal chains—we are invited to introspect and observe the unmistakable phenomenal feel that marks the reality of these acts of volition.[19] However, even if we grant we can be certain that when we inwardly pronounce 'peu' we are acting, how much reason does this certainty provide for the general claim that it is self-evident that whenever I 'exert my body' part of that exertion is an *act* of willing? Upon

---

[18] When one wills something, what one wills is typically an event, not an action. For example, I will my arm to rise. I do not will myself to raise my arm. I shall argue later that when one decides to perform a basic act, the object of that decision is also a bodily movement. This gives some plausibility to the claim that acts of will are events in which one carries out decisions that are reached by deliberation.

[19] It is in this spirit that Ginet introduces 'the actish phenomenal quality' of volitions. I take this appeal to introspection to be Ginet's way of suggesting that he has reasons for offering his simple acts of volition as basic actions.

introspection I may feel some 'actish phenomenal quality' when I exert my body to open a heavy door, but without making the theoretical commitment that Ginet has made, I do not find within my act of bodily exertion a distinct act of volition with its own intrinsic actish quality revealed to my introspective inner eye. Even if introspection may be a reliable indicator of the presence of feelings, it is notoriously misleading as to the source of these feelings.

At this stage of the defence for the existence of such *sui generis* acts of volition, a discussion of the paralytic case is invariably introduced. When one's body is paralysed, and one wills one's arm to rise, one might be surprised to find that no such thing has happened: one has not raised one's arm. But, the narrative goes on to maintain, in these situations we certainly *do* something—we in fact do *exactly the same thing* that we do when we successfully raise our arm. So much, it is claimed, is phenomenologically transparent. So there is a kind of act that we perform whether we actually raise our arm or merely try to raise our arm and fail, and that act is an act of volition. It is in this spirit that Ginet asserts, 'To try to act is to act' (1990: 10). As will become clear later, I tend to think that to try to act and not succeed is to fail to act.

All things considered, the suggestion that the best way of satisfying the base clause of the foundationalist theory of action is to posit volitions as irreducible basic acts commits us to quite an unwieldy commodity, and I will devote the remainder of this chapter to developing further reasons as to why we should not take volitions as paradigm actions.

DIFFICULTIES WITH IRREDUCIBLE BASIC MENTAL ACTS

Mysteries of Agency Causation

It may very well be true that when we attend to our powers, we find that we are capable of doing things 'readily' and that this capacity presents itself to us as a basic fact about agency.[20] But is it a transparent

---

[20] I personally find these invitations to introspection quite baffling: I know how to raise my arm, but do I really know how to will that my arm rise? What counts as knowing how to will such a thing? If I clench my teeth and issue a mental command to my arm and my arm

fact that our alleged acts of volition are among the (or *are* the) foremost things we do so 'readily'? In contrast, do I know just as transparently that I do not have the power to acquire a belief 'readily'? Maybe I do. But when I form an intention to do something, do I have an equally clear-cut knowledge of whether I am performing an action or some sequence of events is taking place in me? If I cannot know with certainty about my intendings, does this not place into jeopardy my alleged knowledge about willings?

But epistemic uncertainties do not really come close to the heart of the mystery about agent causation. The Cartesian claim that there is nothing any *more* mysterious in agent causation (in interactionism) than there is in one (material) event causing another does not allay one's worries: if anything, it revives one's already present worries about event causation. It seems more prudent to live with one unanalysed concept of causation rather than two. And since we seem committed to event causation in making sense of the material world, unless we propose to offer a general agency theory of causation to cover events, too, agent causation appears as a superfluous mystery.

C. D. Broad has remarked that if enduring entities like agents are designated as causes, they cannot help explain why actions occur at one time rather than another: 'How could an event possibly be determined to happen at a certain date if its total cause contained no factor to which the notion of date has any application? And how can the notion of date have any application to anything that is not an event?'[21]

More recently, agent causation has been defended in much more sophisticated forms than were found in Reid (1969), Taylor (1966), or Chisholm (1966). O'Connor's (2000) sustained argument in favour of agent causation is an excellent example.[22] O'Connor discusses Broad's objection and argues that, since the things that are true of an agent are true at given times, it is no mystery that an agent causes her action at the time she does. He admits that in the agent causation view there is

---

goes up, have I raised my arm *by having willed* it to rise? Is the difference between a successful paranormal spoon-bender (if such creatures exist) and me just that the spoon-bender knows how to will the spoon to bend, and I don't? Here Anscombe's lovely comment is quite apt: 'People sometimes say that one can get one's arm to move by an act of will but not a matchbox; but if they mean, "Will a matchbox to move and it won't", the answer is "If I will my arm to move that way, it won't," and if they mean "I can move my arm but not the matchbox" the answer is that I can move the matchbox—nothing easier' (Anscombe 1957: 52).

[21] From C. D. Broad 1952: 215, as quoted with approval by Ginet (1990: 14).

[22] Another example is to be found in Clarke (1996).

no account of why an act occurred at one time moment rather than at some other time moment. O'Connor adopts the causal powers view about causation, as defended by Harré and Madden (1975). By endorsing what he describes as a non-mechanistic species of that view, 'involving the characteristic activity of purposive free agents' (O'Connor 2000: 72), he maintains that he can defend his version of agent causation against most of the traditional objections. I am not confident that I understand how invoking 'the characteristic activity of purposive free agents' demystifies the traditional notion of immanent causation. The causal powers view was originally designed to account for mechanistic causation. When O'Connor says that his agent causation is a species of that view, he might be ignoring this fact. As I see it, what he has introduced is a *new* genus of causation. I tend to think that the mechanistic event causation account of action I develop in the following chapters is closer in the spirit of Harré and Madden's view of causal powers than O'Connor's agent causation is.

In any case, this is not the place to enter into a detailed criticism of modern agent-causation views like O'Connor's. It would be hard to do justice to their subtleties in the limited space. My interest in this chapter is to argue that it is a mistake to posit irreducible acts of volition that are supposed to initiate all voluntary actions on the grounds that such acts are introspectively transparent.

History of philosophy should have taught us by now that, if a thinker is willing to embrace agent causation, which to me seems aesthetically unsightly and ontologically unnecessary, there is little that can be said to dissuade him. Chisholm (1978: 623) seems to be confirming this point when he says,

Now if you can analyze such statements as 'Jones killed his uncle' into event-causation statements, then you may have earned the right to make jokes about the agent as cause. But if you haven't done this, and if all the same you do believe such things as that I raised my arm and that Jones killed his uncle, and if moreover you still think it's a joke to talk about the agent as cause, then, I'm afraid, the joke is entirely on you. You are claiming the benefits of honest philosophical toil without even having a theory of human action.

I hope to pick up the gauntlet Chisholm throws down, and in the following chapters attempt to show how we can analyse action sentences into event-causation statements. But even if such an attempt is not successful, that in itself does not warrant subscribing to agent causation without proving that there is some theoretical need for it.[23]

I suggested earlier that a condition of adequacy for the items that are proposed as 'basic' in a foundationalist theory of any concept is this: the items must be paradigm instances of the concept in question. So if acts of volition are to be the *basic* acts, they must be shown to be paradigm *acts*. But as I shall argue, there are good reasons for doubting that they are. My argument will have two branches. First, there is a strong parallel between the reasoning we get from the proponents of volitions-as-basic-acts and that used to arrive at an erroneous position in the theory of perception. If the parallel is real, and if the position in perception is accepted as involving an error, this will place volitions in jeopardy. Second, According to a view about reasons for actions, the reasons one has for *willing* that one perform an act are always identical to the reasons one has for *performing* that act. If this view is right, then it seems that it is a mistake to offer an act of the will as a separate act from which all other actions are generated.

Analogy with Visual Perception

A blunder transformed into official doctrine by empiricists like Locke and Berkeley seems poised to repeat itself in contemporary action theory. Locke, who had the beginnings of a causal theory of perception, maintained that, in seeing an external object, say a tree, one enters into a vision-like relation to an internal object, the idea of a tree: one's 'immediate' object of perception is the idea, and through the intermediacy of the idea one sees the tree. The external tree, by it primary qualities, causes the idea of the tree, which consists of a complex of primary and secondary quality ideas, and the perceiver, by becoming aware of this complex idea 'mediately' sees the tree. One can schematically represent the analysis that was implied by Locke's view in the following way:

> The Causal Theory of Perception (CTP)
> S sees object o if and only if

---

[23] Agent causation is sometimes defended on the grounds that without it we cannot show where our freedom as agents, or our control over our actions can come from. (See e.g. O'Connor 1993.) Nothing I say in this chapter is in response to this kind of alleged theoretical need. I shall take up the issue in Ch. 7 and argue that the concept of acting out of one's own free will is analysable within the confines of the causal theory of action.

There is a mental object, I, such that
  (i) I is a bundle of ideas of primary and secondary qualities, and
  (ii) I is caused by the primary qualities of o, and
  (iii) S stands in some relation R to I.

Here the temptation, which few empiricists seem to be able to resist, is to maintain that the relation, R, in question is a species of seeing. In fact, Berkeley, cleverly exploiting this temptation, argued, in the reckless and daring way we have come to love and hate, that all we really *see* are our ideas. What the imagined astronaut sees at different points in his journey from the Earth to the Moon are all different things. They cannot be aspects of what is ordinarily called the Moon; they are totally disparate entities, to which the relation of unity is arbitrarily imposed by the mind.[24] Berkeley uses an analogy that captures the spirit of this type of view very well.[25] The analogy involves the way we are supposed to 'see' Caesar by looking at a picture or a statue of him. What we really see is the statue, and we infer from its features what Caesar must have looked like. In this analogy, the statue stands to Caesar as our idea of the tree (our percept) stands to the tree itself: we see the former and make an inference, based on custom, to the latter. Without some reason we can give in support of Berkeley's view, the view would appear to be totally implausible and gratuitous. Our untutored gut reaction in this matter would seem to be on the side of the naive realists (or perhaps 'the vulgar' as Hume liked to call them). What reason then can support such a view? One reason that is pertinent to the analogy between perception and action comes from cases of illusion and hallucination. When we see an oar half submerged in water as a bent oar, *what* we see cannot be the oar out there in the water, the argument goes; hence it must be something else. When Macbeth has the vision of the dagger with the handle towards his hand, *what* he sees cannot be a real dagger out there. So he must be seeing an 'imaginary dagger'. Furthermore he has exactly the same experience as a person who is *actually* seeing a dagger. This means that, regardless of

---

[24] 'For, in case I am carried from the place where I stand directly toward the moon, it is manifest the object varies still as I go on; and by the time that I am advanced fifty or sixty semi-diameters of the earth, I shall be so far from being near a small, round, luminous flat that I shall perceive nothing like it—the object having long since disappeared, and, if I would recover it, it must be by going back to the earth from whence I set out' (Berkeley 1709: §44; in 1965: 301).

[25] Berkeley (1713: dialogue I; in 1965: 166–7)

whether we are having a veridical perception or we are suffering from a case of illusion or hallucination, there is some aspect of our experience that is the same: we enter some mental episode, which constitutes our perceptual experience; in this experience we stand in some relation to a mental object that resembles, or fails to resemble, as the case may be, the mediate objects of our perceptions. (Hume, in his typical insightful way, calls this 'the dual object theory', and condemns it as a 'monstrous offspring of two principles which are contrary to each other'.[26])

The Dual Object Theory of Perception has two components. The first component, going back to Locke's causal theory of perception (CTP), is the need to posit the existence of some mental entity, I, which may possess, or fail to possess, the qualities of the external object—the percept (the immediate object of our perception) with a distinctive shape, a size, a colour, etc.[27] Modern sense-data theorists have perpetuated belief in this component by insisting that the predicates that are applicable to objects are also applicable to sense-data.[28] That this is a mistake should be evident to anyone who realized that endorsing it commits one to the existence of things like ideas of garbage that smell like rotten flesh! The mistake consists in thinking that, since we need to speak of the qualities objects *seem* to have, and sometimes fail to have, we have to posit some entity that *actually* has those qualities. Representational structures have representational qualities, but such qualities are not the extensional qualities of the structures; they are rather the qualities of the objects represented.

The second component, which involves perhaps a more transparent mistake, pertains to the nature of the relation, R, in which S is supposed to stand to the mental entity, I. As long as we envision this relation on the model of *perception*, and require that in visual perception, for example, S see I, or S be (visually) aware of I, we invite an infinite regress of nested representations, and nested acts of vision performed by nested 'inner eyes'. And the invention of 'immediate' seeing is the brute force with which the infinite regress is supposedly blocked. The alleged justification for the claim that the device of immediate perception stops the regress is that the argument from

<hr />

[26] Hume (1740; in 1978: 215)
[27] Indeed secondary qualities like colour are sometimes maintained to be properly speaking qualities of ideas (percepts) *only*.
[28] Robinson (1994).

illusion is inapplicable to the 'objects' of immediate perception—the nature of these objects is incorrigibly transparent to our introspection.

These two components are not wholly independent of one another. For if we can resist the suggestion that there exists some entity (an idea, a percept, or a sense-datum) whose determinable properties are the sorts of things that are perceived, then the temptation to view the relation between the subject and the entity as some species of perception would vanish.

Analogy as Applied to Action

Each of these two components finds its counterpart in action theory. If we think back to the way the argument from paralysis is supposed to work in justifying volitions, we can immediately see the parallel to the arguments from illusion that were used to justify the introduction of a special kind of perception—that is, the immediate perception of the idea. When my arm is paralysed and I try to raise it, I have the distinct *feeling* that I am doing something. In fact, just as Macbeth has the distinct feeling that he is seeing a dagger, a feeling indistinguishable from what he has when he does see a dagger, I, too, judge that what I do when I try to raise my paralysed arm is one and the same thing that I do when I successfully raise my arm. Since this thing that I do cannot be raising my arm, it has to be some other *action* that I *perform*. But as we saw earlier, to stop the infinite regress, it has to be a special kind of action. So as a counterpart to *immediate seeing*, we end up with performing McCann's most basic action or Ginet's simple act, that is, the act of volition that I perform when I try to raise my arm, as well as when I successfully raise my arm. Here, too, the alleged unmistakable actish quality that accompanies these special acts parallels the certainty that immediate perception supposedly enjoys: just as there is no argument from illusion for the objects of immediate perception, there is no paralysis of the will that can reveal a more 'immediate' mental act!

I submit that the conclusion to be drawn from this comparison is this: the reasons for thinking that when we perform the act of raising our arm, we perform a mental act, and it is *through* the performance of this mental act that, all other things being equal, we succeed in performing the bodily act are no better than the reasons we have for thinking that when we see an oar, we 'see' a mental entity, and it is through this episode of the immediate perception of the mental entity that, other things being equal, we succeed in seeing the oar. So we should conclude that, just as we do not see a real dagger-like mental object *both* when we actually see a dagger *and* we hallucinate it, we do not perform a bodily-act-like mental act *both* when we actually raise our arm *and* when we try in vain to raise it when it is paralysed.[29]

We can now return to what I claimed was the first component of a Dual Object Theory of Perception, which was the need to posit the existence of a mental object, which instantiates the properties that are attributed to external objects in ordinary speech. An oar may seem to be bent and not be bent, but if the oar *seems* to be bent, the mental image of an oar cannot, by its very nature, fail to be bent because being bent is the *actual* quality of the mental image. The analogy with volition is this: an act of arm raising may seem to be voluntary and yet not be so (as might happen when I will my arm to rise at the same time a scientist stimulates the appropriate neurons in my motor cortex that make my arm rise), whereas an act of willing, which has the proper phenomenological quality, cannot fail to be voluntary. This way of defending the paradigmatic act status of willings is no better than the defence for the special status of mental objects of immediate seeing.

Objections

A volitional theorist may want to resist the arguments I have been developing in one of two general ways. The first way might be to point out that one important task of a theory of action is that of explaining how action is possible, how agents initiate their acts, and to suggest that no satisfactory explanation can be provided by reductive theories. All theories that try to eliminate the first acts of agency in favour of a sequence of causally connected events end up eliminating agency altogether. As a result, they fail to carry out their task.

The only way to respond to this way of resistance is to develop a non-volitional theory and to argue that there is room for agency in that theory. That is what I propose to do in subsequent chapters.

---

[29] It is important here to use paralysis as an analogue to hallucination. Trying to raise one's arm when it is strapped to one's waist is a different affair. In the latter case, we do something that is distinct from what we do when we successfully raise it. We exert our body with a greater force than we would normally need. Even the phenomenology of forcing one's arm unsuccessfully under constraint is very different from trying to raise it when it is paralysed.

The second way of resisting might consist of objecting to the analogy. I can imagine three types of objections, each of which I will briefly consider here.

Sense-Data Theories of Perception

It could be held that my rejection of sense-data theories of perception is unjustified; that Locke and Berkeley were right in arguing that the only way we can make sense of perceptual illusion is to maintain that, every time we perceive something, the immediate objects of our perception are mental. The objection would continue by insisting that such mental objects necessarily possess the properties that external objects seem to have. And it would point out that, as the argument from paralysis demonstrates, the analogy with perception is perfect: the ontological status of acts of volition is as secure as that of the mental objects of perception.

It is true that this type of move undermines the main thrust of my arguments above because it denies me the main premise of those arguments, that is, it denies me the claim that these things that we are said to immediately *see* in our minds whenever we see some external object are ontologically suspect. But it is important to appreciate the price at which such a denial is purchased: one has to insist that, when one sees a tree, one *sees* a tree-like entity in one's mind, and it is through the perception of such an entity that one succeeds in seeing the physical tree. I do not think this is a price one should be willing to pay. The history of philosophy contains sufficient evidence for the inadvisability of paying it. Epistemological infelicities that ensue are too well known to describe at length here: the difficulty of explaining how one gets to the knowledge of the external object from the knowledge of one's percept, and the Berkeleian immaterialism one is forced into in the attempt to avoid sckepticism are just two of the many ills familiar to all.

One need not, of course, subscribe to a Berkeleian theory of perception in order to defend a volitional theory of action. A volitionist may simply reject the analogy. But what would such a rejection be based on? Actions are different, the volitionist might insist; they are events in which the *agent* is *active*; whereas in perception the *subject* is *passive*; she is acted upon. However, this way of dismissing my arguments would beg the whole question. For the question at issue is whether there is any reason to think all actions are grounded in irreducible acts of agency. And merely asserting that they must be because it is obvious that they are does not swing the scale in favour of the volitionist.

Going back to the analogy, I grant that a sense-data theorist need not insist on *seeing* the mental entity. The perceiver may be said to *have* the percept (or be aware of it), and she may stand in some computational relation to this object of awareness. But now this kind of a sense-data theory of perception ceases to provide an analogy to acts of volition. The volitionist is not content to have some willing taking place in the mind. She must insist that this willing be an *action*. If like the more tempered sense-data theorist, the volitionist were to allow that there be a non-actional relation between an event in the agent (say, the formation of an intention) and the willing's occurrence, then she would be allowing the viability of a reductive account of action. My rejection of volitional theories was not directed at views that are compatible with such reductive approaches.

Limited Sense-Data Theories

A limited volitionist may not insist on there being an act of volition embedded in *every* action one performs, but only in those special cases in which 'exerting the will' is the only thing one can do, or the only way in which one can get the intended thing done. Otherwise, in our typical routine actions, in things we do with ease, the volitionist may admit, there is no need to invoke volitions. The partial domain where acts of will are said to be the agent's 'first', 'direct' actions may also find its analogue in perception. There are two types of case here.

1. *Paralysis and hallucinations.* Suppose Smith is paralysed, and he is in denial of his paralysis. Smith attempts to raise his arm. The arm does not move. A volitionist might say, in such cases, that in spite of the fact that he did not raise his arm, there *was* something Smith *did*. He *tried* to raise his arm.[30] The tryings in these cases are nothing other than original acts of will.[31] In the same way, when one sees a tree, there need not be any mental entity one 'first' *sees*. But when one hallucinates a tree, the limited sense-data theorist may propose, there *is* something that one sees—the mental image of a tree. This view, it may be said, conforms to the way we actually speak: Macbeth did see a

[30] As we have seen in discussing Ginet, for some philosophers, trying to do something, even when the trying is unsuccessful, is *always* doing something.

[31] Hornsby (1980) and O'Shaughnessy (1979) argue for this view for all acts of agency.

dagger, and since there was no *real* dagger for him to see, what he saw must have been an imaginary dagger.[32] I think that the claim for the perception case is just false. 'S sees o' logically entails 'o exists'. And the existence conditions for a dagger are *not* satisfied by an imaginary dagger. One may be said to *have* the visual image of a dagger, to *seem* to see a dagger, but to say that one actually *sees* a dagger is to use at best a short hand for the more careful formulations.

If the limited sense-data theorist is willing to concede this point, then a similar concession should be forthcoming on the volition end. When Smith tried to raise his arm, there is no theoretical pressure to say that he *did* something. 'He tried to do something and failed' is logically consistent with 'He couldn't do anything'. Certainly it is true that Smith's mental world did undergo a series of changes when he tried to raise his arm—changes that were absent when he was not trying to do anything. In fact a good portion of the sequence of events that takes place when a normal person raises her arm must have taken place in Smith's mind (for example, a desire to raise the arm, causing an intention to raise the arm, and so on). All these changes may be used in unpacking the claim that Smith exerted energy to raise his arm. But this picture does not require that we leave room for an original act of will as the terminus of such a sequence of events. Consequently paralysis examples do not warrant a commitment to a limited volitional theory.

2. *Strength of will.* It is maintained in some quarters that some acts we perform require a special effort on our part so as to overcome the temptation to take the easy way out.[33]

I need to shovel the snow off the sidewalk. I would much rather stay indoors and read in front of the fireplace, but I 'screw [my] courage to the sticking place', as Lady Macbeth advises her husband to do, and put on my parka, pick up the shovel, and go out to deal with the elements. The act may be said to have taken a *resolve* on my part, an act of will, so to speak, without which I would be sweetly dozing in front of the fire. It might be maintained that a volition needs to be posited to account for the undeniable difference between such cases and cases where one may

---

[32] Shakespeare has Macbeth describe his experience in a much more sensitive way than our limited sense-data theorist is inclined to. Although in addressing the dagger Macbeth says over and over, 'I see thee', he also questions, 'Art though but a dagger of the mind, a false creation proceeding for the heat-oppressed brain?'

[33] Nahmias (2000) gives a sensitive discussion of such cases. See also Mele (1987) on self-control.

look forward to shovelling the snow, and go out and do it willingly, gleefully, without any resistance.[34]

It is certainly true that there is a difference between the two types of cases. It is a difference I hope to capture in my account of the causal processes that underlie deliberation, and of the role played by strong desires the fulfilment of which is incompatible with the ultimate goal of an act plan. But at this point, an analogy may be sufficient to show that positing an original act of will is not the only way to account for the difference.

Imagine the contrast between opening a well-oiled gate and a rusty heavy door. The first can be done in an effortless swift arm motion, almost simultaneous with stepping through the gate. The other, though, requires straining against the door with one's whole body, tensing one's shoulder and leg muscles, and pushing with all one's strength. If one were to know the state of the respective doors, one's planning for the two acts would involve quite different considerations. Clearly, to make sense of the contrast between them, there is no need to posit a special act of will for one of them. The contrast can be captured in terms of the difference between the two act plans that are put in motion. The same can be said for the strength of will cases. One does know oneself; one knows the 'resistance' there will be to going out to shovel. So one plans for it. One throws an extra log into the fireplace before going out, one decides to have hot chocolate after the deed, one thinks of the neighbour's scornful look, and so on, making the whole package more 'attractive' than just sitting in front of the fire and reading.

In summary, although these limited applications of volition do not involve the philosophical infelicities of foundationalist volitionist theories of action, invoking volitions as irreducible mental acts is not warranted by the phenomena we have examined.

Reasons for Acting and Reasons for Willing

In addition to what action theory should learn from epistemology, there is a second type of consideration that should make us sceptical of the category of acts of will. The consideration involves proposing as an

---

[34] I am indebted to David Sanford and Güven Güzeldere, who pressed this point on me during discussion.

essential criterion of voluntariness of acts that they be performed for a reason, and showing that the sorts of reasons for which acts are normally performed do not apply to acts of will.

I now take up the second branch of my argument. When I do something voluntarily, my action typically conforms to a pattern of the following sort. There is a goal I wish to accomplish. In deliberating, I consider the different means of achieving the goal; I try to anticipate the consequences and the side-effects of these different means; I weigh the pros and cons of each and settle on one of them. What I settle on is a plan that links, through my means–end beliefs, the achievement of the goal to some proximal act that is immediately accessible to me. In this plan, a sequence of anticipated acts are strung together in a chain, starting from the proximal act and ending at the goal, where each link has been designated as the means to the subsequent links.[35]

For example, when Sam settles on going to see his doctor as his goal, he picks up the phone. Picking up the phone is an action that is immediately available to Sam, and it is the act that is designated in his act plan as a means to his goal. Here his reason for picking up the phone consists in the fact that he conceives it as a means to some intermediate or final end that is along the chain of actions that appear in the act plan. Sam's reason for picking up the phone was to dial the doctor's office, to make an appointment, to visit the doctor, and so on. And his reason for making an appointment with the doctor was to visit him, to consult him about his blood pressure medication, and so on. Each voluntary act can in this way be placed in a pattern in which the agent's reasons for performing that act are revealed.

I maintained above that the chain of projected means–ends relations that make up this pattern terminates at some proximal act that is immediately accessible to the agent. The question that is of importance to the present concern about acts of volition is this: is the terminus of such chains always a mental volitional act or is it typically an overt bodily act? I suggest that one way of approaching this question is to see if it is possible to find reasons for performing the alleged volitional act that are distinct from the reasons for performing any of the overt actions in the act plan.

Recall that the candidate for the volitional act is a mental act that is allegedly basic and irreducible to event causation. As such it could be an

---

[35] The details of this simplified picture of an action that is undertaken after deliberation are worked out in greater detail in Ch. 5.

act of willing, an act of deciding or intending. So we want to see if one can have reasons for willing one's hand to grasp the phone, or one's deciding (intending) to pick up the phone that are distinct from the reasons one has for picking up the phone. The target I am aiming at here is that, if these reasons are not distinct, then the thesis that these mental activities are basic acts that initiate all voluntary actions will lose its plausibility.

It seems clear from a common-sense point of view that Sam's reason for *deciding* to pick up the phone is one and the same as his reason for picking up the phone: he wanted to call his doctor![36] The same point may be extended to the alleged act of willing: if Sam willed his hand to grasp the phone, could his reason for willing this be different from his reason for grasping the phone? One thing seems clear to me. Sam could not have thought that an effective means of satisfying his desire to grasp the phone was to will his hand to grasp it. It is not as if the act plan that was settled upon included such an act of will that was the means for Sam to grasp the phone.

An act of volition, whatever it may be, is surely not regarded by the agent as a means to some desired end, the way, say, picking up the phone is regarded as a means to making a phone call.[37]

So much gets me only part of the way to my target, which is the thesis that the reasons an agent has for an action are the same as the reasons she has for willing, deciding, or intending to perform that action. It only establishes that, if the reason for deciding to do A is distinct from the reason for doing A, it is not because deciding to do A is conceived as a means for doing A.

---

[36] Davidson notices this feature with respect to intentions. He points out (in 1985: 213–14) that the reasons an agent has for intending to do something are the same sort as the reasons an agent has for *doing* that thing.

[37] This is what McCann (1974: 467) asserts in an unguarded moment: 'when a bodily change is brought about by performing a mental act, the act serves as the means by which voluntary control over the change is exerted'. I would wager that a moment's reflection would persuade him to withdraw this assertion. But Ginet (1990: 30), expresses a similar view: 'It [the volition] is the means by which I cause my body's action'. Pink seems to think that there is some means–end relation that holds between agents' second order actions (like deciding or willing) and their first order (bodily) actions. He maintains that these second order actions require a 'capacity for active self determination—a capacity to cause oneself to perform actions *by performing* second order actions in the mind' (Pink 1996: 24; my emphasis). The pervasiveness of this teleological view among friends of the basic acts of volition, which view I maintain to be a mistake, strengthens my argument: it seems that, in order to support their false conclusion concerning the existence of such acts of volition, these authors find themselves committed to a false premise about their teleological role.

However, there exists a different way in which the reasons for intending to do something are said to be different from those for doing A.[38] The clearest example for this claim is found in the much-discussed toxin puzzle, originally introduced by Kavka (1983).

In the example a person is offered a million dollars if he intends to drink a toxin that will make a person sick but will not have any long-lasting effects. Between the time at which the intention is formed and the time at which the toxin is to be drunk, the million dollars will be irreversibly deposited in this person's account. It is claimed that, in terms of beliefs and desires that justify an action, there is a very good reason for forming the intention to drink the toxin at the designated (later) time. But, the claim continues, when the intention *is* formed and the money is in the bank, there is an equally good reason not to drink the toxin.

I find the example very unconvincing. What is the deliberation that results in the person's intention to drink the toxin? Presumably it is one in which the advantages of becoming a millionaire are weighed against the drawbacks of drinking the toxin, and the former are found to be stronger. For the deliberation to show that *intending* to drink the toxin is the rational act, it has to be able to show that *drinking* the toxin is the rational act. Otherwise one would not be forming the intention to drink the toxin; one would be merely forming the intention to *appear* to have formed the intention to drink it. A simpler way of making the same point is to see that, if one believes that one will *not* drink the toxin, one cannot genuinely intend to drink it. So the person cannot sincerely intend to drink the toxin if his plan is not to drink it after he gets the money. And he cannot sincerely consider whether to intend to drink the toxin if he does not consider whether to drink it or not. If he has formed the genuine intention to drink the toxin, and received the million dollars, he has now exactly the same reasons for drinking the toxin as he had for intending to drink it. His reasons cannot change after he gets the money because all the circumstances that weighed in favour of his decision have remained unaltered in the interim.

In saying this, I am not denying that one *can* change one's mind by going through a new deliberation with the old information. One does change one's intentions even when the circumstances remain

---

[38] I confine the discussion at this point to intending. But the considerations raised apply equally well to willing or deciding.

unaltered. But this fact does nothing to support the view that in special cases (like the toxin example) the deliberation can be about *intending* to do something as opposed to *doing* something.

Bratman (1987: 101–6), in discussing the toxin case, agrees that the deliberation that will result in an intention to drink the toxin is a deliberation about whether to drink the toxin. But he suggests that, if one can act so as to cause oneself to have the intention to drink the toxin (say, by self-hypnosis), then the reason for so acting may not be the same as the reasons for drinking the toxin. Bratman's suggestion does not damage the present thesis, but I will argue later in Chapter 5 that such 'artificially' induced intentions, which bypass a deliberative process and lack an act plan as part of their content, are not genuine intentions.[39]

In summary, I remain convinced that in the relatively simple structure of the toxin puzzle, we do not have a case in which reasons for intending (deciding, willing) to do something are distinct from the reasons for doing that thing.

Literature subsequent to the original appearance of the toxin example has concentrated on cases that have a more complex structure. The complexity is partly due to the conditional content of the mental act that is focused on. These involve situations that have been named the 'paradox of deterrence'. Suppose the alleged mental act is deciding.[40] And suppose that the content of the decision has the form 'R if A'. The application of this structure to rationalizing nuclear armament is to show that one can be justified in deciding to retaliate if attacked. Justification takes the form of pointing out that the net effect of the act of *deciding* this conditional (and making the decision known to the other side) is to minimize the chances of being attacked. But the reasons that thus justify the decision, it is said, do not justify the *act* of retaliating if attacked because retaliation will have disastrous effects for the whole world.[41]

---

[39] For additional discussions of the toxin puzzle, see Lewis 1984; Mele 1992a, 1995b; Pink 1996.

[40] Deciding is a better candidate because there seems to be a better case to be made for the claim that deciding is a mental act. (See Mele 2000; Pink 1996; for arguments to this effect.) In the causal theory I shall develop both reaching a decision and coming to have an intention will, except in extraordinary situations, turn out to be mental acts.

[41] For interesting and thoughtful discussions of this claim see Pink 1996; Kavka 1987; Gauthier 1990; Lewis 1984; McClennen 1990. No unanimous agreement exists on what conclusion to draw from the puzzle or whether there is a genuine puzzle.

Leaving the game-theoretic and ethical subtleties to one side, we first need to notice that the complication that emerges from the 'paradox of deterrence' is not just due to the conditional form of what is decided upon. To see this, consider a simple conditional decision. Suppose Joe decides to go to the party if Sally goes too. Such a decision simply makes the act of going to the party contingent on the fulfilment of some condition (Sally's going to the party) and thus presents Sally's company as a reason for the projected act of going to the party. In other words, Joe's reasons for going to the party include, among other things, Sally's going too. Ordinarily, in arriving at such a decision through deliberation, Joe would consider one and the same factors that are the pros and cons of going to the party with or without Sally, and the reasons for the final *decision* will be the same as the (conditional) reasons he has for going to the party.

To appreciate the complication that resides in the 'paradox of deterrence', we need to consider two scenarios of a different conditional decision. Here are the elements that are common to both scenarios. A bank robber has killed two of the security agents in the bank and has taken some hostages inside the bank. The police have surrounded the building. The robber's ultimate goal is to go unharmed and escape with the money.

Scenario 1. The robber thinks, 'They will either let me go with the money, or else, to get even with them and to avenge my eventual death, I will kill all the hostages.' So he decides to kill the hostages if the police do not meet his demands, and announces his decision to the police. The decision is similar to Joe's in that the robber's reasons for his decision, at least as he has conceived them, are the same as his reasons for killing the hostages if his demands are not met.

Scenario 2. The robber thinks, 'I have control over something that is of value to the police. I will try to convince them that I will kill the hostages if they don't let me go with the money. I am not sure I will carry out my threat if they refuse because *if* they refuse, being captured with just two killings against me may have less disastrous consequences for me than having a dozen deaths on my hands.' So he announces, with the same conviction of the robber in Scenario 1, that he has decided to kill the hostages if his demands are not met.

In Scenario 2 we have moved into the territory of the 'paradox of deterrence'.[42] But if this scenario captures the salient aspects of the deterrence example, what we find is *not* both that the agent has good reasons for *deciding* to R if A (kill the hostages if the demands are not met, or retaliate if attacked) and lacks good reasons for *doing* R if A. It is rather that he has good reasons for making people think he has decided to R if A, and no good reasons for doing R if A. If the robber's thinking in Scenario 2 makes it irrational for him to *decide* to kill the hostages if his demands are not met, given the facts of the matter, a nation's *deciding* to retaliate if attacked would be equally irrational. What *might* be rational is to convince the other side of what is actually false—that is, that one has decided to retaliate if attacked. And towards this deceptive end, the act of stockpiling nuclear weapons (provided that one can be confident of one's prediction that they will never be used) may be a rational means.

Skyrms (1996: 38–42) contrasts two decision-theoretic strategies. The first one, which he calls 'modular rationality', is the one that favours making a decision to act at a later time on the basis of what information is available at the moment, and leaving the execution of the act to the time at which more information is presented. This strategy, Skyrms maintains, is more rational than one he calls 'the theology of commitment'. But he worries whether evolution has promoted this second strategy at the expense of modular rationality. Whatever the decision-theoretic considerations may favour here, I maintain that the psychological structure of intending and deciding does not make the modularity of reasons a viable alternative.

If I am right, then neither the toxin puzzle nor the deterrence example shows that the reasons for deciding (willing or intending) can be distinct from the reasons for what is decided (willed or intended). This leaves us with the conclusion that what is essential to *action*, that it be done for the reasons the agent has, does not carry over to making a decision. It does not carry over to them because there is no room for having reasons for deciding to do something that are separable from the reasons one has for doing the thing that is decided. And this observation should make us sceptical of the claim that whenever we perform an overt action voluntarily, we also perform an antecedent act of will. The claim's mistake becomes apparent when one realizes

---

[42] I have been placing quotes around the label because I do not think there is a real paradox involved.

that the volitions do not share with ordinary actions any of their reason related properties.

Pink (1996: 7), in setting up the thesis against which the proposes to argue, puts the point I have been developing in this section eloquently:

It is a serious question whether there really is an agency of the will.

It is not hard to see where the skepticism comes from. The actions which our actions explain are purposive...We perform these actions, then, in the belief that they will attain desirable ends. And that is connected with the fact that the practical deliberation which explains our actions is precisely deliberation about how to act...

But the forming of intentions to act does not seem to be purposive. It does not seem to be motivated by beliefs about what ends it will further. We perform intentions to do A because we believe *doing A*—the action decided upon—will attain desirable ends, and not because we believe that *now intending to do A* will attain desirable ends. The deliberation that explains our intentions to act, then, is simply deliberation about which actions to perform. Our intentions are not generally based on practical deliberation about which intentions to form.

LIBERTARIANISM AND VOLITIONAL THEORIES

I have argued that a volitional theory of action, a theory in which volitions are introduced as irreducible actions that initiate a causal chain, subsequent links of which are attributable to the agent as further actions, does not do well upon close scrutiny. The foundationalist programme, which seems to be the best motivation for the volitional theory, does not carry to action theory gracefully because only unreliable intuitions seem to support the thesis that in any action, volitions (or decisions) are the most basic actions we perform.

Having said this, the task that remains now is to offer some explanation as to why volitional theories are so prevalent. And the explanation is not difficult. An account of action that lacks irreducible volitions—volitions, which are, by their very nature, under the agent's control, and which are posited as the ultimate source of voluntary actions—seems to many incapable of capturing the essence of agency. It is said that if action is reduced to event causation, then the difference between one's doing something and something happening to one will vanish.[43] If we see the freedom of an act to consist in our ability to do or not to do an act when we keep unchanged the past history of the universe as it includes our personality, character traits, our desires, beliefs, values, and preferences, that is, if we think that a necessary condition for a free act of mine is that I could have done otherwise even if nothing were different about me or the circumstances, then (on the assumption that the class of voluntary actions is not empty) it becomes very attractive to introduce a faculty that acts 'forthwith' and thus initiates action, and to require that the acts of this faculty are not reducible to event causation. If the acts of volition are nothing other than certain events in us causing other events in our bodies, then it would not be possible to maintain consistently that without any change in our total psychological state and the circumstances we find ourselves in, we can *non-arbitrarily* perform or refrain from performing some actions.

On the other hand, if we can show that a coherent account of voluntary acts is viable on a causal theory of action, then there would be no need to introduce the mysterious and ontologically ill-formed category of agent causation—what some action theorists deprecatingly call 'the standard view' would suffice. I shall be defending this 'standard view' in subsequent chapters.[44]

---

[43] O'Connor (1993) and Velleman (1992) have expressed this sentiment very well.

[44] It seems to me that issues of freedom and control should not drive one's ontological commitments in action theory. The correct strategy should be to begin with the most plausible account of action and then see how one can resolve questions about the will, about what makes some acts voluntary or autonomous, and what constitutes the freedom of the agent. Action theorists like Kane, Mele, and Ekstrom are to be commended for conforming to such a strategy.

2

Basic Actions

THE FIRST PROBLEM OF ACTION THEORY

The force of Chapter 1 was on the whole negative—a form of exorcism, as I conceived of it. The thesis I sought to defend there was that any view of action that requires the existence of an unanalysable mental act as the initiator of all (voluntary) acts will have to face serious problems. And I ventured the suggestion that philosophers who embrace such acts in spite of these problems are likely to do so because of their commitment to a libertarian view of free action. In this chapter I begin to develop an alternative view of action.

The arguments that were examined in Chapter 1 had as their ultimate objective that of distinguishing the class of things that we do as rational agents from things that happen to us, or of things that our bodies do in the course of their physiological functioning. The expressions 'rational action' and 'mere doing' or 'mere happening' are not the happiest or the clearest labels we can use for these respective classes, but I do not know any other label that does the job any better.[1] The labels 'voluntary' or 'intentional' behaviour, as opposed to 'mere' behaviour are in fact worse for the job. From now on I will refer to the task of distinguishing between these two classes as the First Problem of Action Theory.

It might be useful to reiterate the question which began Chapter 1, the question which presents the First Problem of Action Theory. Let us suppose that we witness the following: Pat, standing in front of his house, kicks the basement window with his foot and breaks the glass. Several scenarios can be imagined that will fill the details of this event. The simplest three are: (1) Pat had locked himself out and figured that the most expeditious and least costly way of getting into

---

[1] Here 'rational' is not to be taken to mean 'reasonable'; it is more in the spirit of 'rationalizable by the agent'. The more precise one makes these labels, the further one moves away from a neutral description of the phenomenon for which a theory is being sought, and the closer one gets to committing oneself to a particular theory.

the house was breaking the basement glass and crawling in through the basement window; since he was wearing heavy boots, he decided to kick the glass in. (2) Pat was standing in front of his basement window and inspecting the siding of his house to see if it needed a paint job this year, and an uncontrollable spasm on his knee jerked his foot forward, and his foot broke the glass. (3) Pat saw through the basement window something going on in the house that shocked and infuriated him, and he kicked in anger. As his foot was close to the window, it broke the glass.

In the first scenario, it is easy to judge that Pat's behaviour was a case of rational action. In the remaining two, what Pat did was the result of something that *happened* to him: the physiological spasm, or being gripped by the psychological state of anger. In (3) certainly Pat *did* something, that is, he broke the glass, but he did not do it for any reason he had; it was not a rational act. The question that poses the First Problem of Action Theory is: 'What is the general criterion of action, which generates such judgements?'

THE CAUSAL THEORY

The First Approximation

The contrast between the first and the remaining two scenarios is so clear that one may be tempted to think the answer to our question is simple: when an agent does something, it is a rational action just in case the agent wants to or has decided to do it—or more generally, just in case the agent has some appropriate propositional attitude towards doing it (e.g. intending it, willing it, having reasons for it). The types of psychological states that will fill the bill here are restricted to a small set. Blushing is the reddening of the face when embarrassed. (Reddening of the face that follows physical exertion or the application of heat is not blushing.) But the fact that to be embarrassed is in response to a psychological state (even perhaps to have a propositional attitude) is not sufficient to make blushing an *action*. Even if we can specify the proper set of psychological attitudes by restricting them either to the class of psychological states that comprise the agent's reasons or to decisions and intentions, and thereby exclude happenings like blushing, we still will be far from solving the First Problem of Action Theory. The first difficulty with this simple answer, as Davidson's ground-breaking arguments in his 'Actions, Reasons, and Causes' have shown, is the fact that merely having the psychological attitude towards the act in question is not sufficient; *the attitude must cause the act*. Pat's breaking the glass is an action only if Pat's decision to break it actually caused what happened. If, immediately after deciding to break the glass, a spasm occurred in Pat's knee, his breaking the glass would certainly *not* be an action. This obvious amendment to the simple answer naturally invites a casual theory of action. It seems that the First Problem of Action Theory is best solved by making reference to the aetiology of the events in question. But now subtler and more difficult problems emerge. Suppose that a fourth scenario was in place. Suppose that Pat thought the basement window was unlatched and intended to push it open with his foot, and then climb and retrieve his keys that he had locked in the house. Since the window was latched, he kicked the window gently, but he broke the glass unintentionally. Now the amended answer gives the wrong judgement. It is false that Pat broke the glass because he wanted to (or intended to) break it. Pat had no reason for breaking it. But in spite of the fact that it was unintentional, his breaking the glass was still an action of his. The reason that Pat's breaking the glass was an action, as opposed to something that happened to him, was just that his kicking the window was an action (he had decided and intended to kick the window), and that action (unexpectedly) caused the glass to break. The internal structure of the scenario is easy to describe. There is something, A, the agent does that is caused by the right kind of psychological state the content of which involved doing A. A brings about some event E. Our amended answer correctly identifies A as an action, but fails to identify the bringing about of E as an action because no psychological state of Pat's had as its content the bringing about of E.[2] So we see that our amended answer gives at best a sufficient but not a necessary condition for something's being an action. To make it necessary we need to relax the requirement that the relation between the proposition that describes the content of the psychological state (e.g. the intention or the decision to do A) and the action of the agent (A) be one of identity, and merely demand that there be 'an appropriate relation' between them, recognizing that identity is just one among

---

[2] At this point we do not need to decide whether 'A' and 'bringing about E' are different descriptions of one and the same action or not. The question will be taken up later.

many such 'appropriate' relations.[3] So the answer to our original question may be revised to read as follows:

> A, something that an agent, S, is said to have done is an action if and only if A is a causal consequence of some psychological state of S's, and the content of this psychological state stands in some *appropriate relation* to A.

For the sake of simplicity, I will take the psychological state in question here to be the agent's decision (or intention) to do the thing that stands in this appropriate relation to A. As I shall argue in Chapter 5, both the decision and the intention to do A are causal consequences of the reasons the agent has for doing A. The problem now is reduced to the problem of specifying the nature of the appropriate relation.

At first glance it might seem that an elegant solution to this problem can be found in Davidson's principle of act individuation. For Davidson, one and the same act can have many descriptions. So Pat's moving his foot, kicking the window, breaking the glass, gaining access to the house are all descriptions of just one action. On this view, one can attempt to cut the Gordian knot by declaring that what an agent does is an action if and only if there is some description of what he does under which it is intentional. So in our fourth scenario, Pat's breaking the glass is an action because there is a description of *that* action, 'his kicking the window', under which the action is intentional. But deciding what counts as a description under which an act is intentional, and which descriptions of what Pat does are descriptions of one and the same thing are not distinct from that of deciding what counts as an appropriate relation.

It has seemed to many philosophers who are inspired by Aristotle's view of practical reasoning that one natural way of solving the problem is to try to specify the relation in question in that context. In its roughest form, practical reasoning is a process of deliberation in which one reasons from targeted ends (the ultimate goals) to the means of achieving them. The means to the ultimate goals, the means to the means, and so on, are strung together until one arrives at a means that is within one's immediate reach, a means that one can bring about 'forthwith'.[4]

---

[3] The term 'appropriate relation' comes from Brand's formulation of the causal theory of action.

[4] I intend to fill out the details of this model of deliberation in Chapters 5 and 6. At this point only this rough outline will be sufficient to make the point I am after.

Using the technical notion of *result* introduced in Chapter 1, we can now specify the *appropriate relation*.[5] Starting with the thing one does forthwith, we can confidently say that there must be an identity relation between *its* description and the propositional content of *some* psychological state. (Whatever else Pat may have decided to do, if he did not decide to kick with his foot just that way, and if his decision to kick that way did not cause his kick, his kick would not be an action of his.) Now the event that is the *result* of what one does *forthwith* (call this *result*, R) will bring about many other events. These may be things that the agent has aimed at, by bringing about R; they may be things that are not among the goals of the agent but are the anticipated side-effects, or consequences, of what he has decided to bring about; or they may be totally unexpected. The cluster of events that spread out from R, like ripples in a pond, are formed by generative relations, such as causal, constitutive (simple), or conventional.[6] Then any member of this cluster of events will be an event the bringing about of which will constitute an action (intentional or non-intentional) of the agent. So the class of actions that are attributable to an agent is not confined only to internal facts about the agent. The class is constituted by objective causal and other generative relations that obtain in the world as well. These relations all trace back to one privileged action of the agent. The privileged action is defined by two features: (i) it is an action that is caused by the intention the agent has formed to perform that action, which intention is a consequence of the agent's reasons for performing it; and (ii) it is an action the agent can do forthwith, that is, it is an action such that the deliberative process involved in practical reasoning does not need to search for a *means* of achieving its *result*.

In other words, the causal theory of action requires a solution to the problem of specifying the *appropriate relation*. And the solution introduces the need to posit a set of privileged acts that are nothing other than the *basic acts* that were discussed in Chapter 1.

---

[5] It will be remembered that an event is the *result* of an action, A, if and only if the sentence that ascribes A to an agent entails that the event occurred; but the assertion that the event occurred, by itself, does not entail that an agent performed an *action*—with the added proviso that the description of the *result* carries all the information about what was done in the action that is carried by the sentence that ascribes the action *minus* the fact that it was the consequence of an action.

[6] If one may speak of a 'makes-it-the-case-that' relation as the genus under which all generative relations are subsumed, then for any member, E, of the cluster of events that are generated by R, it would be true that R made it the case that E happened. See Ch. 3 n. 17.

We can summarize the argument up to this point as follows. Starting with the question, 'What is the criterion of action?', I suggested that a natural answer to the question is to offer a causal theory, according to which, something an agent does is an action only if it is caused by some psychological state that contains the agent's reasons for doing that thing, or if and only if it is caused by a decision or an intention.

But the causal theory will not do the required work until the nature of the relation between the expression that states the content of the intention and the description of the putative action is fully specified. It was shown how requiring this relation to be an identity is too strong. And it was suggested that a solution could be found if some privileged set of acts, the so-called basic acts, was posited. This approach towards solving the First Problem of Action Theory may be expressed by the following rough formula:

> *Causal Definition of Action 1 (CDA1)*
> S's behaviour, B, is an action if and only if:
> (1) (i) B is basic, and
>   (ii) B is caused by S's intention to perform B, *or*
> (2) The *result* of B is generated by the *result* of something, B', that S does, and B' is an action of S's.

This is a first approximation. Before a full answer can be formulated, a number of issues need to be addressed. First, the sense in which B is 'basic' needs to be made precise. Secondly, what makes a basic behaviour an *action* should be explained. Thirdly, the notion of generation needs to be fully explicated. And finally, the causal relations between the contents of the psychological states that comprise the agent's reason for acting (what Davidson calls 'primary reason') and the action must be specified. However, since this first approximation will set the tone of the discussion for the rest of the book, it may be useful to stop here and evaluate the price one would have to pay if one resisted this approach.

Ways of Resisting

First, one may try to reject the causal theory that underlies CDA1. One type of view of action that does not rely on a causal account takes action as an unanalysable simple. Examples can be found in the simple acts of

Ginet, or in Wilson's teleological view (Wilson 1989). In my opinion, this type of view does not go beyond putting a label on a genuine philosophical problem.[7] It is not something that a naturalist about human action can happily endorse.

It seems clear that if we are to be naturalists about action, other alternatives look very unattractive.[8] It is clear that merely saying 'what counts as action is self-evident, and any further analysis of action is unwarranted', will not do. I suppose one can start with the deliberative schema that is implicit in practical reasoning and maintain that everything an agent does in the course of enacting the end-result of practical reasoning is *in accordance with the agent's will*, and, as such, counts as action, and then go on and include those side-effects and consequences, foreseen or unforeseen, of such actions also among the actions of the agent. In this proposal there is no explicit appeal to a causal condition and no mention of a basic action. However, when pressed, the proponent of the proposal would have to admit that things an agent does that are 'in accordance with his will' may sometimes be things that he does, not *because* he wills them, but because he is physically coerced into doing them, or that sometimes what an agent does 'accords with his will' by mere luck. These fortuitous matches between the objects of one's will and one's non-actional doings can only be unmasked by introducing some causal clause into the account.[9] This may in fact be the explanation for why so many action theorists, who may appear to be resisting a causal theory, pack the causal clause into the content of the mental act (or mental state). They require that when one decides (or intends), one decides that (or intends that) one's very decision (or one's very intention) cause one to perform the action.[10] I find the self-referential content of these mental acts theoretically inelegant.[11] But more to the point here, the proposal now becomes isomorphic to the causal theory. For when the match is fortuitous, the behaviour of the agent will be declared not to be an action because the behaviour will have failed to conform to the agent's

---

[7] For a criticism of these views, see Mele 1992*b* or 2000.

[8] Brand, who gives a taxonomy of action theories in a two-by-two matrix, in which one dimension is determined by whether the cause is a mental event or a mental action, and the other by whether the effect is an action or 'mere' behaviour, has no room in his map for an account that does not conform to a causal theory.

[9] This kind of pressure is basically the Davidsonian consideration mentioned above.

[10] Compare Harman 1986*a*: 85–8

[11] See Mele (1992*b*: 197–227), who argues convincingly that we have little reason to accept these self-referential views about the contents of intentions.

decision or intention. It failed to conform to the decision (or the intention) simply because the decision required that the behaviour be *caused by the decision*.

In short, I see no satisfactory way of avoiding a causal element in the formulation of a criterion of action.[12]

A more reasonable and more common way of resisting CDA1 is to reject its allegiance to basic acts. It may be suggested that the foundationalist tenor of CDA1 is unwarranted by the problems it is designed to solve. This suggestion may be accompanied by a proposal for an alternative account that seems to eschew basic acts altogether.

> *Causal Definition of Action 0* (CDA0)
> S's behaviour, B, is an action if and only if:
> (1) B has among its causal antecedents some set of psychological attitudes that comprise the reason S has for doing B, *or*
> (2) The *result* of B is generated by the *result* of something, B', that S does, and B' has among its causal antecedents some psychological state that contains the reason that S has for doing B'.

Going back to our original example of scenario 1, we can say that *breaking the glass* was an action of Pat's because it satisfies clause (1) of CDA0. (Let us assume that his reason for breaking the glass was that he wanted to get in the house and he figured that breaking the glass was the least objectionable way of getting in.) Also his causing himself the cost of later fixing the window, and his waking up the dog were actions of his because they satisfy clause (2) of CDA0: the dog's waking up stands in a generative relation to the breaking of the glass, and Pat wanted to break the glass.

In the same vein, we can see that Pat's *kicking at the window* was an action of his because, again by clause (1) of CDA0, his kick was caused by his decision to break the glass and by his reasoning that it was easier and safer to use his heavy boot than to resort to other alternatives.

The picture that is emerging here is what was alluded to in the brief discussion of practical reasoning. At the planning stage the reasoning

---

[12] It is interesting that action theorists like Melden, who maintain that causes and reasons are mutually exclusive elements in our explanations, and would thus reject causal theories as products of gross conceptual confusion, were never in the business of formulating a criterion of action.

starts with some ultimate objective, and utilizing a sequence of instrumental beliefs, it strings together a course of action: get into the house
—crawl through the basement window, break the glass, kick the
window…And if the beliefs involved are true, the items in the string
get enacted more or less as projected. And if some of the beliefs are
false (as was the case in scenario 4, when Pat thought the window was
not latched and that he could push it open with his foot), the action
takes a course that diverges from the anticipated one. But in either case,
there is at least one thing that the agent does because he has reasons for
doing it and hence intends to do it. Typically, in successfully enacted
scenarios, things that an agent does because he intends to do them
make up a long list. And for each item on such a list, it would be true
that the agent had a reason for doing it and did it *for* that reason. The
existence of such a list is what CDAo exploits.

What is important to notice here is that the string of actions that are
anticipated by practical reasoning in the planning stage has a natural
stopping point. Barring very unusual scenarios, the dots in the example
above are not filled with items like, 'send nerve signals to leg muscles'
or 'activate such and such neurons in the motor cortex'. And what
makes something like 'kick the window' a *natural* stopping point is a
fact about normal human agents. Kicking is something the agent can
readily do; there is nothing that he needs to identify as a means in
figuring out how to kick, in the way he needed to identify kicking as a
means in figuring out how to break the glass, simply because, in some
intuitively graspable sense of the expression, the act of kicking is
'immediately accessible' to him.[13] So I admit that CDAo does not
invoke basic acts, and is extensionally equivalent to CDA1. But when
we look at the underlying pattern that connects an agent's reasons with
his actions, we have to admit there the existence of a set of basic acts. In
other words, it seems possible to solve the First Problem of Action
Theory by formulating a definition of action that makes no explicit

[13] The discussion up to this point is designed to be a *general* argument for the need for a
causal theory of action that requires reference to a set of basic acts. So strictly speaking,
I should ignore the case made against mental acts in Ch. 1, and allow the possibility that
basic acts may be constituted by *acts* of willing or deciding. So if *willing* to kick were where
practical reasoning stops, it would stop there, and not, say, at willing to will to kick, because
willing to kick would be tagged as being 'immediately accessible' to the agent. Hence the
attempt to avoid basic acts would fail here for the same reasons. I have run the argument by
assuming that practical reasoning stops at some bodily act first because that is the way
practical reasoning is traditionally formulated, and second because, as it will become clear
later, this is where I think it does stop.

reference to basic acts. But since such acts are an undeniable reality in the architecture of rational action, a definition of action that acknowledges them would seem to be more informative.

The conclusion to be drawn from all this is that the formulation given in CDA1 should be preferred to that of CDA0 because CDA1 makes reference to two elements that are central to action: (i) a causal element, and (ii) the recognition of a set of privileged acts that are basic in the sense that they provide a natural stopping point in practical reasoning.

But this conclusion is the beginning point of a major project. In looking at the set of the basic acts that CDA1 forces on us, we need to ask, 'what sorts of things are these "basic acts"?' and 'in virtue of which features do these basic acts provide a stopping point in practical reasoning?' And if we recall the arguments of Chapter 1, we might worry that these questions are quite difficult to answer.

It would seem that the defender of basic acts will have to face a dilemma: either endorse the thesis that basic acts are constituted by bodily movements, as proposed by Danto, and suffer the effects of McCann's regress, or place these basic acts in the mind of the agent in the form of volitions or what not, and then be beaten down by the criticism that there are no adequate reasons for thinking that such mental episodes are *actions* that precede every action.

In this chapter I propose to defend a notion of basic acts as overt bodily actions, which is not too far in spirit from Danto's notion. So I need to show that it is possible to develop such a notion that will not be vulnerable to McCann's regress, and also I need to argue that other legitimate complaints about positing bodily basic acts will not apply to the notion developed.

Traditional Views on Basic Acts

Annette Baier in her 1971 essay, 'The Search for Basic Actions', makes an excellent case in support of her scepticism about basic acts. She takes it to be an implicit assumption of most proponents of basic acts (*a*) that whenever there is any action, there is a basic action, and (*b*) that basic acts are all bodily movements. She also supposes that there is a clear intuitive sense of 'basic' to which we can appeal in most situations in deciding which act is the basic one. This sense is coincident with what we see ourselves as doing immediately, readily, forthwith. And she uses this intuitively graspable sense to test general formulas that are offered as defining basic acts. Baier's targets are two formulations of basic acts: Danto's and Chisholm's. Using examples that appeal to our intuitive sense of 'basic', she argues, convincingly to my mind, that neither of these formulations deals with the examples adequately.

As will be recalled from Chapter 1, Danto's formula was as follows:

> S's act A is basic if there is no action of S's the *result* of which causes the *result* of A.[14]

Baier (1971: 166) gives an example designed to show that this formula is inadequate. She describes a physiologist 'who knows that when he straightens his fingers, his arm muscles tense, and a lot of other things happen, including the firing of neurons$_{1-n}$ in his brain. He is then able to perform the task of firing neurons$_{1-n}$ by straightening his fingers.' When the physiologist straightens his fingers with the intention of firing those neurons, a sequence of causally related events occurs. The intuitions guide us to the act of straightening the fingers as the basic act, but the causal definition of basicness forces us to regard the agent's firing his neurons as the basic act because that neural event is distinct from, and is the cause of, the event in which the fingers are straightened. So the agent's action of bringing about the neural event has a *result* which is the cause of the *result* of his action of straightening his fingers.

This type of example emphasizes the teleological underpinnings of whatever intuitions we may have about basic acts. And indeed these teleological factors are lodged firmly in expressions like 'doing B *in order to* do A' or 'doing A *by* doing B' that are traditionally used to test to see whether an act is a basic act or not.

---

[14] It is interesting that in an earlier version Danto (1965) had asserted, as he himself puts it, 'due to a certain infelicity of formulation and a corresponding insufficiency of understanding' that a necessary condition for something to be a basic act was that it (the *act*, rather than the *result*) have no causes. The error in this can be seen by noticing that the usual way in which an agent causes the gun to fire is one where the *action* of moving the finger causes the *event* of the gun's going off; *not* one where the action of moving the finger causes the *action* of firing the gun. For the latter to occur a more Byzantine scenario is required: the agent moves her finger (say, of her left hand), which generates in her an overwhelming desire to fire the gun, which desire she then proceeds to satisfy by pulling the trigger (say, by moving forefinger of the right hand). In this scenario the agent performs *two* distinct acts, the first of which is the cause of the second; whereas in the usual setup, only one action exists which has different properties (or, as Danto would have it, different components). The literature is full of essays in which Danto is taken to task on this issue. (See e.g. Margolis 1970; Brand 1968; Baier 1971.)

In this respect, Chisholm's characterization comes closer to capturing the intuitions. He says, ' "A is performed by the agent as a basic act" could be defined as: the agent succeeds in making A happen in the way in which he intended, and there is no B, other than A, which he undertook *for the purpose of* making A happen' (1966: 39). Chisholm's definition of 'undertaking B for the purpose of A' is roughly that the agent undertakes to do B *and* to make this undertaking itself cause A (1966: 36). Leaving aside the self-referential apparatus that is packed into the notion of undertaking, we can see that the purposive element in Chisholm's definition gives the right answer in cases like that of Baier's physiologist: the physiologist succeeds in making his fingers move in the way he intended, and there is nothing that he undertakes for the purpose of making his fingers move (certainly his firing his neurons is not something he *undertakes* for this purpose). This definition also focuses on two features that I think are essential to the intuitive sense of basicness that is at issue: the intention with which the act was performed, and the means–end relations built into the planning of the act by the agent.[15]

The element of teleology in Chisholm's formulation is better suited to define a class of privileged actions. The account I will offer below is closer in spirit to Chisholm's than to Danto's. However, when the commitment to the thesis that basic acts be constituted by simple bodily motions is added to Chisholm's account, it becomes vulnerable to a different type of counter-example. These examples involve actions of some complexity. It is assumed that the agent has acquired the capacity to perform them as a whole unit, without being aware of the bodily movements that comprise the whole act. Examples are the man who knots his own tie (Brand 1968: 188), 'the gestalt lace-tier, who can successfully tie his laces, but could not show you the movements by which he did so except by actually retying the laces', 'the smiling savage who has never seen his face mirrored and so does not know exactly what his face does when he smiles', or the analytic adolescent who has perfected a world-weary wave of the hand as a greeting by studying each component of his arm movement carefully (all three from Baier 1971: 166). In each of these cases, the teleological

---

[15] In Chisholm's definition of a basic act there is an explicit requirement that the act that is to be basic be *intended*. As we saw in Ch. 1, this requirement has the net effect of disqualifying basic acts from helping us formulate a general criterion that separates actions from mere doings. Since this task was not part of Chisholm's goal, the point is not a criticism of Chisholm's formula.

formula identifies the complex act as the basic action involved. But this is regarded as a violation of the assumption that basic acts are always 'mere bodily movements'.

The force of these examples is clear: we must either abandon the idea that definitions of basic acts are going to conform to our intuitive understanding of basic as that which is immediate, that which we can do forthwith, *or* reject the assumption that basic acts are mere bodily movements. Here, it seems, the choice is easy. I argued above that the pattern of practical reasoning presupposes that there are certain things we *can do readily*. In other words, pressures from the theory of rational deliberation force on us a class of actions to perform, and these actions are such that we do not need to figure out the means for performing them; we can perform 'forthwith'. This class roughly conforms to the intuition that guides Baier's counter-examples against Danto and Chisholm. So the natural move here ought to be to reject the assumption that basic acts must be mere bodily movements, and to take the intuition seriously.

Indeed the move is so natural that one wonders why the friends of basic acts have embraced this implausible assumption so fondly. My conjecture is that the assumption was mistakenly believed (and is still believed in some quarters) to secure the autonomy of psychology, to legitimize psychology as a science. Developing this conjecture will take the discussion of this chapter too far off on a tangent. But briefly the idea is as follows. If psychological states, like beliefs and desires, are to be functionally defined, then part of their identity conditions will be constituted by the types of actions they cause. But if some of the things they directly cause are actions 'broadly construed', like waving hello, then they cannot be defined in terms of mere bodily *actions*, which, coupled with conventions, norms, or causal connections among events, constitute these broad actions. This in turn would mean that the identity of psychological states will violate the autonomy of psychology, sometimes referred to as the principle of methodological solipsism, that is, the identity conditions for the concepts used in psychology will then be partly derived from social norms or conventions or laws of physics. The only way to avoid this is to insist that basic acts must be publicly observable bodily movements. Kim gives expression to this worry in the following passage. (The example he refers to in the passage is one in which he wants to turn on the stove to start cooking his dinner.)

It is true that whether or not my action succeeds in bringing about the intended result normally depends on whether the belief involved is true. Thus, whether my action results in the burner being turned on depends on whether my belief that it would go on if the knob is turned is correct. However, it is not part of the object of *psychological* explanation to explain why the burner went on; all it needs to explain is why I turned the knob. It might be objected that not only did I perform the action of turning the knob but I also performed that of *turning on the burner*, and that this latter action does involve—it logically entails—the burner's going on. That is correct; however, the action of turning on the burner, insofar as this is thought to involve the burner's going on, is not an action that is the proper business of psychological theory to explain or predict. The job of psychological explanation is done once it has explained the bodily action of turning the knob; whether or not this action results in my also turning on the stove, my starting cooking dinner, my starting a house fire, and so on is dependent on events and facts quite outside the province of psychology, and are not the proper concern of psychological theory. Only *basic actions*, not 'derivative' or 'generated' actions, need to be explained by psychological theory.[16] (Kim 1982: 62)

I propose to argue that this worry, which, I assume, can be traced back to the tenets of behaviourism, is unwarranted. I hope to show that both evidence from ethology and evidence from operant conditioning support the view that the study of animal behaviour must recognize certain 'broad' behaviours as their proper explananda. I will then suggest that the view is equally valid in cognitive psychology and action theory.

First Definition of Basic Acts

When we look at the pattern of practical reasoning, which, I have been urging, is the real source for the need to introduce basic acts, we see that the series of means–end linkages that are laid out in practical reasoning must end with an act to which the agent has immediate access. Exploiting this notion of immediate access, I propose to define basic acts in terms of knowing how to do something. The deliberative process involved in practical reasoning generates a string of instrumental beliefs of the kind, 'If I do B, then I will have succeeded in doing A'.

---

[16] I assume that identifying *turning the knob*, as opposed to *moving one's wrist*, as the basic action is merely an oversight on Kim's part.

The string terminates as soon as the value of B involves something the agent knows how to do without having to resort to yet another instrumental (conditional) belief. For example, if Sam's set goal is to whisk the egg whites to a soft peak, Sam may very well know how to do this without resorting to a mental manual that describes how to achieve this goal. Once the act is started, Sam's expert hands start moving, the left rotating the bowl slowly, and the right holding the whisk moving in a downward circular motion. Sam may now release her conscious control of her hand movements. I intend the way Sam, in whipping the egg whites in this scenario, uses her knowledge of how to whip the egg whites *without* using her knowledge of how to move her hands to be the defining feature of basic acts. It is worth remarking that in each case in which our intuitions urge identifying some token action as a basic act, the agent performs that act using her knowledge of how to do it, and even if this knowledge of hers is constituted by her knowing that in order to perform that act, she will need to do a series of other things each of which she knows how to do, in the token performance of the act in question, she does not utilize any of this latter knowledge.

Some examples may make this point clearer. When Baier's analytical adolescent waves his hand, he knows exactly which arm and wrist motions go into the wave. After the wave has been mastered by him, when at some moment he decides to issue the greeting, he does not consciously consult a mental manual and follow its instructions as to which movements to produce in which sequence; he knows how to wave 'directly'. Similarly, when I raise my arm, whether I know which muscles will contract, whether I know that nerves will be carrying signals from my brain to those muscles, and so on, is irrelevant to my ability to raise my arm. When I decide to raise my arm, I raise it without having to consider how exactly I should go about doing it, and without having to use any knowledge I may have about the physiology of arm raisings. In contrast, when an actor has to shed tears at a certain point in the play, he knows that bringing his handkerchief that was carefully soaked in onion juice to his face will achieve this result. He may use this knowledge in order to make it look like he is weeping. Here, the actor's making himself shed tears is not a basic act of his. Also, when someone genuinely weeps, this is not a basic act because typically one does not know how to obey the command 'Weep!'—except by doing something else first.

When we think of basic acts from such a perspective, we have to realize that each person has slightly different capacities; some of us can wiggle our ears, others do not know how to, some of us can sing a tune, others cannot, etc. In addition, there are times when a person may do something 'immediately', without using her knowledge of how to do something else that will generate that thing, and yet at other times, the same person may deliberately attend to each component of that thing and perform the components one by one with the knowledge that the components will collectively generate the act. For example, an accomplished pianist may play a whole musical phrase on the piano without attending to the finger movements that go into the production of that tune, and yet when she is teaching a novice pupil, she may move each finger intentionally, thereby producing the complete phrase. So if we are going to look for a definition of basic acts, the definition can at best give us *token* basic acts. It is true that each person will have a repertoire of basic acts. And this repertoire will change through time: we all acquire new capacities, and eventually end up losing some of them through disuse or through old age. But what will determine that some act is basic in the circumstances in which it was produced as a *token* is the fact that the agent did not use her knowledge of how to do something else *in order to* produce that token.

These considerations suggest that it may be possible to define the notion of a basic act token in terms of the twin concepts of knowing how to do something and using one's know-how in order to do something:

First Definition of Basic Action
The token act of S's doing B is basic if and only if
   (i) S knows how to do B,
  (ii) In the token act of doing B, S uses her knowledge of how to do B, and
 (iii) There is no action A of S's such that
      (a) S knows how to do A, and
      (b) in order to do B, S needs to use her knowledge of how to do A.

I think the definition adequately captures the intuition I have been trying to develop concerning basic acts. However, the definiens may be no more informative than the intuition itself, that is, it may be just as easy to judge directly whether an act is basic or not using Baier-type intuitions as to decide whether clause (iii) of the definition is satisfied.

I propose to approach the concept of basic acts from a different perspective, with the aim of providing a naturalistic gloss to the notion of *using one's knowledge of how to do something*. The plan I shall pursue will appeal to certain facts about animal behaviour. These facts will serve as a model for the basic acts that initiate rational actions. To set up this model it will be argued that the smallest units relevant to the explanation of the goal-directed behaviour of simple animals are coarse-grained—they are not properly described in terms of mere limb trajectories. The model then will serve as an analogy for how certain intentional states of rational agents control macro outputs, such as a smile, the tying of a knot, the playing of a tune on the piano, or running fast, rather than particular sequences of muscle or limb movements.

In order to set up the analogy, I will take a lengthy digression to discuss two considerations, each of which provides independent evidence for the existence of hierarchically ordered systems and subsystems that control the behaviour of organisms.[17] The picture that will emerge from this digression will be one in which organisms have command centres that trigger coarse-grained behavioural outputs, whereupon certain subsystems take over and determine the specific limb trajectories that will be executed in the course of realizing these coarse-grained outputs.[18]

UNITS OF BEHAVIOUR

Hard-Wired Behaviour

Simple organisms are capable of achieving their long-term goals, like feeding or mating, in virtue of possessing certain built-in subsystems. When the conditions are right, these subsystems kick in and execute their function. For example, avoiding predation by bats is one of the standing goals of the moth, and it achieves this goal partly due to the activities of its auditory system, the function of which is to detect

---

[17] The reader who chooses not to attend to the details of animal behaviour may skip the next section without significant loss of continuity.

[18] A more detailed discussion can be found in Enç (1995). Also see Peressini (1997) who puts these considerations to good effect in his discussion of explanation of behavior.

the high-pitched sounds of the sonar systems of the bats. These organisms may pursue a multitude of specific goals, and each of these goals may have sets of behaviours exclusively reserved to help the organism achieve that particular goal—the quick diving behaviour of the moth when it detects the tell-tale high-pitched sound is one example. But there may also exist items in the organism's behavioural repertoire that may be recruited to subserve different goals at different times, for example, the walking behaviour of the cockroach, or the ciliary motion of the protozoan. So when I speak of the behaviour of an organism, I will be typically referring to the specific tokening of a behavioural type, and that token will be expected to be directed at some goal (or be the causal consequence of some behaviour that *is* directed at some goal).

Scientists who have studied movements of relatively simple animals have come up with fascinating accounts of the mechanisms that are responsible for the production of these movements. One striking fact is that each piece of goal-directed behaviour, like the dive of the moth, the walk of the cockroach, or the song of the cricket, contains an immense amount of variation in its execution. The output behaviour is elicited by an environmental input registered in the organism. The input activates some 'command' signal. However, the specific movements that constitute a token output are controlled by subsystems whose internal workings are impenetrable to (are incapable of receiving signals from) the centres that register the input and issue the command to execute the behaviour. One way of describing this division of labour is to say that the behaviours in question have considerable plasticity and that how the token of some behaviour is to be crafted, the decision as to which specific limb movements are to be produced, is left to lower subsystems, which, like servo-mechanisms, adjust to variations in the environment that are transmitted to these subsystems directly.

Just a few examples will have to suffice to illustrate the point here.[19] The way the cricket's song is structured is perhaps the clearest case of a unit being triggered endogenously:

The wings are under the control of a set of muscles under the thorax of the cricket. These muscles have connections to a network of nerve cells in the thoracic ganglion. Signals from some cells in the thoracic ganglion activate

---

[19] For a wealth of additional examples, see Gallistel 1980.

motor neurons, which in turn cause the wing muscles to contract in ways that result in a song. The trick is to get the motor neurons to fire as an integrated unit (because many muscle fibers are involved) with the appropriate timing pattern. This can be achieved by a single cell that runs from the brain in the head of the cricket to the thoracic ganglion. A neuro-anatomist can find the *command interneuron* in its characteristic location in male cricket after male cricket. If a stimulating electrode is attached to a command interneuron, and the cell is stimulated by a weak electric current from the electrode, it produces a train of impulses with the correct timing. These signals reach neurons in the thoracic ganglion causing them to relay the right temporal pattern of orders to the wing muscles. The result is a perfect calling song, even in a brainless cricket. Presumably, in an intact cricket sitting by its burrow, cells in the brain integrate information about such things as the time of day and weather conditions. If the setting is correct, the brain cells fire...
(Alcock 1979: 37–8)

There is some similarity between these units of behaviour, which are called 'motor programmes' or 'fixed action patterns' by ethologists, and (involuntary) reflexes: (i) when these units are triggered, just like reflexes, they are triggered as a whole package, (ii) they both incorporate circuits that allow a specific type of input to generate a co-ordinated set of neuron firings that controls a muscle or a group of muscles, and (iii) they both contain a degree of plasticity in their production (or variation among their tokens).[20] However, differences are significant. For one thing, reflexes have external stimuli as their immediate causes, whereas the motor programmes are internally triggered by higher centres of the central nervous system. For example, the immediate cause of the song of the cricket is the output from the brain to the command interneuron. The second difference is that the degree of plasticity involved in a motor programme is of a higher order of magnitude than that of the reflexes. Gallistel (1981: 612) expresses this very well:

A cockroach's walking straight ahead may seem a simple and unitary act, but the close observer of cockroaches will note that they have a great many

---

[20] For example, the wiping reflex of the hind leg of the frog can apparently be triggered by applying a stimulus on the shoulder of the frog. The plots of the motion of the hind leg show a spectrum of trajectories. The variation from one complete wipe to another seems to be built into the circuitry and is not correlated with any external stimulus. In fact, neuro-ethologists conjecture that, even when external conditions do not vary, the system's ability to generate a set of solutions for one and the same motor task may have been selected for because it provides the organism with a more effective strategy against unpredictable perturbations (Birkinblitt et al. 1986).

different ways of doing it. There are so many different leg-stepping patterns that it is only a slight exaggeration to say that the cockroach never walks in exactly the same way twice in its life. By 'exactly the same way' I mean an exact duplication of the timing and magnitude of contraction and relaxation in every one of the many muscles involved, over several complete stepping cycles.

These motor programmes act as *units*, so that the higher centres of the animal have no access to the *components* of these units. This feature is best revealed by Weiss's experiments on salamanders (1941). Weiss exchanged the right and left forelimbs of larval salamanders. When the limbs were re-innervated by regenerating nerves, the limbs resumed function. But since the adductor and abductor muscles, as well as the extensor and flexor muscles had traded places, the sequence of nerve signals which would normally produce forward locomotion, now ended up producing backward locomotion. So a hungry salamander, when shown food, ended up running away from it.[21]

Some of these motor programmes, like those of the salamander or the cockroach, come prewired; some develop upon maturation, but others are learnt during the lifetime of the individual organism. The last category is the least well-known. But ethologists are fond of speculating. For example, Gould (1982: 176) says,

Who thinks about which muscles to move when during walking, running, or crawling? It is as though these coordinated muscle patterns have become 'hardwired', incorporated into the brain just as firmly as any wholly innate motor program....And it seems clear that even motor tasks learned without any apparent innate guidance also become hardwired with time and practice: most of us can, after the months of arduous learning as children, tie our shoes with our eyes closed.

Behaviour in Skinnerian Learning

A second reason for accepting the distinction between macro-units of behaviour controlled by higher centres and micro limb trajectories controlled by subsystems is to be found in the structure of operant and reflex conditioning. In the Skinnerian learning paradigm, it is

---

[21] Although many of the motor programmes are *unmonitorable* by the higher centres, I do not intend their total impenetrability to be a necessary condition for these units of behaviour. Just *the fact* that they are unmonitored (or the fact that they need not be monitored) *in the context* is sufficient for the purpose.

maintained that the probability of the production of a piece of behaviour of an animal can be altered by creating a correlation between the production of that piece of behaviour and an event that affects the animal in some way. When the probability is changed in this way, the behaviour is said to become an *operant*. For example, the key pecking behaviour of a pigeon becomes an operant when the behaviour is reinforced by food pellets when a light is on.

An operant, as Skinner defines it, is a class of responses which 'operates on the environment [of the organism] to generate consequences [for the organism]. The consequences define the properties with respect to which responses are called similar' (1965: 65). The general idea is simply that an organism's behaviour is shaped, and frequencies in operants are determined, *because* the behaviour causes certain changes in the environment of the organism and these changes affect the organism in certain ways. Or to express the same idea, an input to the organism (a stimulus) elicits a response from the organism *because* in the past that type of response, when the same type of stimulus was present, has had certain consequences for the organism.

The force of these 'because's is clearly causal. (In saying this, I am departing from the letter of Skinnerian behaviourism.) What we are here requiring is that a correlational fact (the correlation between key pecking under the stimulus conditions and food) become part of the cause of the key pecking behaviour. When such a causal structure gets established, then the mere chance muscular movements that were occurring in the neck of the pigeon prior to the conditioning cease to be *chance* movements; These very movements are transformed from 'pointless motion' into 'behaviour *for* some result'. The difference between 'pointless' motion and behaviour *for* some result is not a difference in the type of *motion*; it is rather a difference in the causal ancestry of a type of motion. That is, whether a pigeon has pecked a key (so as to get food) or just moved its neck in a random way and accidentally happened to hit the key with its beak depends on whether its neck movement was caused by some correlation between key pecking and food or not.

We can now ask an important question. What exactly is the pigeon conditioned to do? What *is* the behaviour that we just said was behaviour *for* some result? Is it moving the neck muscles in a specific way when the visual signals indicating the presence of a key-like object are received and processed? Is it pecking the key? Is it getting the key depressed? Is there a unique correct answer? When we try to answer these questions in the context of operant conditioning, a problem emerges. To see this let us go back to our original observation about the causal structure involved in operant conditioning:

> S: In operant conditioning, the fact that responses of a certain kind have in the past been correlated with certain consequences to the organism causes an increase in the probability of that kind of response.

In the context of Skinner's theory, this is close to a definitional truth. But the uncertainty about the precise nature of the behaviour involved raises in one's mind the possibility that the first occurrence of the word 'response' in this claim need not refer to the same type of behaviour as the second occurrence of that word.[22]

In order to set up the problem clearly, we first need to ask, 'what exactly is the mechanism that results in an increase in the probability of key pecking under stimulus conditions?' In spite of Skinner's abhorrence of causes, as I suggested above, it is hard to make sense of changes in probabilities unless something causes these changes. And I think the kind of causal story that is probably involved here is not a very unusual one. What we want is the past correlation between key peckings and food to become a causal factor in the causal link between the light flash and the pigeon's pecking the key. The process may be pictured in the following way. Before the conditioning, the light flash is not part of the cause of the pigeon's pecking the key. After the conditioning, the light has become the cause of the pigeon's pecking the key. What causes the light to be the cause of this behaviour is just that past instances of this behaviour have had certain desirable consequences to the pigeon. So the past correlation between key pecking and food is a second order cause; it is that which causes the light to elicit (cause) a key-pecking behaviour. The second order causation need not be anything mysterious; it may indeed be reducible to the establishment of a particular state in the pigeon. After all, the fact that peckings have been correlated with food in the past may have induced some internal neuro-chemical state in the pigeon. And it may be the presence of this state that makes it possible (i.e. becomes a causal condition)

---

[22] In a seminal essay, A. C. Purton (1978: 655–6) says, 'the great defect of behaviourist psychology lies in its lack of attention to the task of classifying and making less ambiguous the use of the term "behaviour"'.

for this flash now to cause this pecking. (Such a picture is developed in some detail by Dretske (1988) in his discussion of structuring causes.)

If this is the correct causal picture behind Skinnerian conditioning, the puzzle about the reference of the word 'response' in (S), above, may be stated more clearly now. Let us grant that the pigeon can peck that key in any one of a vast number of ways, that is, let us grant that there is a vast number of sequences of muscular movements each of which is within the pigeon's repertoire and each of which will trigger the mechanism that sends the food down the chute. Now consider this neuro-chemical state of the pigeon that was said to have been caused by the past correlation. A correlation between *what* and food is the cause here? Suppose the pigeon randomly produced 1,000 sequences of muscular movements, a dozen of which got the key depressed. If the correlation is between each of these dozen movements and food, then we cannot expect the pigeon to peck the key in any way *other* than one of those twelve sequences. But it is a physiological fact that pigeons do produce *different* (new) sequences of muscular movements that get the key depressed *after* the conditioning. So what the pigeons learn is to do something that gets the key depressed. We may not know yet what the correct description of that thing is, but we do know that what they learn is *not* to exactly reproduce one of the dozen sequences that were used during the conditioning. So when the light flashes and the pigeon pecks the key with a *new* sequence of muscular movements, how did each of those dozen sequences of muscular movements being followed by food increase the probability of this thirteenth *different* movement to be elicited by a light flash? I suggest that the only satisfactory answer will have to come from assuming that the units of behaviour that are relevant to the explanation in operant learning are macro-behaviours, somewhat analogous to the motor programmes of simple organisms. This assumption, already supported by evidence reviewed in connection with motor programmes, is tantamount to recognizing that organisms have what we might call a basic behaviour repertoire that consists of packaged 'large' units of behaviour, which cannot be identified with any of the various limb trajectories that may implement them. Which trajectory gets to realize such a unit is not controlled by the centres that control such units.

When one identifies operants with the 'large' units of behaviour that the assumption invokes, the puzzle about the 'new behaviour' that gets elicited in operant conditioning dissolves. All we need to do is move away from a picture where the centres that are involved in learning by operant conditioning are assumed to record and remember which specific muscle movements are correlated with the reinforcers. Instead, we adopt a picture where we view these centres as representing and controlling larger units of behaviour (perhaps *pecking* in our example). We recognize that correlations are represented as holding between, say, food and the production of these larger units of behaviour. Once we acknowledge that the features in virtue of which the muscular movement sequences are classifiable as *different* outputs are features that are not accessible to the centres involved in operant conditioning—that such differences arise from the role played by reflex circuits or servo-mechanistic devices that under the conditions are not monitored by these centres—we see how the organism was literally and truly being reinforced to do *one and the same thing* each time it produced one of these 'different' sets of muscular movements.[23]

A similar conclusion forces itself in some experiments involving reflex conditioning. A phenomenon that is sometimes called 'response generalization' is again best understood in terms of the picture where the units of behaviour that are picked for conditioning are the 'large' units that cannot be identified with limb trajectories.

One of the most fascinating cases of response generalization is reported by Wickens (1938). In this experiment a number of subjects had their arm trapped to a board with the palm downward. The subject's middle finger rested on an electrode capable of delivering mildly painful shocks. Wickens conditioned an involuntary finger withdrawal response to a buzzer by giving several trials in which the buzzer preceded a shock to the finger. The response was involuntary in the sense that subjects could not inhibit the conditioned response when instructed to do so.

---

[23] Needless to say, this is not the only way operants are shaped. There is a second scenario, which requires the subjects in Skinnerian learning to 'project', 'generalize', and compute which of the many *different behaviours* that are available to them will yield the distal goal. For example, organisms, like mice, can be conditioned to learn tasks (like getting to the cheese at the end of a maze) which may require them to recruit any one of several such programmes (e.g. running, crawling when their legs are amputated, swimming when the maze is flooded). The point about the basic behaviour repertoire of organisms is rather that, as a matter of fact, operant conditioning rarely, if ever, works by reinforcing the organism to produce one specific set of muscular movements, because there is little evidence to think that specific muscular movement sequences are commonly under the control of the higher computational centres when learning by operant conditioning is in progress.

Here the same question that was asked about the pigeon's key pecking response may be repeated: what is the response that is conditioned? Is it, for example, withdrawal from the surface? Or is it an excitation of the extensor muscles accompanied by an inhibition of the flexor muscles? The fact that there is a correct answer to these questions is revealed by the next stage of Wickens's experiment. When the involuntary response was thoroughly conditioned, Wickens unstrapped the subject's arm and then strapped it back onto the board again. Only now, the arm was turned over. The palm faced upward and the *back* of the middle finger rested on the electrode. Under these circumstances, the two descriptions of the subject's conditioned response—'withdrawal' versus 'extensor excitation and flexor inhibition'—make opposite predictions about what will happen the next time the buzzer sounds.

In fact most (all except for one) of Wickens's subjects made a rapid withdrawal response the next time the buzzer sounded. In other words, the buzzer triggered extensor *inhibition* and flexor *excitation*. The nervous systems of the majority of the subjects somehow seemed to know what to generate in order to withdraw the finger from the table.

It seems as if the reflex circuit is wired to move the finger *away from the surface* that normally produces the unconditioned stimulus. *That*, as far as the reflex response to an electric shock is concerned, is the 'smallest' unit of behaviour that the body is producing; individual subcomponents of that unit, that is, individual muscle movements, are not independently accessible in the circumstances of this conditioning process.

Explanatory and Causal Relations

Each of the two considerations above, the units that are involved in motor programmes, and the units that are targeted in learning by conditioning, suggest the need to distinguish between the behaviour that is directed at the goal of the organism and the specific limb movements that are produced in the course of playing out that behaviour in some specific instance. The issue here is partly an explanatory one. When we want to explain how the cricket attracts its mate, the explanatorily relevant bit of behaviour is its producing the species-specific chirp, not its moving its wing muscles in the specific way it does at a given time. The reason seems to lie in a principle of explanation that Putnam made famous by requiring that explanations be invariant under perturbations in parameters that are irrelevant to the explanandum. In his example of a peg-board, Putnam rightly pointed out that the question why a peg goes through one hole and not through another is answered better by describing the respective geometries of the pegs and the holes than by writing the wave-mechanical equations of the peg-plus-board system. A different peg, or a different board, with the same geometric properties, would most likely require a different quantum mechanical explanans. And this fact speaks in favour of the geometric explanation.

This point, however, is only an epistemic one and does not speak to the causal (ontological) concerns.[24] However, when we turn to the contrast between the goal-directed behaviour of animals and their specific limb trajectories that constitute a token of such behaviour, it may be argued that certain causal facts form the basis of this contrast. When the cockroach issues the command 'walk', the lower servo-mechanistic centres take over and continue to carry out the task until a new command is received, determining in which sequence the legs are to be activated, adjusting for the terrain, balancing the force with which the legs are to be moved, while the command-issuing centres 'turn their back' on the task and 'attend' to other matters, like obstacles looming in the way, scents detected in some direction, and so on.

Stripping the narrative of its anthropomorphic imagery, we are still left with a distinction that is best expressed in intensional vocabulary. And this is as it should be because descriptions of goal-directed (or purposive) activity invariably involve intensional contexts. The distinction can be stated as follows. (i) The token walking of the cockroach is its goal-directed behaviour (suppose that in a given instance it is directed at food gathering). (ii) That token walking is identical with the multitude of sequences of specific leg movements following specific trajectories (because the type, walking, is supervenient on a set of limb movements). But it does not follow from (i) and (ii) that the *specific* sequence of leg movements that comprise the cockroach's walk at a given time is directed at the goal of food gathering. Indeed, I would venture the suggestion that it is *not* directed at food gathering—it is

---

[24] The fact that Putnam's claim rests only on an epistemic distinction has been rehearsed in various forms by philosophers writing on the causal role of supervenient properties. It is said that although supervenient properties may yield better explanations than those given in terms of their base properties, when it comes to causal questions, it is clear that they have no causal role to play over and above that played by their bases.

rather directed at, say, negotiating the irregular surface of the terrain. My suggestion is based on the fact that the causal antecedents of the walk are located in different systems with different functions. The causes that trigger the walk are events that occur in a system the function of which is to determine, given the environmental and internal signals the system receives, what goal to set. This system has the resources to specify the behaviour that is directed at the goal it has set: to walk, as opposed to run, to walk in one direction, as opposed to another, etc.; but it does not have the capability to select the individual limb trajectories that are to realize the behaviour so specified. In contrast, the causes of each member of the particular sequence of leg trajectories are located in a different system, the function of which has nothing to do with the selection of the goal of the behaviour. The function of this latter system includes that of responding to the inputs from the features of the terrain. It is as if the goal-directed system commands a package behaviour, the way one orders a packed lunch from a hotel for a day's hike, being confident that what goes into the package will be selected by competent personnel.

A mechanistic example for the distinction may be found in the operation of some cordless phones. When the talk button in the handset is pressed, a randomizer selects one among many preassigned channels of a given set (each defined by a different frequency band), and the handset starts transmitting on that channel. The base phone then activates one by one each and every one of the channels in the given set until a 'handshake' between the base and the handset is established. In this example, pressing the talk button causes the establishment of a connection between the handset and the base, but it does not cause any one particular channel to be selected as opposed to another. Furthermore, even though establishing communication is token-identical with selecting one out of the many available, the function of selecting the particular channel that gets selected is not the same as the function of establishing the communication between the handset and the base.[25]

The Basic Behaviour Repertoire

If my suggestion has any merit, it immediately yields a corollary. When we ask, 'what is the first, most basic, goal-directed behaviour

[25] I owe this example to Ellery Eells.

of the cockroach?' the correct answer will have to lie in the proper description of the 'package' that is triggered by the causes located in the system, the function of which is to set goals and to select the means for reaching those goals. In this way, the *basic* behaviour of the cockroach will be *walking*, and not, for example, the sequence in which its muscles are contracted and relaxed.[26]

The thesis involved in this corollary will be central to my claims about basic acts later on. So I will label it the 'Thesis of the Basic Behaviour Repertoire of Organisms'. Using the analogy of the motor programmes of simple organisms, this thesis may be characterized in the following way.

> *The Thesis of the Basic Behaviour Repertoire of Organisms (TBBR)*
>
> The Basic Behaviour Repertoire of organisms consists of macro-units of (types of) bodily outputs such that:
> (i) the higher centres of the organism have the capacity to directly trigger these units, and
> (ii) these higher centres have no causal access to the inherent plasticity that these units possess.[27]

THE ANATOMY OF BEHAVIOUR

This long narrative that led to the Thesis of the Basic Behaviour Repertoire of Organisms was designed to give substance to the notion of needing one's knowledge of how to do something. I can summarize the result of the preceding pages by characterizing behaviour in the following way.

The basic behaviour repertoire of an organism consists of the set of units of behaviour that can be elicited by an event occurring higher up in the central nervous system of the organism. The event in question is typically one that is directed at subserving some goal of the organism and occurs in response to some information from the environment or some change in the inner states of the organism. The units of behav-

---

[26] The proper description of this behaviour is to be discovered by empirical investigation into the construction of the systems and the subsystems in question. It is quite probable that our pre-theoretic categories of walking and running will turn out to be ill suited for the cockroach.

[27] In an earlier essay (Enç 1995), inspired by the terminology of chemistry, I called these units 'molar units of behavior'.

iour in the set possess a high degree of plasticity (or mere variability) that is unmonitored by the centres in which the triggering event takes place.[28] I should emphasize here the fact that the behaviour types that make up the basic behaviour repertoire of an organism are not ontologically a different category from that of events. Behaviours are not primitive versions of the unanalysable, *sui generis*, acts of agency that were criticized in Chapter 1. Indeed, *behaviour* is to be given a *causal* account. Suppose we take the simplified schema to represent the causally linked set of events involved in a piece of basic behaviour (Figure 2.1). In this picture, the compartment labelled 'Command Centre' integrates the information provided by EI and IS, picks a goal, determines the BO directed at the goal, and in consequence of this computation, the event labelled 'C' occurs, which, in turn, initiates the subprogramme that is executed by the Subsystem.

Members of the basic behaviour repertoire, then, are the bodily outputs that are caused by a C. And the bodily outputs are the 'large' units that cannot be reduced to a specific set of neuron firings, muscle movements, or limb trajectories. To be precise, I should say that behaviour is some event—in the schematic representation of Figure 2.1, the bodily output labelled 'BO'—that has a specific type of causal ancestry. So in this precise way of talking, to say that behaviour is caused by some event in the higher centres of the organism is to utter a tautology. Strictly speaking, one should say, behaviour is some *event*, identified as *bodily output* with a certain type of cause. However, I will

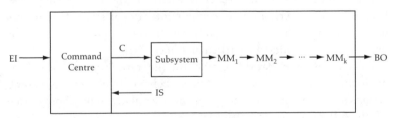

Fig. 2.1. *Anatomy of behaviour* (EI: environmental input; IS; input from the inner states of the system; BO: bodily output; MM: specific muscular movements)

---

[28] This characterization of the basic behaviour repertoire allows for reflex behaviours like salivating upon sight of food, or pulling the hand away upon touching a hot surface, to be members of the basic behaviour repertoire. This will not be of any significance in our discussion of actions.

often ignore this refinement and conform to the general way causal theories of action are formulated in the literature—except in those rare occasions where precision is called for.[29] A definition of *token* basic behaviour readily follows:

> Definition of Token Basic Behaviour (DB):
> B is a token behaviour of organism O, if and only if:
> B is a member of the basic behaviour repertoire of O, and it is endogenously triggered in the way it normally is (as opposed to being externally manipulated by some other agent).

ACTIONS

Difficulties with the First Definition of Action

Having given a naturalistic gloss to behavior in general, what theoretical need remains for *actions*? Is there a *real* distinction to be drawn between mere *behaviour* and *action*? The answer one gives is bound to be linked to one's judgement about the difference between psychology and functional physiology. Like all friends of folk psychology, I tend to think that, although at some level these two sciences may, and do, interact and influence each other, they are distinct disciplines. Psychology acknowledges contentful states or episodes which have a high degree of intentionality not admitted into neuroscience, psychophysics, or physiology. When we move from protozoa, through cockroaches, birds, to mammals, somewhere along the journey, we, friends of folk psychology, encounter intentional states that have a basis in reality—that are not merely constructs of a false theory, or the heuristic instruments of a particular stance.[30]

Once we assume that this is true, the theoretical importance of the distinction between action and 'mere' behaviour becomes apparent: actions are behaviours that are relevant to a science of psychology that admits folk psychological attitudes.

---

[29] For example, Davidson speaks of reasons being causes of *actions*, in spite of the fact that he subscribes to a causal theory of action.

[30] Where in the phylogenetic tree psychology becomes relevant is not my concern here. I tend to think that (*a*) the psyche of cockroaches is overrated, (*b*) animals that do not have a language (like some primates) do have intentional states, and (*c*) intentionality comes gradually in degrees. None of this is of any consequence to what follows, because from now on I will be concentrating on the behaviour of humans as paradigms of organisms with full intentional states. What is of consequence is that we agree that psychology, which admits propositional attitudes, is a *bona-fide* science of human behaviour.

At this point we can go back to our first Causal Definition of Action and note two difficulties with it.

CDA1
S's behaviour, B, is an action if and only if:
(1) (i) B is basic, and
      (ii) B is caused by S's intention to perform B, *or*
(2) The *result* of B is generated by the *result* of something, B', that S does, and B' is an action of S's.

It will be remembered that one (positive) condition for an act's being a *basic* act was that the agent *knows how to do* it. A second (negative) condition was that the agent *does not use* her knowledge of how to do something else in order to do it.

I suggested earlier that one problem with the definition was that for the definition to be informative, two key notions (knowing how to do something, and using one's knowledge of how to do something in order to do something) needed explication. But there is a second problem. The second problem consists in the fact that the definition of *basic* act is to be used as the base clause in the definition of action. Consequently, basic acts cannot contain in their definiens a reference to action: the definition cannot state, 'an act is a basic act if and only if...' because identity conditions for what is to count as an *act* are to be given partly by reference to *basic acts*.[31] One might attempt to address this second problem by defining *action* in terms of basic *behaviours*. However, instead of attempting an explication of *basic behaviour*, I will try to approach both of these problems by introducing a notion of *basic *results** on the model of the 'bodily outputs' of organisms as schematized in Figure 2.1.

Basic Result Types

We can give a definition of basic *result* types in a way analogous to the earlier definition of basic acts.[32]

Definition of Basic Result Types (BR)
An event type E during time period T and under circumstances C is a basic result type of S's if and only if:

---

[31] It will be recalled that it was exactly for this reason that Danto's definition of basic acts could not be used in a foundationalist theory of action.
[32] I am indebted to Greg Mougin for the key idea in this section.

> During T and under C, S knows how to bring about E, and S does not need to use her knowledge of how to bring about a different event in order to bring about E.

Human agents have the capacity to bring about a variety of movements (physical movements in their bodies), changes of state (either in their environment or in themselves). For example, they can sweat, they can sneeze, they can fall in love, they can form the image of a friend's smile, they can raise an arm, they can pull the chain, they can walk, and so on. Each of these behaviours has a result. In searching for the subclass that constitutes the *basic results* of an agent in this large class of event types, we ask, which of these events does the agent know how to bring about when she wants to bring it about, without having to rely on her knowing how to bring about something else first. This is basically a question about the capabilities of an agent. Its answer does not require our knowing yet whether anything is an action or not. The answer is relative to the specific agent. The sequence of bodily events involved in walking, or in raising an arm, are two obvious candidates for basic results for most agents. A sneeze or sweat are things that we can bring about in our bodies, but normally only by first doing other things we know how to do (like taking snuff or exercising heavily). So these two would not count as basic results for most agents.

The familiar underlying intuition that supports relativizing basic results to particular agents at a certain time and under certain circumstances is that the types of things agents can do forthwith change with time. Tying one's shoe laces is something one could not do (did not know how to do) as a child, and one may lose the ability to do it (may cease to know how to do it) because of a partial stroke. Shoe laces getting tied, then, is a basic result type for certain people at certain stages of their lives, under certain circumstances, that is, if their hands are free and fingers not frozen, etc.

The notion of a basic result type for subject S (during time period T and circumstance C) exploits a distinction. On the one hand, there is S's higher cognitive centre, which deliberates, decides, and issues intentions, that is, a centre where practical reasoning takes place. On the other hand, there are S's lower systems whose function is to 'translate' those intentions into physical activity. One can now restate the notion of a basic result by means of an alternative definition that does not depend on the notion of needing to use one's knowledge:

Alternative Definition of Basic Result Types (BR')
E, a type of act-neutral event or state of affairs, is a basic result
type for S (during T and in circumstances C) if and only if:
A command by the higher cognitive centre to make E the case
issued to the lower (subdoxastic) systems would be effective
during T and in circumstances C (i.e. the command to make
E the case is sufficient in circumstances C to bring about E).

The cognitive centre, where practical reasoning takes place and
where an intention is formed, is the analogue of the control centre in
simpler animals. The conjecture here is that this centre is *not* the place
where the causal antecedents of the limb trajectories that realize the
intended macro behaviour are located. This conjecture is based on the
fact that practical reasoning never goes 'beyond' the decision to produce such macro behaviour. Once the intention to tie one's shoe lace is
formed, no subsequent practical reasoning is required to figure out
how to satisfy the intention. If the content of the intention matches an
item in one's repertoire of basic acts, and if the conditions are right, the
formation of the intention becomes sufficient for its execution by the
lower subsystems. On the other hand, the condition of BR' will not be
satisfied for most values of E because the lower behavioural systems
only 'know how' to make good on certain commands. For example,
'Sneeze!' is not executable by the lower subsystems, but 'Take snuff!'
is. That is why the result of sniffing the powder between one's fingers
is a basic result type, but a sneeze is not.

Furthermore, since the commands issued by the deliberative faculty
have a high degree of intentionality, the *result* of opening a jar lid
may be basic, whereas some sequence of events identical to that token
event, such as the contraction of a set of muscles, may not.

In summary, knowing how to do something, B, without needing to
use one's knowledge of how to do something, A, in order to do B boils
down to a capacity rational agents have of getting B done without
needing to cognitively control how it is done.[33] The fact that we have
this capacity seems intuitively clear. But at this stage of our knowledge, what particular facts about our internal wiring give us this
capacity can only be an informed guess. In the Alternative Definition

---

[33] Such a capacity in reverse is also found in our perceptual systems. For example, in
visual perception the mechanisms that yield size constancy also operate without the need
for input from the doxastic systems.

of Basic Results (BR') I have offered a conjecture as to how this capacity may be realized.

What I need to emphasize here is that the two definitions of basic result are intended to capture a type of behaviour that is defined, on the analogue of the elements of the basic behaviour repertoire of organisms, as a macro-unit. The different tokens of this type of behaviour may all be produced by different sets and sequences of muscle movements, and limb trajectories. *Which* of these tokens is actually produced in some performance of the basic act is not decided by whatever mental state it is that selects the basic result. Suppose that my desire to whip egg whites is what causes my wrist motions with a wire whisk in my hand. Let us also suppose that a considerably large number of these motions makes up one unit of the basic result. Each motion is a circular movement of the wrist, and the angular velocity, the radius of the arc produced by the whisk, as well as the exact location in the bowl at which the whisk will make contact with the egg whites will vary within certain limits, from motion to motion. This variation is likely to be random—if it is not random, which movement is to be tokened at a given time in the performance of the basic act is certainly *not* under the control of the psychological states that cause the whipping. (If we had taken walking as our example, in addition to the random selections that might be involved, the differences would also have been controlled by subsystems that integrate proprioceptive signals and compensate, without any psychological interference, for the variations in the terrain.) We can represent the general picture as in Figure 2.2. Here the psychological state, S, causes the basic result, BR. The Ps of the different stages represent the different muscle movements (or limb trajectories) that are available to the agent for the act in question (say, each P designates one circular movement of the wrist with a specific angular velocity, radius, and so on). At each stage one of the Ps gets selected (indicated by asterisks). Although S is the cause of the macro output BR, and although BR is token identical with a sequence of Ps, members of which are selected from each of the m stages, S does not cause P_i, as opposed to P_j in stage k. To say this, of course, is not to deny that S does cause whichever P gets selected at each stage—it just does not determine which Ps get selected; it does not cause one P *as opposed to* another.[34] This contrast is what makes it possible to say that the

---

[34] Here I am relying on the judgement made in the context of the cordless phone example.

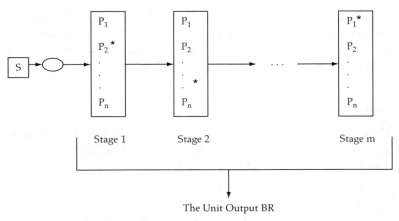

Fig. 2.2. *The internal structure of a basic result*

agent knows how to do the basic act, to cause the BR, and in so doing she does not require the exercise of her knowing how to do any of the Ps in the different stages. In the example of my whipping egg whites, although I do know how to bring down my hand while rotating my wrist, when I start whisking, while reading on the recipe for the soufflé, my arms are on automatic pilot, and I do not utilize *that* knowledge, say, in the way I would need to if I were showing a child how to whip egg whites properly, demonstrating the act slowly one movement at a time, or the way I would need to if the rotation of the bowl met some obstacle and I had to free the bowl. In these latter cases the circumstances would make my whisking dependent on my knowledge of how to move my wrists, and thus my act of whisking would cease to be basic. So there are some basic result types, like the *result* of whisking, that are not *essentially* basic. In contrast, the snapping of my fingers, or the wriggling of my toes are basic result types of mine that cannot typically be rendered non-basic by attending to the muscle movements or neuron firings that generate them simply because I do not know how to bring about such events directly. But this contrast does not make a difference as to whether a *token* act is basic or not. If in the tokening of some act one does know how to bring about the component *results* of the act and yet this knowledge is not being used, then the token will be a basic act. It can also be a basic act if such knowledge is not available. If such knowledge is not available (as it is not in the example of wiggling my toes), then it is a trivial consequence of BR that the agent does not use her knowledge of how to bring about a different event in order to bring about that *result*.

Causal Theory of Action

We can now attempt an improvement on CDA1 by first defining basic act tokens in terms of basic result types, and then giving the final formulation of the Causal Theory of Action.

> *Definition of a Basic Act Token (BA):*
> A is a token Basic Act if and only if:
>   (i) the *result* of A is a token of a Basic Result type of S's;
>   (ii) the *result* of A is caused (in the way it is normally caused) by an intention of S's which includes an explicit reference to bringing about that type of result; and
>   (iii) in the particular circumstances in which S brings about the *result* of A, S does so without using her knowledge of how to bring about any other event in order to bring about the *result* of A.

Conditions (i) and (ii) together play two crucial roles. Condition (ii) places basic acts within the framework of a philosophical causal theory. Philosophical causal theories are typically designed to formulate a necessary condition for falling in the extension of a category. If we label the category to be defined by a causal theory Ψ, we can describe the general logical structure of a causal theory as follows. We take a category φ that already has a definition, usually in terms of some non-relational properties of its members. We then stipulate that for a member of φ to count as a member of Ψ, it must also possess a relational (external) property. For the account to constitute a *causal* theory of Ψ, the relational property in question must be that the member of φ has a particular type of causal history.[35] A few examples may illustrate the point.

Seeing an external object is (identical with) entering a mental state of 'seeming to see' that is caused by o. *Knowing that p* is having the fact that p cause one's belief that p. Being *cognac* is (identical with) being a

---

[35] See Ch. 5 for a detailed discussion of causal theories in general.

distilled liquor made out of grape juice that is produced in the Cognac region in France, etc.

And all causal theories end up having to appeal to a qualification about the nature of the causal path to exclude the so-called deviant chains. This is done by including a clause about 'the normal way' in the definition. I take up this issue in detail in Chapter 4.

True to the logical structure of causal theories, clauses (i) and (ii) define *basic acts* (category Ψ) as non-actional neutral events of a certain kind (category φ) that have been caused by the intention of the agent.[36] The content of the intention includes an explicit reference to bringing about such an event.[37] This satisfies the need for some privileged set of acts that are caused by certain intentional states the content of which corresponds to the description of the act—the description here being the bringing about of a *result*.[38]

The role of condition (i) of BA is to narrow the class of event types that will constitute the non-actional neutral event. For, as the category of basic results has been defined, for most agents, a sneeze, a blush, weeping, sweating, nerve signals being sent to the muscles do not count as basic results. Accordingly, even if they satisfy the causal condition (even if the agent intended to bring about a sneeze and the

[36] Myles Brand (1984: 17) claims that the Causal Theory of Action is a non-reductionistic theory, and thinks that this is to the theory's credit. This is because he takes the theory to define (intentional) action as an *action* that is caused by an appropriate mental event. But strangely enough, his notion of an action is reductive, for he says, 'Richard's clapping his hands is an event (*sic!*) consisting of a causal sequence, part of which happens inside Richard's body, such as events in his nervous system, and part of which is publicly observable, namely his hands moving together. That entire complex causal chain is an action according to the C[ausal] T[heory], in virtue of being caused by a non-actional mental event, say a desire plus belief' (1984: 16). Brand's Causal Theory is very similar to that formulated by BA, with the exception that what is identified with action is not the *sequence* of physiological events that leads to the basic result that is caused by the mental event; it is rather the *result* that is caused by the mental event. To say this is not to deny that the whole sequence *is* caused by the mental event. The parallel with the causal theory of seeing is instructive: seeing is identified with the *percept* caused by an object, not with the causally connected sequence of events starting with the light rays emanating from the object and terminating in the percept as caused by the object.

[37] The state of intention in question here is envisaged as having a holistic content, which includes all the foreseen consequences of one's actions. Also, cases of trying to do something, when one does not believe that one will be able to do it, will also count as cases of having an intention the content of which includes an explicit reference to doing that thing. I will offer a detailed discussion and an argument for this view of intention in Ch. 6.

[38] For the sake of generality, the earlier discussion for the need of such privileged acts was conducted in terms of the agent's reasons for bringing about the event in question. I have now moved to the formation of an intention as the cause in the definiens. This does not exclude reasons from the picture because, as will be shown in Ch. 6, reasons are the antecedent causes of intentions.

intention was the cause of the sneeze), they will not qualify as basic acts (one's sneezing will not be a basic act).[39]

It should be clear by now that this second role of the first two conditions blocks McCann's regress. It was suggested in Chapter 1, in discussing Danto's conception of basic acts, that Danto could not stop at bodily movements as the 'first things' one does, if he insists on defining 'first thing' by saying there is nothing one does the *result* of which causes that first thing: sending nerve signals is clearly one such thing *one does* the *result* of which causes the bodily movement. And Danto could not disqualify sending nerve signals from among actions if he were to use his definition of basic acts as the base clause of his definition of action. It will be recalled that observation of this difficulty is what sent McCann in search of actions that had no action-neutral events as their results. In the way it is formulated in clause (i) of BA, events that are not basic results cannot be basic acts *even if* they are caused by the intentional states of the agent. And travelling nerve signals, or any of the events further upstream in the production of a macro behaviour, do not qualify as basic result types for most agents simply because the deliberative faculty does not 'know' how to send nerve signals directly in the sense explicated above—perhaps because the subsystems that receive the commands from the intentional centres are not equipped to respond to commands like 'Send nerve signals!' Accordingly, sending nerve signals to one's muscles will not be a candidate for basic acts.

The force of condition (iii) is different. Agents typically have a large repertoire of basic results in which certain *results* are hierarchically related to each other. For example, the downward motion of the forefinger, and that of the middle finger of either hand are all basic results as these are defined. But the light switch's being flipped as one walks by it may also be a basic result. One may be in a position in which one does not need to use one's knowledge of how to move one of those four fingers in bringing about the *result* of flipping the switch. One may decide to flip the switch and let the subsystems 'figure out' the most convenient means. Serving at a game of tennis is another (perhaps more convincing) example. Whether the individual limb movements or the compound event is to count as the basic act, when both qualify as the basic result types of the agent, will be determined,

---

[39] Actually sneezing is also disqualified by condition (iii) of BA.

in the token case, by condition (iii). If the tennis pro is serving in a competitive match, the serve may be a basic act. But if the pro is demonstrating the proper serve technique to a novice, the individual component arm movements may each count as basic acts.[40]

One consequence of a BA is that the 'by' relation which is sometimes used in eliciting intuitions about basic acts ceases to be an effective measure. As flipping the switch example illustrates, even if one does B *by* doing A, in the circumstances B may still be a token basic act.[41]

Basic acts as defined by BA can now, without further elaboration, be used in the recursive definition of *action*.

> *Causal Definition of Action (CDA)*
> A is a token act of S's if and only if:
>   (i) A is a token basic act of S's, OR
>   (ii) The *result* of A is generated by a token basic act of S's.

Putting together all the definitions developed so far, we can unpack CDA as follows:

> *CDA*
> At time t and in circumstances C, A is a token act of S's if and only if:
>   (i) A satisfies the following conditions that are necessary and sufficient for being a basic act of S's:
>   (*a*) During the time period T which includes t and in circumstances C' that are consistent with C, S knows how to bring about the type of event, E, a token of which is the *result* of A, and S does not need to use her knowledge of how to bring about a different event in order to bring about E, and
>   (*b*) the token of E that occurs at t in C is caused (in the way it is normally caused) by an intention of S's, the content of which explicitly refers to bringing about that type of E, and

---

[40] If in the absence of an actual tie, I try to go through the finger motions of tying my tie, I find that I cannot complete the mime. For me the proper sequence of the individual finger movements that constitute the act of tying a tie has ceased to be a Basic Result. This shows again the degree of intentionality involved in the notion of a Basic Result, and hence of a basic act.

[41] The same applies to the 'in' and the 'while' relations that Baier discusses.

(c) In the particular circumstances in which S brings about the token of E, S does so without using her knowledge of how to bring about any other event in order to bring about that token of E.

Or:

(ii) The result of A is generated by a token basic act of S's.

At this point a disclaimer is in order. The examples that have been used to illustrate basic results and to show how the recursive definition of action functions may have given the impression that every action performed by agents involves a bodily act. This is not something that the definition of action is committed to. There is nothing in the spirit of the CDA that should disqualify performing these mental operations from being *actions*. I can add 2 and 5 and come up with 7 without even silently pronouncing 'seven'. I can also multiply 43 and 53 and mentally arrive at the result without producing any bodily movement. In these acts there certainly is no limb movement that will be a proper analogue to the bodily output of organisms of Figure 2.1. But the occurrence of number 7 or of 2279 in my mind are, properly speaking, *results*. Furthermore, since the sum of 2 and 5 is something I know how to arrive at (bring about) mentally without needing to use my knowledge of how to bring about another mental occurrence, it should count as a basic result type for me. So when the thought 'seven is the sum of 2 and 5' occurs in my mind as a causal consequence of my intending to add 2 and 5, my forming that thought will constitute a basic act of mine. On the other hand, in order to arrive at the product of 43 and 53, I need, among other things, to use my knowledge of how to add 2 and 5. So the occurrence of 2279 will not be a basic result type for me. But of course, this will not mean that my forming the thought that the product of 43 and 53 is 2279 is not constitutive of an act of mine. It is in fact constituted by the sequence of basic acts, such as taking the product of 3 and 3, the product of 5 and 3, the sum of 2 and 5, and so on.

In short occurrence of certain mental events may also count as *results* of actions. By the same token, preventing certain bodily occurrences, as in suppressing a cough or a burp, may also qualify as action.

I now turn to the task of confronting some objections to the causal theory, and to developing a thesis about the individuation of actions that is in harmony with the causal definition.

3

The Causal Theory Revisited

INTRODUCTION

The Casual Definition of Action (CDA) that was offered at the end of Chapter 2 might seem, on the face of it, totally implausible. How can an action be one and the same thing as a bodily occurrence? Isn't it self-evident that there is a categorical difference between something agents *do* and some physical *change* that takes place in their bodies?

There are two ways of understanding this objection. The first way is to read the objection as issuing a challenge to explain how agency can possibly emerge out of a story that is confined to just causal relations among events. If mental states including reasons and intentions are events and actions are mere causal consequences of these events, the objection would go on to ask, how can there be a difference between the passive role of a chemical 'agent' and the active role of a person who performs *actions*?

Meeting this challenge by giving a positive argument for the way agency is locatable in a world of event causation is certainly something the causal theorist owes to his critics. I attempt to pay this debt in Chapter 5.

But there is a second way in which this objection may be intended. This second way consists in the suggestion that it is preferable to opt for conceptions of action that are different from what the causal definition captures. I shall briefly address myself in this chapter to this second task, and argue against some alternative approaches. I shall then try to make the causal definition more precise; I shall also defend a view about the individuation of action that fits in smoothly with that definition, and discuss some problems said to arise for that view.

SOME ALTERNATIVES

One major alternative to the reductive view of action of Chapter 2 is to be found in a tradition that regards action to be an ineliminable part of rational agency. In this tradition an agent is said to possess the capacity to produce some 'first' act of *willing* (or *trying*), and typically it is required in a foundationalist spirit that anything that is to count as action be related in some specific way to that first act.[1] I argued in Chapter 1 that as long as these views are committed to regarding that first act, which is to form the base of a foundationalist theory of action, as an irreducible, unanalysable act—a brute fact about agency that is introspectively self-evident—they fall victim to a common philosophical mistake. I have nothing to add here to those arguments. And I do not expect to have made any converts away from this approach because subscribers to the dogma on which the approach depends are adamant about the self-evident nature of such foundational acts. I suspect that the readers who have not found my arguments against such an approach persuasive will not have made it to this chapter anyway.

There is, however, a second alternative approach, which deserves to be addressed. This is an approach in which one would deny that the issue I labelled as 'the First Problem of Action Theory' is of any philosophical interest.[2] One would argue that the distinction between *action* and *mere behaviour* is a philosopher's construct; actions are the things we do. And what is of real interest is how we explain the various things we do.[3] I must confess that I have sympathy with this view, *except* that I do not think the programme involved here, as long as it shuns a commitment to irreducible mental acts of the first alternative, is really different from defining action: the two programmes actually converge on the same issues. The difference is just that of

---

[1] Ginet's set of relations (Ginet 1990) are formulated in terms of the 'BY' relation; Hornsby (1980), following O'Shaughnessy (1973), takes all acts to be *identical* with some *trying*; Wilson (1989) takes the relation between desires (reasons) and action to be non-causal but teleological; Pink (1996) has all first acts of agency being *caused* by second order acts of deciding; and so on.

[2] My colleague and dear friend Dennis Stampe, for whose philosophical instincts I have the greatest respect, has often urged me to admit that the 'First Problem of Action Theory' is in fact a bogus problem.

[3] One good way of studying the history of philosophical action theory is indeed to see it as centred around the question of explanation-cum-rationalization of action. The theme then becomes an examination of the nature of practical reasoning, an attempt to understand whether it differs from theoretical reasoning, and if it does how, and it may include a debate over reasons versus causes of action.

deciding where to begin. Were one to begin with the explanatory concern, I wager, one would be irresistibly attracted to the Davidsonian thesis that reasons must be causes, and that rational explanations are grounded in causal relations.[4] This thesis then would immediately invite two questions. (1) What is the nature of the things reasons cause and explain? (2) How do reasons cause? Both of these questions can be answered only if the First Problem of Action Theory is given a satisfactory solution. If one starts with explanatory concerns, one cannot merely offer 'action' as an answer to the first question because unless action is shown to be a category of things that can be caused by events (or occurrences), the thesis that rational explanations are causal explanations will not be at all illuminating. So the first question is basically a request to find a solution to the First Problem of Action Theory: once it is agreed that rational explanations of action have a causal basis, explanatory concerns converge on concerns about act identity. Similarly, understanding the structure of explanations provided by reasons requires figuring out the interrelations among the contents of mental states involved in practical reasoning as well as the relation between these states and the outputs they determine. This, too, is a task the definition of action has to anticipate. I plan to attempt that task in Chapter 5.

In short, what is proposed as a dramatically different programme in action theory is really nothing other than a different way of starting the programme of the previous chapter.

AN ANALOGY FROM BIOLOGY

Clause (ii) of the definition of a basic act token (or clause (i)(c) of the Causal Definition of Action, CDA) identifies a basic act with a special kind of event (with a token of a basic result type) that is caused by some mental occurrence (by the onset of an intention of a specific kind). As I remarked earlier, this identification is in the spirit of philosophical causal theories. However, it might seem that a causal theory of action is specifically objectionable because it has the net effect of identifying an element from one conceptual domain (that of rational psychology) with an element from a categorically different conceptual domain (that

---

[4] Being attracted to this does not, of course, require a commitment to Davidson's thesis of the anomalous nature of the mental.

of physiology). This objection might be encapsulated by noting that the question 'What did he do?' cannot be answered by saying, for example, 'His arm rose'.[5]

It is true that the question, 'What did he do?' is a question that can only be answered correctly by attributing to the agent the performance of an *action*. The point of the objection is that if actions were identical with bodily movements caused a certain way, 'his arm moved as caused by his intention' would be as good an answer as 'he moved his arm'. But it is not. Hence the identity thesis has to be false.

However, it is clear that the reason why one cannot answer the question by using the intransitive 'move' is purely grammatical. The syntax of the question is such that it demands an answer of the form, 'He X-ed', where 'X' is an action verb. And grammar is not always an index to ontology. I agree that if one is asked, 'what did he do?' one cannot answer 'his arm moved as caused by his intention'. But this does not prove that 'his moving his arm' describes something ontologically distinct from 'his arm motion's being caused by his intention'. In fact, there is nothing *grammatically* wrong with the answer, 'he did something which consisted in his intention causing his arm to move'. The point may be illustrated by looking at a different causal theory. Suppose for the moment that the causal theory of perception is correct. Suppose, that is, that 'S's seeing o' describes one and the same thing as 'S's being in a perceptual state of seeming to see o that is caused by o'. We cannot refute such a casual theory by pointing out that the question 'what did S see?' cannot be answered by 'S's perceptual state of seeming to see a tree as caused by the tree'. The casual theory may not be the true theory, but if it is false, its falsehood does not derive, as the objection would seem to suggest, from a conceptual error.

Indeed the identification of elements from different conceptual domains with each other is not unique to the causal theory of action. A similar move in evolutionary physiology provides a very close analogy.

On the causal theory of action, a basic *result* token may be a basic act or it may be a non-actional bodily movement. For example, my arm's motion, as basic results are defined, is a basic result type of mine. On some occasion, when my arm moves as the causal consequence of the formation of an intention in me to move that arm, the motion is a token

---

[5] Hornsby (1980: 3) expresses this objection by pointing out the absurdity of answering the request for act descriptions by describing bodily movements.

basic act. On another occasion, when the arm manifests the same type of motion in reflex response to some input, it is merely a non-actional basic result token. A division that shares a logical structure almost identical to this distinction exists in the taxonomy of traits in biology.

Features of organisms may be viewed in two ways: (i) what the feature does for the organism in its natural habitat, and (ii) what, if any, selection forces have been responsible for organisms of a species to have that feature.[6] The first way is the way functional physiologists study organs of animals; the second way is the way evolutionary theorists speak of traits or features in populations. For example, from the perspective of functional physiology, the short fore-legs of the Tyrannosaurus may have been used to help the animal rise from a lying position. However, according to the second view, these diminutive limbs are *not* adaptive features; they are rather 'the reduced product of conventionally functional homologues in ancestors'.[7] Again, according to the second view, the human *chin* is *not* a feature; it is just 'a product of interaction between two growth fields' (Sober 1984b: 256)

This second view holds first that what counts as an *adaptive feature* cannot be determined purely by anatomical considerations, and secondly that a feature's enabling the organism to do certain things does not mean that the feature is an adaptation for doing those things.

To use one last example from Lewontin (1980: 242), 'Green Turtle, *Chelonia mylas* uses its front flippers to propel itself over dry sand to an egg-laying site above high-water mark, and then digs a hole for the eggs in a slow and clumsy way using its hind flippers as a trowel. But...[these flippers] cannot be regarded as adaptations either to land locomotion or hole digging.'

The flippers are not adaptations for land locomotion because their presence is not causally explainable by the fact that they have enabled turtles to move on sand. The correct causal explanation for their presence in the population has to advert to the fact that these limbs have in the past generations been useful for swimming.[8]

---

[6] Elliott Sober's clear discussion of adaptation (in Sober 1984b: ch. 6) should be consulted for a detailed treatment of this point.

[7] S. J. Gould and Lewontin 1978 in Sober 1984a: 258.

[8] In an earlier paper (Enç 1979) I had argued, with reference to the heart and the kidney, that the typology of these organs quite often reflects what these organs are thought to have been an adaptation for. Similarly here, classifying these appendages as flippers (rather than, say, as hole-diggers or legs) may presuppose a hypothesis that they are adaptations for water-locomotion.

A biological structure made up of tissue and bones is an adaptation only if the frequency with which that structure appears in a population is a causal consequence of the advantages afforded by that structure to earlier generations of the population. This view about what constitutes a significant feature in evolutionary biology may be used as a model for the parallel view as to what constitutes psychologically significant behaviour. Just as a cluster of tissue and bones does not constitute an *adaptive* feature unless that cluster is the causal consequence of certain selection pressures, we can see that producing a packaged unit of behaviour does not constitute a piece of *psychologically* significant feature (that is, it does not constitute *action*) unless those movements have a specific type of aetiology.

The parallel between action and evolutionary biology is illuminating because in both a request for an explanation of why something is there, or why something is doing what it is doing, what its 'purpose' is seems to be pertinent.[9] An anatomical structure is an adaptive feature only because its causal history contains certain selection pressures. It is prevalent in the population because it has conferred advantages on the members of the ancestral species. Similarly, a bodily movement is there because it has a certain type of aetiology: it is caused by an intention, by reasons. In a sense that the identity of that movement is an *action* is due to the fact that its causal history contains such items.

Just as whether an appendage is properly classified as a flipper (an adaptation for swimming) or a leg (an adaptation for walking) may depend on its causal history, so may whether the rising of an arm is to be properly identified as voting in favour of a motion or shooing a fly (or a spasm) depend on the reasons (or lack thereof) that caused the movement.

A related defence for a causal theory of action (or a causal theory of adaptive features in biology) may be found in an argument of Grice's (1962) in favour of a causal theory of perception. Grice notes that when there are two qualitatively identical objects similarly positioned, only one of which is seen, the object of one's perception is not fully determined by the nature of one's perceptual state: which object one is seeing is not always apparent in what one seems to see. The

---

[9] See Wright 1973 or Enç and Adams 1992 for a defence of the thesis that an aetiological account of functions provides an answer to such explanation requests.

answer to the question, 'which object is the person seeing?' is to be found in finding out which object is the *cause* of the perceptual state one is in.

In a similar vein, as we saw, *what action* (if any) a bodily movement constitutes is determined by what has caused that bodily movement. The nature of the action manifested by a bodily movement is not apparent in the features of the movement. The analogy here with Lewontin's thesis is undeniable.

ACT INDIVIDUATION

A puzzle that readers of contemporary literature on action theory are familiar with revolves around the problem of individuating actions. When a basic act is performed in pursuit of some goal, or in expression of some psychological state, the act gives rise to a large set of events. The outcomes of one's basic acts spread wide both spatially and temporally. Each of these outcomes can be referred to in attributing an action to the agent. The set of such doings associated with a basic act is sometimes said to constitute an act-tree. The question that faces philosophers interested in act individuation is that of deciding in what relation the different items of an act-tree stand to each other. One group, which includes Goldman and Kim, maintains the relation is that of one action *generating* many *distinct* actions (the maximizers), and the opposite group, which includes Anscombe and Davidson, argues that the relation among these items on an act-tree is one of identity (the minimizers).[10]

Act-Trees

I find myself in sympathy with the minimizers.[11] Part of the reason for my preference lies in the fact that the minimizing view provides a better fit with the causal theory of action, and with the explanatory

[10] 'Minimizer' and 'maximizer' are Ginet's terms for these competing groups. Ginet himself proposes a compromise solution.

[11] There exists a body of literature devoted to showing that the difference between the minimizing and the maximizing views is merely verbal. Karl Pfeifer's book (1989), which contains the most comprehensive treatment of this issue that I know of, discusses this literature at length, and gives a critical review of the arguments for and against each view.

schemes the theory provides. The fit I have in mind is best described by developing the notion of an act-tree.[12]

Suppose we take the basic act α_o and its concomitant basic result ρ_o. The relation between α_o and ρ_o is *not* a causal one; it is a constitutive one. My raising my arm does not cause my arm's rising. My raising my arm *is* my arm's rising that is caused by my intention the content of which makes explicit reference to my raising my arm. In typical cases, the basic result, ρ_o, will give rise to a large set of events $\{\rho_i\}$. I will say that ρ_o *makes it the case that* each member of $\{\rho_i\}$ occurs. The 'makes it the case that' relation includes, but is not confined to, the causal relation. It also includes relations that have been labelled 'conventional generation' and 'simple generation' by Goldman.[13] Each of these events in the set $\{\rho_i\}$ (with the important exception of ρ_o) are things that I bring about *by doing something*. When the expression α_i attributes an action to me, the action will be canonically identified as my making it the case that ρ_i (i.e. the *result* of α_i) happen. For example, when I *turn on the light*, my action of turning on the light

[12] The notion of an act-tree is used to good effect by Goldman, who is a strong defender of the maximizing view. But it can be adopted by the minimizing view also. Ginet (1990: 19) conceives of an act-tree using his very carefully crafted definition of the general generating relation. That definition relies essentially on the notion of an agent's doing something *by* doing something. I am hoping that my less rigorous discussion will avoid implicitly assuming this notion.

[13] See Goldman 1970: ch. 2. An example of conventional generation is the relation between extending one's left arm out and signalling for a left turn. An example of simple generation is the relation between one's dangling a line in water, and one's fishing. Goldman also includes what he calls 'augmentation relation'. An example of this is the relation between one's running and one's running at 8 mph. Goldman realizes that the augmentation relation is significantly different from the others. It certainly does not fall under ordinary uses of 'makes it the case that'—my running did not make it the case that I ran at 8 mph. Since as a minimizer, I take the more natural position of maintaining that my (token) running is identical with my running at 8 mph, I will not dwell on this problem at length. The augmentation relation, as it holds between action tokens, is a relation of identity simply because it can be argued that the token event of the run is identical with the token event of the run at 8 mph. The same may be maintained for token events related by conventional or simple generation—under the circumstances, the extended arm out and a left-turn signal are arguably one and the same event. So 'ρ_1 makes it the case that ρ_2' may be consistent with 'under the circumstances, ρ_1 is identical with ρ_2', but it is also consistent with 'ρ_1 causes ρ_2', and hence with the two events being distinct. I will not attempt to offer criteria of individuation for events here. But I am assuming that it is possible to individuate them so that (i) 'the exhaust noise produced by the car in front of my house at t', 'the exhaust noise produced by John's car at t' (where John's car is the car in front of my house), and 'the loud noise produced by that car at t' all refer to the same event, and (ii) the motion of my hand, and the light's going on when I turn on the light by moving my hand and flipping the switch, are *distinct* events. Beyond this degree of specificity, whether two descriptions pick the same event token or different event tokens will not make an important difference to the way I individuate acts.

will consist in my making the case that the light goes on. More explicitly, my turning on the light is identical with my doing something which makes it the case that the light goes on. From now on I shall take it as a general formula that my α_i-ing is constituted by my doing something which, in the circumstances, makes it the case that ρ_i.

On the view represented by the schema of Figure 3.1, α_i is identical with α_j if they are actions of the same agent and their corresponding ρs stand to each other in the *makes it the case that* relation—provided that these ρs can be traced back through the makes it the case that relations to some *basic result* of that agent.[14] It is in virtue of their being related to such a connected web of events that the different αs belong to the same act-tree. In accepting this kind of a minimizing criterion of individuation for actions, one conceives of actions as spatio-temporally located entities, which, just like material objects, possess indefinitely many properties. One difference between material objects and actions is that the majority of the properties that actions possess are causal (or at least generational)—they are properties of the form, 'being the cause of φ', where 'φ' typically refers to an event. So when I move my finger, pull the trigger, fire the gun, frighten the birds, shoot Joe, kill him, and start the gang wars that will culminate in my own assassination, I do something

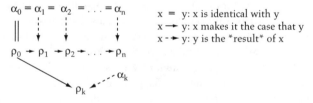

Fig. 3.1. *Actions and their *results**

---

[14] The relation between a ρ and its corresponding α is not easily stated. If ρ_j is the death of Joe, then typically α_j is 'S's killing Joe'. If ρ_j is brought about by S's act, α_i, of hiring a hit man, then α_j will be 'S's causing Joe to be dead'. Also, to borrow an example from Ginet, if, in the course of a walk through a field, Carl picks up a stone and then drops it a few steps further on, and a man, walking through the field a year later, trips over that stone, then ρ, this second person's tripping, has as its corresponding α, Carl's causing the man to trip, not Carl's tripping the man. (Ginet denies that in this scenario Carl caused the man to trip. I do not share Ginet's intuition here. I suspect that he is making an implicit demand that the truth conditions for 'an agent S caused an event E' are different from those that govern 'an event C caused E'.) The fact that there is no easy algorithm for generating the description of a *result* from its corresponding action, or vice versa, makes it clumsy to discuss these relations in general terms. I am assuming that this linguistic infelicity does not flag some deep ontological problems.

that is located at the time and place where the finger's motion occurs, and has the property of causing the trigger's being pulled, causing the gun's firing,…causing Joe's death…

Temporal Concerns

Defining basic acts as events that are caused by the occurrent psychological states of the agent is not the only way a causal theory of action can be formulated. Dretske (1988), in discussing the difference between the paw movement of a rat and the behaviour that consists in the rat's moving its paw, points out that, on a casual theory, *the rat's moving its paw* may be identified with *the paw movement produced by some internal cause*. But he then goes on to argue that the expression, 'a movement produced by some internal cause' is ambiguous between

    (i) a movement *which* is caused by some internal event, and
    (ii) a movement's *being caused by* some internal event.

Appealing to temporal considerations, Dretske maintains that using (i) as the reading for behaviour gives the wrong answer.[15] He says (1988: 15),

It would be an elementary confusion to identify, say, a rat's paw which was moving…with the paw's movement. The first is an object, a paw; the second is an event, a movement. It is the same confusion, though at not so elementary a level, to confuse movements which are brought about by internal events with their being brought about by those events. The former is an event, a movement, something that happens to (say) a paw. The second, I shall argue, is a piece of behavior, possibly an action, something the rat *does*.

One of the arguments Dretske offers for this claim rests on temporal considerations.[16] For Dretske there are two aspects of the time problem. The first involves the time at which a basic act occurs: 'The rat can *start* to depress the lever—efferent signals being sent to the muscles,

---

[15] Other philosophers have been attracted to the process view of non-basic actions. J. J. Thompson (1977) is an excellent example in which temporal views are used in arguing that an act like shooting Joe has parts that are causally connected. Kim (1976) also briefly suggests such a view.
[16] The concern over the time at which acts occur has been a strong source of criticism directed at the minimizing view. One of Goldman's (1970) objections was based on temporal worries. Ginet (1990: 58) finds the temporal problem the biggest flaw of the minimizing view.

muscles contracting, and pressure consequently being applied to the lever—*before the lever begins to move*' (1988: 16). The causal account I have been developing above, on the other hand, must insist that the basic act takes place at the time its basic result occurs. Part of the reason for this stems from my argument that the causal linkage between the internal event (the psychological state), which triggers the limb movement, and the limb movement itself belongs to a subsystem. And the workings of this subsystem have little bearing on psychological considerations. It is true that there is a time-lag between the occurrence of the internal cause and the limb movement. But that time-lag by itself does not require reading (ii) as the preferred reading for *behaviour*, that is, in the absence of an independent argument, there is no reason to insist that the rat's moving its paw *begins* when its motivational force (the internal triggering event) kicks in. A more natural inclination might be to say that the rat's moving its paw begins when the *paw* starts moving.[17]

The second aspect of the time problem for Dretske involves non-basic actions.[18] Dretske says, 'Though Booth did not succeed in killing Lincoln, and hence did not kill Lincoln, until Lincoln died, this does not mean that Booth killed Lincoln at the time of Lincoln's death. The deed began long before the beginning of that event, Lincoln's death, whose occurrence is necessary for the behavior to *be* a killing of Lincoln' (1988: 16). On my reading of 'Booth killed Lincoln', the sentence has the same truth conditions under the circumstances as 'Booth did something which caused Lincoln's death'. One description of what he did is that he pulled the trigger of the gun he was pointing at Lincoln. And *that* act, his pulling the trigger, certainly occurred before Lincoln's death.

---

[17] In saying this, I am not ignoring the crucial role Dretske's vision of behaviour plays in his account of the causal efficacy of the representational content of psychological states. The elegance of that account is in itself a strong point in favour of his vision. Since I have treated myself to the luxury of ignoring problems of mental causation, I can afford to be critical of the time-lag argument. If Dretske's account of mental causation were to be adopted, then my definition of basic acts would have to be revised to read as the *process* in which an intention causes a basic result. This revision would not significantly alter the rest of my claims about action.

[18] In fact, I am not convinced that Dretske needs the extension of his process view of behaviour to non-basic acts for his account of the causal efficacy of content. I tend to think that his theoretical needs would be fully met if he applied his process view to a set of basic behaviours and then adopted the minimizing account of non-basic behaviours. On the other hand, the position I defend could not, without major revision, be altered to adopt the process view for non-basic acts.

When we look back in time to the act of Booth's pulling the trigger of the gun, we see that, as the causal consequences of the trigger's being pulled spread out in time, more definite descriptions that refer to that act become available. So when the trigger's being pulled causes the gun to fire, it becomes possible to refer to Booth's act as an act of firing the gun; when it causes Lincoln's being shot, the expression 'Booth's shooting Lincoln' also secures reference to that act, and so on. The principle operating here is that the agent performs a basic act token α_0. That basic act has associated with it a basic result token ρ_0. Both the basic act and the basic result take place at the same time, say at t_0. The basic result starts a sequence of causally connected events, each of which qualifies as the *result* of an act of the agent. Thus when the basic result causes some event, ρ, ρ occurs at a time later than t_0, say at t_1. Now ρ is the *result* of an act α of the agent. What the minimizing view maintains, namely that the agent did α at t_0, is counterintuitive because at t_0 the fact that ρ_0 would cause ρ was not known. This fact may not be epistemically accessible until t_1. On the other hand, at least it is arguable that, given that ρ_0 was to cause ρ, at t_0 ρ_0 did have the property such that it *would cause* ρ. In other words, it can be maintained that the sentence 'ρ_0 will cause ρ' uttered at t_0 is true just in case ρ_0 does at t_1 cause ρ. And the truth of this sentence has nothing to do with whether the causal connection between ρ_0 and ρ is deterministic or indeterministic. If this is right, then the reason 'Booth's killing Lincoln' cannot be used to refer to Booth's act of pulling the trigger *before* Lincoln dies is epistemic, not based on any thesis about the ontology of properties. Booth's doing something that caused Lincoln to die *is* his pulling the trigger, except that we may not know that it is, until Lincoln dies. It is only in this epistemic sense that Booth's pulling the trigger was not yet his killing Lincoln.[19] This is a specific instance of a general problem about external (causal) properties of events. For example, we can refer to an event as the event that occurred ten years ago and made Sam's sole heir rich. That event was Sam's uncle's death, which did occur ten years ago, but the description, 'the event that made Sam's sole heir rich' could not be used to refer to Sam's uncle's death until Sam died yesterday—until yesterday it was not known (say, due to the volatility of the market in which Sam's fortune was invested) that the description referred to Sam's uncle's death.

[19] If a doctor can tell that with that wound Lincoln is going to die, he can justifiably say to Booth at the time he shoots Lincoln, 'You have killed him!'

Actions as Things an Agent Does

I have been insisting that the physiological processes that mediate between the intentional psychological cause and the basic result consist of a sequence of events that typically have little relevance to the explanation of action or to concerns about the identity of basic acts. This compartmentalization has been the main instrument in showing how McCann's regress can be stopped and how the *result* problem can be solved. The causal structure of behaviour is such that in explaining action, one is justified in ignoring the activation of neurons in the motor cortex, the nerve signals being sent to the muscles, muscle contractions, specific limb trajectories, and even in some cases, single limb movements, and in focusing on structured complex *results* as the basic building blocks of action. Owing to this feature of the causal structure of action, practical reasoning does not go beyond these large building blocks. Or to put the same thought in terms of the notion of an act plan, performing these physiological tasks is not typically included in the act plan. However, a question that has been suppressed up to this point needs to be confronted: when an agent performs a basic act, say, turns on the light, does he not, in the course of performing that act, move his right fore-finger in certain ways, contract and relax certain muscles, send nerve signals, and so on? Would it not fly in the face of common sense to deny that he *does* all those things?

The question may be approached from a different angle. Going back to Figure 3.1, we can appreciate that it is only a partial picture of the anatomy of a single act. It is necessarily a partial picture because the generational consequences of the *results* are indefinitely many. Each ρ in turn stands in some generational relation to a huge number of events. Some of these events may have been anticipated in the deliberation process and taken into account in the construction of the act plan. But many others may be expected, yet ignored; still many more may be totally unexpected. Each of these *results* is something the agent brings about; hence the description of these *events* may be reformulated in describing the thing the agent *does*. The switch's being flipped produces a click; the click makes the blind dog lying in front of the fireplace perk an ear; the light's going on alerts the prowler, and so on. So the agent produced a clicking sound; he made the dog perk up an ear; he alerted the prowler. Many of these things that he did were not part of what he may have intended. But that does not acquit him from being an agent in all of these doings. In the way I have been conceiving actions, all of these things that an agent is correctly said to have done are *actions*—whether they are intended or not.

In the same spirit, when I tie my shoe laces, the finger movements that I produce constitute an action of mine: I move my fingers a certain way, and I do this even if I do not intend to move them in the particular way I move them. The reason for including them among actions as opposed to *mere* behaviours, such as sneezing or blinking, which are also things that I can be correctly said to have *done*, is simple: the things that I do in the course of executing an act plan are all consequences of my intended objective. In contrast with a blink, they arise from a plan that is reached by deliberation. Even if they were not included in the deliberative process, if they had been, the result of the deliberation might have been different. *In that sense* they could have been avoided. (In *that* sense, a blink could not be avoided.) This simple fact about such actions allows us to hold the agent responsible for unexpected, undesirable side-effects of her intended actions— especially when we think she could have anticipated them if she had been more attentive. So if one particular sequence of finger movements in my tying my shoe laces opens up a stitch in my left middle finger, and I knew about this but had merely forgotten, it could be argued that I am the responsible agent to be blamed for causing my finger to bleed, as opposed to bleeding of the finger being something that happened to me. In this example, although my tying my shoe laces was a *basic* act of mine, moving my fingers in the particular way I did should also count as an action, albeit a non-basic action, of mine. This judgement makes it possible to answer the questions with which I started this section. When an agent performs a basic act, like raising an arm, her sending nerve signals, her contracting her muscles, and so on are all actions of hers. But they are not basic acts. Furthermore, except in special circumstances, the fact that the agent will be performing these acts in the course of performing the intended basic act is of no significance whatsoever, and need not be taken into account in the deliberative process. But we may imagine an extraordinary case. Suppose a robot's arm is controlled by signals from a computer programme that in turn receives signals from the electrodes planted in one's brain to anticipate one's arm movement, and is designed to move the robot's arm along the same trajectory as the intended movement of one's own arm.[20] Furthermore, suppose that the robot's arm moving along that trajectory will do some harm to someone. In this case, knowing the scenario, upon deliberation, one may well reach the decision not to move one's arm. The decision will be governed by the recognition that in moving one's arm, one will be acting *as an agent* to cause harm to that person. Doing harm to that person would be a non-basic act if one raised one's arm. By the same token of reasoning, one ought to recognize that activating the neurons in one's motor cortex that causes *both* the basic result of the arm's rising *and* the harm to the person is also a non-basic act.

As a matter of fact, we can imagine a scenario in which a physiologist, who, knowing what nerve signals are sent to the muscles in fist clenching, decides (intends) to send those signals, and he clenches his fist in order to send those signals. (Suppose he has a gauge hooked up to his hand muscles that registers the nerve impulses arriving at the muscles, and he wants to see when they arrive.) In this scenario, the physiologist's sending the nerve signals to his muscles would be an intentional (non-basic) act.

Thus whether the things an agent does, the *results* of which occur upstream of the basic result, are intentional or not makes no difference to the fact that these are non-basic acts of the agent. And consequently, using the general formula offered above, the physiologist's sending of signals to his muscles is his doing something which generates the event of the signals being sent.

This discussion brings into focus the need to include among the generative relations the relation in which the clenching of my fist stands to the signals being sent to the hand muscles. That relation is quite different from the family of relations catalogued by Goldman and subsumed above under the 'makes it the case that' relation. For when we look to the causal connections that hold among the *events* involved, it is quite clear that the clenching of the fist does not cause, but is *caused by*, the signals being sent to the muscles. However, the characterization of a basic result picks the clenching, and not the signals being sent, as a basic result: I cannot bring about the event of the

---

[20] Such a scenario was reported in the *New York Times* (16 Nov. 2000). A neuroscientist doing research in prosthesis at Duke University had connected electrodes to the brain of an owl monkey and had developed a programme that transformed signals from the monkey brain to reproduce its arm movement in the arm of a robot.

signals being sent to my muscles without using my knowledge of how
to clench my fist.

Figure 3.2 represents the anatomy of action a bit more fully than
Figure 3.1 did. Again ρ_0 is the designation of the event that constitutes
the basic result in the token basic act α_0. Here under the circumstances
ρ_0 makes it the case that a series of ρ_i occurs. But also, again under the
circumstances, there is a sequence of physiological events that are the
causal antecedents of ρ_0. And each member ρ_{-i} of this sequence is
associated with an action: I send signals from my motor cortex through
the nerves to the muscles, I exert my body, I contract my muscles, etc.
ρ_0 is located in the middle of a causally connected sequence. The appeal
to 'know-how' was designed to identify the proper member of this
causal sequence as the basic result. Once the basic result is thus
identified, we can define all non-basic acts by defining a notion of a
generative relation and using this extended notion in the second clause
of the Causal Definition of Action.

> *(GR)*
> λ_0 generates λ_i if:
>> *either* (i) λ_0 makes it the case that λ_i happens,
>> *or*   (ii) λ_i is a physiological event (or a limb movement) that
>>   makes it the case that λ_0 happens.

In this definition λs typically take events as values. But by extension,
acts also generate events. For example, my pulling the trigger certainly
makes it the case that the gun fires. Thus in clause (i) λ_0 could either be
an action or the *result* of an action, and in (ii) λ_i may be the *result*
of the action that makes it the case that λ_0 happens. The action will
generate an event if the *result* of the action generates the event in

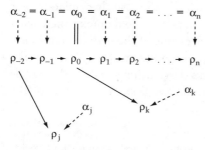

$$\alpha_{-2} = \alpha_{-1} = \alpha_0 = \alpha_1 = \alpha_2 = \ldots = \alpha_n$$

$x = y$: x is identical with y
$x \rightarrow y$: x makes it the case that y
$x \dashrightarrow y$: y is the *result* of x

$$\rho_{-2} \rightarrow \rho_{-1} \rightarrow \rho_0 \rightarrow \rho_1 \rightarrow \rho_2 \rightarrow \ldots \rightarrow \rho_n$$

Fig. 3.2. *Things that one does and their *results**

question. In some cases it might be necessary to cite the *action* as the thing that generates the event. Such cases would arise when the *result* would not be causally efficacious unless it was the *result* of that action.[21] For example, Carl's committing robbery causes him to be thrown in jail. The event of Carl's being in put jail would not have been caused by the removal of the goods if the removal were not the *result* of an action of Carl's. In this case, it was Carl's *act* of committing the robbery, as opposed to the event of the removal of the goods, that made it the case that Carl was put in jail.

Aggregate Actions

Philosophers writing on action have noticed that many action designators designate actions that extend over time and require the performance of a set of actions.[22] Baking a cake, reading Dante's *Inferno*, playing a hand of bridge, are obvious examples. The definition of action should be expanded to cover such actions:

> *Final Version of the Causal Definition of Action (CDA)*
> A is a token act of S's if and only if:
> (i) A is a token basic act of S's, *or*
> (ii) the *result* of A is generated by (the *result* of) a token basic act of S's, *or*
> (iii) A is an aggregate of several *distinct* token acts, each of which is either a token basic act or is generated by (the *result* of) a token basic act of S's, and the aggregate is represented in some act plan of S's.[23]

Clause (i) of the definition is unpacked at the end of Chapter 2. As it will be recalled there, basic acts were defined in terms of basic result types. Since the notion of basic result types recognized macro events that agents know how to bring about 'directly', some token actions like typing 'by' on the keyboard, walking, whisking egg whites, and so on,

---

[21] I owe this point and the following example to an anonymous reader of an earlier draft.

[22] Ginet and Goldman are two notable examples. Ginet conceives of them as an aggregate of component actions. Goldman calls the relation between the component acts and the aggregate compound generation. But neither seem to be worried about regarding an aggregate of totally unrelated acts (e.g. my chewing gum yesterday and my building a fire today) as an action. See Sara Chant's dissertation (in progress, University of Wisconsin, Madison) for a sustained discussion of aggregate acts.

[23] This final clause involving an act plan is needed to prevent a set of totally unrelated acts from counting as an action. Act plans will be discussed at length in Ch. 6.

are accepted as basic acts, and not as aggregate acts that have basic acts as components.

The causal definition of action also implicitly recognizes the minimizing principle of act individuation. Consequently, on this definition to identify an act *as* a basic act is to identify an action with reference to some basic result token. That token act can also be identified with reference to any *result* that stands in some generative relation to the basic result token. Thus to say that Booth's pulling the trigger was a basic act, and his killing Lincoln was not a basic act is *not* to attribute to Booth two acts; Booth performed one action which had many consequences, and each of these consequences may be used in describing what he did.[24] He fired the gun (= he did something that caused the gun to go off); he shot Lincoln (= he did something that caused Lincoln to be shot); he killed Lincoln (= he did something that caused Lincoln to be dead); he surprised the people who witnessed the shooting (= he did something that caused the people who witnessed the shooting to be surprised); and so on. And there was only one action that he performed that had all these consequences. This fact also matches the fact that one and the same set of reasons that Booth had will play a central role in the explanation of all these things that Booth did in connection with his pulling the trigger.

I will postpone describing how the set of reasons the agent had stands in a causal relation to the agent's action to Chapter 5. There, I hope to meet the challenge mentioned at the beginning of this chapter, and argue that, given the unusual causal role which reasons play in the deliberative process, rational agency differs categorically from the 'passive' objects that are causally efficacious, as well as from the agency involved in built-in patterns of animal behaviour.

I now turn to a problem any causal definition needs to confront. The next chapter will be devoted to an examination of the conditions under which the simple causal account of a basic act token fails. These are the conditions that warrant the qualifying phrase, 'caused in the right way', or 'caused in the way it is normally caused' in the definition— the so-called 'deviance conditions'.

---

[24] 'What Booth *did*' may be ambiguous between 'the action that Booth performed', and 'the consequences of the action Booth performed'. In the first sense, Booth did (in the example at hand) just one thing. In the second sense, Booth did many things. So in this sense, the minimizing view of act individuation is compatible with claiming that when one raises one's hand one *does* many things.

4

Deviance

INTRODUCTION

In the previous two chapters, I have been bracketing an issue that is supposed to be one of the two insurmountable problems that face causal theories of action. The issue concerns the nature of the causal path that connects the reasons of an agent with the execution of the action that is done for those reasons. The bracketing is typically achieved by introducing the qualifier, '...causes...*in the right way*'. According to many authors, giving a *general* gloss of this 'right way', showing what conditions *in general* make a causal path from the intention to the behaviour deviant (or, as some authors call it, 'wayward') is an impossible task. These authors maintain that this impossibility, in turn, undermines any attempt to ground the necessary and sufficient conditions for some act's being an action (as opposed to mere behaviour) in the causal connections among mere events. Davidson, who, in my mind, has given the best reasons for subscribing to a causal theory of action, himself confesses to being defeated by this problem.[1] And friends of agent causation gleefully dismiss causal theories of action by providing a catalogue of past failures in the attempts to solve this problem.[2]

The failures are said to arise from the fact that such attempts have to appeal implicitly to notions like 'control' or to whether it is 'up to the agent', which beg the question by rendering the causal theory of action dependent on an unanalysed notion of agency.

It is to John Bishop's credit that he fully appreciates the significance of this challenge to any causal theory of action.[3] He devotes one-third

---

[1] In fact, I tend to think that Davidson's arguments for the thesis of the Anomaly of the Mental rely in an essential way on his view that if the problem of wayward causal chains cannot be solved, then all attempts to have a genuine science of psychology are bound to fail. For a defence of this interpretation of Davidson, see Enç 1985.

[2] One of the earliest sources of this type of criticism that I know is to be found in Richard Taylor 1966: 249. For a more recent version, see Moya 1990: 115–28.

[3] Bishop 1989.

of his book, *Natural Agency*, to coming to grips with the problem, and emphasizes the need to solve the problem of deviance without appealing to notions that implicate agent causation. His is the most sensitive treatment of deviance that I know of in the literature.[4]

I am in full agreement with Bishop, Brand, and Moya that the success of a causal theory of action is conditional on solving the problem of deviance, simply because, without it, a causal condition that involves only event causation will not adequately address what I have called the First Problem of Action Theory.

This chapter will be devoted to a solution by providing a general requirement of non-deviance in the causal chains that are required by all philosophical causal theories. I propose to proceed as follows: I will first look at the structure of causal theories in general. Their generalized structure will present a good clue to the source of deviance, and it will help explain why a certain breed of attempted solutions to the problem of deviance has been unsuccessful.[5] Although this is rather a circuitous route to my proposed solution to the problem, it is hoped that it will ground the proposal on a sound foundation. Finally, I will give a somewhat comprehensive catalogue of cases that have been diagnosed in the literature in connection with causal theories of action, and run some typical ones through my solution as a way of testing it.

FOUR CAUSAL THEORIES

Consider the following as a minimal condition for what is to count as a philosophical causal theory:

> *Minimal Condition:* If a causal theory is to apply to a category of things, Φ, then by definition something (some structure, or state) will be a Φ if and only if it is caused by a C-type event (or a C-type object).

---

[4] Other authors who have treated the problem of deviance in causal theories, though not always in the context of the causal theory of *action*, include, among others, Davies (1963), Woodfield (1976), Tuomela (1977), Bach (1978), Peacocke (1979), Searle (1983), Brand (1984), Thalberg (1984), Audi (1986), Mele (1992b), Gibbons (2001). The problem of deviance in action theory has also been addressed outside the context of causal accounts. Both Ginet (1990) and Mele and Moser (1994) offer necessary and sufficient conditions that define intentional action without invoking a causal theory, and these conditions are designed to block deviant chains.

[5] Some of the material for this part is taken from my 'Causal Theories and Unusual Causal Pathways' (Enç 1989).

Here are the four applications of this schema:

    I. S sees object o if and only if o causes S to be in a perceptual state of seeming to see o.[6]

    II. S knows that a is F if and only if a's being F causes S to believe that a is F.[7]

    III. R's being G represents o as being F if and only if under conditions of fidelity o's being F will cause R to be G.[8]

    IV. S does A intentionally if and only if S's intention to do A causes S's bringing about an event that is the *result* of A.[9]

One feature of this minimal condition is that, according to the definition, what counts as a Φ depends not on the *intrinsic* (physical, physiological, or chemical) structure (or properties) of Φs, but rather on its aetiology (an *extrinsic*, relational property of Φs). Hence of two *physically identical* entities, one may be a Φ, and the other may not. This feature is distinct from the fact that, in all the four theories mentioned above, Φ admits of multiple physical realizations. This latter fact is not an immediate consequence of the minimal condition. Multiple realizability of a Φ by different physical properties is consistent with supervenience. But the minimal condition violates (local) supervenience. In other words, things of kind Φ are not locally supervenient on the physical properties of their realizations.

Supposing that philosophical causal theories are all of the form exemplified by the schematic versions of (I)–(IV), one can write a single master recipe which will generate counter-examples to any causal theory. The recipe is very simple: take a causal theory that defines a Φ as a state or an entity that is caused by a C-type event; concoct a physically possible scenario in which a C-type event results in something that is, in its intrinsic or structural properties, indistinguishable from clear cases of Φs; however, make the causal chain take so unusual or extraordinary a path that we would decline to call the product a case of Φ. The idea is that it is often possible to find unusual

---

  [6] Grice 1962.

  [7] Compare Goldman 1967. Also see Dretske and Enç 1984. Goldman himself is explicit in stating that the causal condition is only a necessary condition for knowledge, but to make my point I consider the biconditional.

  [8] Stampe 1977. For the purposes of highlighting the parallels among these four theories, I have simplified Stampe's view considerably. Part of the simplification involves the relation between o's being F and R's being G. For Stampe this causal relation must be lawful, but governed by *ceteris paribus* conditions, which make up the conditions of fidelity.

  [9] Again, I simplify the causal theory that I developed in the previous two chapters so as to focus on its basic structure and to draw attention to the similarities among the four theories.

enough causal paths which start with C's, but which end in entities (or events) that are obviously not Φs.

It is a simple matter to follow this recipe and concoct counter-examples to the four causal theories mentioned above.

1. Suppose a man is under the influence of a hallucinogen. He is in a redwood forest with his eyes open, but the neural activity in his eye is drastically slowed down by the drug. The scent of the redwoods causes him to have a vivid hallucination that involves the visual image as of redwood trees which happens to match precisely his surroundings. The man is clearly not *seeing* the redwoods.[10] If we operate with a naive version of the causal theory of perception, which maintains that an object's causing the agent to have a visual percept of the object is sufficient for seeing the object, then this example would show that version to be mistaken.

2. Suppose a man is looking at a yellow object through a blue filter, but he has no reason to think that there is a coloured filter in his field of vision. The appropriate cluster of rods and cones in his retina fires and the man has the percept as of a *green* object. However, due to the optical properties of the filter, the light rays reaching the man's retina affect the man's nervous system in such a quirky way that the percept of a green object causes the belief that the object is yellow. In this case the belief that the object is yellow has been caused by a yellow object. It is arguable that the man does not *know* that the object is yellow (although he sees a yellow object, he does not see *that* the object is yellow), but, again, an unsophisticated casual theory of knowledge may not be able to accommodate this result.

3. Suppose that the temperature in a room drops from 70 to 30 °Fahrenheit. Its being 30° causes a crack in the wall; and a coil thermometer hanging on the wall, which was stuck at 60° falls to the floor; its coil breaks, and by coincidence its pointer reads 30°. Now although the temperature's being 30° is what causes the thermometer to read 30°, the thermometer does not *represent* the room temperature as being 30°.[11]

4. An actor has been criticized in the past for not doing nervous scenes well. On the opening night of a new play, since his part requires it, he intends to appear nervous, and yet his intention causes him to

---

[10] Borrowed from Peacocke 1979: 55.

[11] Stampe's counterfactual condition is satisfied in this case: under *conditions of fidelity*, the room temperature's being 30° *would* cause the thermometer to read 30.

be nervous, and as a result of his nervousness, he ends up appearing nervous. I think it is clear that, at least on the opening night, his appearing nervous was not intentional.

Causal theorists typically invoke the standard qualification and try to avoid the problem of deviance by saying that it is assumed the causal chain takes the right, the ordinary, or the characteristic path.[12]

REVIEW OF SOME ATTEMPTS

It is clear that if the causal theory of action is to constitute a naturalized account of rational agency, the qualification needs to be cashed out by providing an account of the conditions that generate non-deviant chains. Such accounts typically require that some specific type of *structural* relation must hold between the links of the causal chain.

Perhaps one of the earliest and the most careful attempts comes from Peacocke's general treatment of causal deviance (1979). He imposes three conditions that must be satisfied by the cause–effect relations if these relations are to be non-deviant. He takes these conditions to spell out the requirement that there be a *sensitivity* relation between the cause and the effect.

   (i) Differential explanation: when the effect's having some property is explained by the cause's having some property, the explanation should be supported by a law that includes a mathematical functional relation between the degree to which the cause has that property and the degree to which the effect has that property. (p. 66)

  (ii) Recoverability: the cause should be necessary for the effect. (pp. 79–80)

---

[12] For example, Grice, in discussing this point, says, 'I suggest that the best procedure for the causal theorist is to indicate the mode of causal connection by examples; to say that, for an object to be perceived by X, it is sufficient that it should be causally involved in the generation of some sense impression by X in the kind of way in which, for example, when I look at my hand in a good light, my hand is causally responsible for its looking to me as if there were a hand before me...*whatever that kind of way may be*; and to be enlightened on that question, one must have recourse to the specialist' (1962, in Swartz 1965: 463). Goldman's analysis of intentional action reads: 'If this action plan *in a certain characteristic way*, causes S's doing A_1, then A_1 is intentional' (Goldman 1970: 57, my emphasis). Goldman, too, suggests that a physiologist ought to be able to describe what constitutes that 'characteristic way'.

(iii) Step-wise recoverability: the requirement of (ii) should apply to each pair of consecutive links of the causal chain. (p. 80)

Peacocke's condition (i) does seem to capture one important feature of the causal pathways envisaged by some causal theories. Both perception and representation seem to require such a functional relation between certain magnitudes associated with causes and other magnitudes associated with effects. It might be claimed, for example, that the thermometer of example (3) above fails to represent the temperature of the room *just because* there is no function which maps different increments of room temperature into different changes of the pointer reading.[13] Furthermore, quite a few of the counter-examples to the causal theory of perception do violate the condition of differential explanation.

A more general view of the type of structural constraint that Peacocke's differential explanation condition seeks to capture is provided by what Bishop has called the sensitivity condition. This condition requires that the behaviour be responsive (or sensitive) to the content of the intention that causes the behaviour. But it has been argued that the sensitivity requirement cannot be met by the condition of differential explanation because differential explanation is not necessary for non-deviance in a causal theory of perception. To show this, Davies (1963) gives an example that involves a creature who has evolved to have discrete generators, each capable of producing a visual experience of one among a number of scenes. (We are to suppose that this creature's survival partly depends upon its ability to tell any one of these scenes apart from the others.) The retina of the creature that receives information from the scene in view activates one of the pulse generators, which in turn stimulates the appropriate one of the experience generators. The fact that the mechanism operates without satisfying the differential explanation requirement (there is no *continuous* mathematical mapping function) does not make the causal path from the scene to the visual experience deviant. As Bishop suggests, a similar example could be used to the same effect in causal theories of action.

---

[13] Such a function may be what Stampe has in mind when he says, 'The causal relation we have in mind is one that holds between a set of properties $F(f_1,..., f_n)$ of the thing O represented and a set of properties $\Phi(\varphi_1,..., \varphi_n)$ of the representation (R)...The relevant causal relationship between O's being F and R's being Φ will be one that normally, if not necessarily, preserves an isomorphism between structures thus defined' (1977: 46). Strictly speaking, isomorphism can obtain when differential explanation fails, but I take it that Stampe means more than just extensional isomorphism here.

A second way of explicating the sensitivity condition, according to Bishop, is to use a requirement that there be a counterfactual dependence between the behaviour and the content of the intention: if the content of the intention had been different, the resulting behaviour would correspondingly have been different, too.[14]

At this point it would be instructive to note that the four causal theories mentioned above should be considered under two categories. In the first category, which includes knowledge and representation, the mere existence of a causal relation between the appropriate thing and the causally defined entity is not enough. That is, it is not sufficient for knowledge that the fact that p cause the belief that p. If the belief that p can also be caused, under relevantly similar situations, by the fact that q, then the belief will not qualify as knowledge. For example, suppose that the wall I am looking at is blue, and I am caused by the colour of the wall to believe that the wall is blue. If I could easily be looking at the wall to the left, which is white illuminated by a blue light, and could have equally been caused by *that* wall to believe that the wall is blue, then my actual belief does not constitute knowledge. So the causal theory of knowledge must at least have an additional counterfactual requirement: if the fact were relevantly different, then the belief would have been different. Or more generally, the causal theory that applies to this category of concepts must stipulate not only that there be a causal relation, but also that the effect be nomically sufficient for the cause (that is, the cause must be 'recoverable' from the effect) or, to put it in more familiar terms, it must be true that if the cause event had not occurred, then the effect event would not be the case.[15]

In the second category all that is necessary for the causally defined entity to emerge is that the structure be caused by the appropriate thing. This category includes perception and intentional action. Take perception. For me to see an object, all that I need to have is a perceptual state of seeming to see an object which perceptual state is caused (in the right way) by the object. I need not ask, 'Would I be in that perceptual

---

[14] Although Bishop does not mention it, this requirement is basically Peacocke's recoverability condition, which Peacocke offers in addition to the condition of differential explanation.

[15] Dretske (1971) uses such a counterfactual in his version of the reliability theory of knowledge and argues persuasively that Goldman's (1967) causal theory is not sufficient for knowledge.

state even if the object were not there?' because the answer to that question does not have any bearing on whether I am seeing the object. The same is true of intentional action.

A *general* account of non-deviance in causal theories must therefore not require a counterfactual dependence between the cause and the effect. Otherwise some *normal* causal chains that arise in the context of theories in the second category would be excluded. This is illustrated by the example of the censor that Lewis (1980) originally offered. A censor is poised to intervene whenever what is in view of the perceiver is different from a predetermined scene, X, and to cause the person to have a visual (hallucinatory) experience as of an X. But when the viewer is viewing X, the censor does not interfere. Although it is false that if the scene were different the visual experience would be different, it is clear that when the scene viewed is X, the person is *seeing* the X.[16]

An identical issue arises in the causal theory of action as illustrated by Frankfurt's (1969) example of the counterfactual contravener. In this example we are to imagine that there is a neuroscientist who would interfere and make me do A if I were to fail to intend to do A. In spite of this, when I intend to do A, and do A as a causal consequence of this intention, my doing A is clearly intentional. Following the same logic as in the case of the censor, we can arrive at the conclusion that the counterfactual contravener does not make the actual causal chain from the intention to do A to doing A deviant.[17]

---

[16] Lewis originally maintained that the person under these conditions would not be able to see the X. Bishop draws attention to a paper by B. Le Catt (1982), in which the counter-factual condition has been extended to include a *step-wise* counterfactual dependence with *a ban on backtracking counterfactuals.* (Peacocke's third condition of step-wise recoverability may have been designed for the same purpose.) Le Catt's move does effectively restore sight to the viewer of X and renders the extended counterfactual dependence reading of the sensitivity condition applicable to both categories.

[17] Just as the censor (or the counterfactual contravener) is designed to show that a simple counterfactual reading of the sensitivity condition is not necessary for normal chains, an example called 'the reverse censor' (see Davies 1963: 412) shows it not to be sufficient. In the reverse censor, the censor allows a *deviant* chain to have a specific scene to cause the visual experience of that scene, but 'interferes' when the scene is different and lets the visual system function normally. So the condition that requires that, if the scene were different, the experience would be correspondingly different is satisfied in the case of the specific scene. But by hypothesis, the chain is deviant. This example shows the importance of the differential explanation requirement because although the counterfactual requirement is satisfied in the reverse censor cases, the differential explanation requirement is not.

A GENERAL CRITIQUE

Impressive as these moves are in rendering some revised version of Peacocke's conditions necessary for non-deviance (at least for causal theories in the second category), they fall short of giving us a satisfactory theory that explains the origins of deviance. To see this, let us take *any* requirement that describes the causal structure a normal chain must satisfy. Call this requirement R. Now consider two scenarios of the nervous actor example above. In the original version, it was agreed that on the opening night the actor did not appear nervous intentionally because the causal chain that connected his intention to appear nervous to his behaviour was deviant. Let us say that it was deviant *because* it violated some clause of R. In the second scenario, the actor can exploit the way in which R was violated in the original scenario and incorporate it into his action plan. He will know that just forming the intention to appear nervous will result in his thinking of delivering his lines as if he were nervous, whereupon his personality will make him nervous, and this will yield the intended result.[18] In this case, the actor's appearing nervous will be caused by his intention to be nervous and the causal path will be *identical* to the causal path of the first scenario, and yet in this second version, he will be appearing nervous intentionally. One and the same path is deviant in the first scenario and non-deviant in the second.

This pair of examples suggests a general argument. Suppose we are given a theory of non-deviance that imposes the requirement R to be satisfied by the structure of the causal pathway, either in terms of some mathematical functional relationship, or in terms of step-wise recoverability. We can always find two systems with identical causal pathways which violate some clause of R, one of which is deviant, and the other of which is normal. This general argument exploits the intuition that when a system contains a deviant causal path, it achieves what it is *supposed to do*, but not *in the way* it is supposed to do it. And the argument proceeds by showing that for some system doing what it is supposed to do by violating R is not that system's doing it in the way it

---

[18] The basic act in the act plan that supports the second scenario is *thinking of* delivering the lines as if he were nervous. But this difference between the scenarios is not reflected in the causal path: the same events are linked in the causal chain in both scenarios. It is just that in scenario 1, his appearing nervous is a basic act type, which gets tokened by a behavior that is not a basic *act* token, whereas in scenario 2, appearing nervous is an *intentional* non-basic act.

is supposed to do it, whereas for another system doing that same thing by again violating R *is* that second system's doing it in the way it is supposed to do it. And conversely, a system's operating in the way it is supposed to by conforming to R does not guarantee that a different system that also conforms to R will be operating the way it is supposed to operate. In summary, *the way* a system is supposed to do something is not capturable by stipulating certain structural requirements on the causal path.[19]

The proper response to the general argument is to turn to the *system* in which the causal chain is being evaluated, and develop a theory of what should count as a normal chain, *relative* to the well-functioning of the system.[20]

The four causal theories we have examined have a common feature. Each involves a system, and the system has the function of bringing about a result or a final product. The normal path that connects the input to the final product is one that subserves the function of the system. More specifically, when causal theories offer a causal analysis of a type of entity, the type of entity is the output produced by the system *when and only when* the system's producing that output is part of what counts as the system's properly executing its function. In other words, the 'right', 'ordinary', or the 'characteristic' ways in which the required type of event causes the output are nothing other than the ways in which the system normally executes its function.[21] On the other hand, if a token causal chain assumes a path that is not 'normal', the system may end up doing what it is its function to do without actually *functioning* at all, that is, it does 'what it is supposed to do', but not '*in the way* it is supposed to do it'.

---

[19] This point is acknowledged by Searle: 'Some people have thought that the problem in all these cases has to do with the oddity of the causal sequences, but the oddity of the causal sequence only matters if it is part of the Intentional content of the intention in action that it should not be odd' (1983: 109) Searle's way of identifying some cases of deviance is to notice that they lack what he has called 'the intention in action'. (An earlier expression of this type of approach to deviance is to be found in Bach 1978.) Elegant as this device is, it does not give a *general* account of normal causal chains even in the causal theory of action because in other cases Searle has to appeal to 'a good match between the act and the act plan'.

[20] The importance of teleological considerations for deviance was anticipated by Davies 1983. When I defended the appeal to the functions of systems in Enç 1989, I was regrettably ignorant of Davies's essay.

[21] The notion of a system's executing its function is perhaps too vague to be illuminating. I shall make this notion more precise below. But I think there is an intuitively clear sense in which the broken thermometer is not executing its function (is not functioning) when its pointer reads 30°.

For example, the thermometer represents the room temperature *only when* the causal path through which the temperature changes in the room bring about changes in the pointer position is the same as the causal path that was anticipated in the design of the device. This representational relation *is severed* if a change in the room temperature causes a corresponding change in the pointer position through a *different* causal path (as it does in the example of the thermometer that falls off the wall). Such a different path interferes with the functioning of the device: it causes it to malfunction. That is perhaps the clearest example of a case where a system does what it is supposed to do (have its pointer reading correspond to the room temperature) but not *in the way* it is supposed to do it. What a system is supposed to do is determined by its function, and the way it is supposed to do it is determined by its design.

It is important to keep the class of cases in which the thermometer fails to (correctly) indicate the room temperature (fails to do what it is supposed to do) separate from cases under discussion. In the former class of cases the pointer reading fails to indicate what the room temperature is just because the room temperature is *not* what the reading says it is. And this may happen in one of two ways: (i) because the thermometer is malfunctioning (e.g. the pointer is stuck), (ii) because although the thermometer is operating exactly as it was designed to operate, the environment does not co-operate (e.g. the thermometer is placed, by mistake, on top of a radiator).[22] The issue of distinguishing deviant causal chains from normal ones does not arise in this class of cases simply because the distinction between deviant and normal is made against the background supposition that the system in question *is* doing what it is supposed to do.

However, just as a system may fail to do what it is its function to do in one of two ways, by malfunctioning or by the environment not co-operating, a causal chain that subserves a function may, in general, end up being deviant in one of two ways: by the system's *malfunctioning* or by the environment's providing *haphazard* co-operation. In the first way, in spite of its malfunctioning, the system fortuitously brings about the expected result. In the second way, the system may not be

---

[22] The difference between these two ways is of interest to the causal theory of representation because those cases in which the device is *not* malfunctioning are the typical cases of *mis*representation, but when the system begins to malfunction, it becomes unclear whether the device is representing at all.

malfunctioning, and yet, outside the system, a sequence of events may occur and these events may serendipitously 'cancel each other' in a way that renders the chain deviant. The account I propose to develop starts with the basic intuition that a key to understanding what counts as a 'normal' causal chain is the concept of executing a function—the concept of a system's doing something that it is supposed to do *in the way* it is supposed to do it. When we move away from designed artefacts to natural systems, these concepts become harder to apply. However, I shall argue that they can be extended to the cognitive systems of higher organisms by an appeal to the theory of natural selection. If the basic intuition is right, though, then the correct account of non-deviance should focus on an explanatory context in which we explain why the system is capable of producing this type of output under these conditions *in this particular way*.

A DEVIANT CAUSAL PATH IN BIOLOGY

In order to give substance to the notion of a system's executing its function, I will take a short digression and describe a natural system which does not involve a causally defined concept, but one which illustrates the notion of deviance very simply.

The flower of a plant has the function of reproduction. On some plants the flower performs its function by producing pollen in its stamen and ovules in its pistil and by having the pollen carried to the stigmas of the pistil by external means, for example, wind or insects. Some flowers effect cross-pollination by emitting a scent that attracts the bees to the stamen. In the case of subtropical orchids, each species of the orchid has its own peculiar fragrance and attracts only one species of the so-called 'golden bees' (see Dodson 1975). In such orchids, the causal chain which leads from the presence of the fragrance through the attraction of the bees to the cross-pollination of the orchid clearly subserves the function of the flower. In such flowers, no causal definition of any output is at issue. But still, an intuitively clear distinction can be made between the 'normal' way the fragrance leads to pollination (or the way in which it is 'supposed to' lead to pollination), and 'deviant' ways in which it may result in pollination. For an example of a deviant way, we can imagine that I find the scent of the orchid offensive and pluck it and throw it away before any bees get to it; the wind carries the pollen to other plants of the same species, and fertilization is achieved. In this example, the scent does initiate a causal chain and the end product of this chain is an event that the flower has the function of bringing about. However, in the circumstances described, this event is brought about fortuitously; it is brought about in such a way that the flower cannot properly be said to be executing its function.

The difference between these two chains, the one normal, and the other deviant, is in many ways analogous to the difference between normal and deviant chains that arise in causal theories. The point of analogy that is of immediate interest here is that no *general* account of this difference seems to be expressible by attending *merely* to the type of lawful regularities in conformity with which the causes are connected to the result. In the case of the orchid, one can imagine a scenario in which the particular species of bee which is attracted to the fragrance dies out; the offending nature of the scent causes human beings to keep plucking the flower and tossing it away. And the forces of selection retain the scent just for the task of offending human beings. In the context of such a scenario, my causing the plant to be pollinated by tossing away the flower would be an instance of the 'normal' way the fragrance causally contributes to pollination.

If the analogy between the right chains in causal theories and biological functioning is basically correct, then a general account of the intuitively clear difference between the normal and deviant ways biological systems bring about that which it is their function to bring about will, *ipso facto*, be a general account of what it is for a causal chain to be the right kind of causal chain for the purposes of a causal theory. And the roots of such a general account (at least for cases of malfunctioning) are to be found in the evolutionary process that has shaped these organisms. More specifically, the basis of the intuition according to which my tossing the flower is a deviant chain lies in the fact that the fragrance of the orchid is an adaptation *for* attracting the golden bee, *not* an adaptation for offending me.[23] From one perspective, adaptation is a causal concept: whether a feature is an adaptation for X depends purely on the aetiology of that feature, or,

---

[23] See Sober 1984b: 196–211, for a clear and illuminating discussion of adaptation and 'adaptedness'.

more accurately, on the forces that have led to the feature's being retained in the population.[24]

In more general terms, we can think of the flower as having the *function* of attracting the golden bee (or having the *function* of promoting pollination). Function assignments to systems can be analysed by the following clauses:[25]

> The *function* of subsystem B in system S is F if and only if:
> > (i) In response to the onset of a certain set of specifiable internal or external conditions, C, B produces output O, and
> >
> > (ii) O results in F, and
> >
> > (iii) The causal chain from C to O and from O to F is such that for any intermediate link, X, in the chain, the fact that C causes X is explainable by the fact that X causes F.

A simpler way of parsing the third condition is to think of O as the most proximal output that is produced by B when an internal state C′ obtains, or when an input C″ is introduced. (In the case of action, this O will be the basic act, and C′ will be the formation of an intention.) We can suppose that F is the event the production of which constitutes the function (or one of the functions) of B. The causal chain involved here can be represented schematically as in Figure 4.1.

One consequence of the third condition in the simplified diagram of Figure 4.1 is that bringing about F is a function of B only if the fact that C′ (or C″) causes O is explainable by the fact that O causes F. Applying this consequence, we can conclude that attracting the golden bees is a function of the flower because the fact that the internal state of the

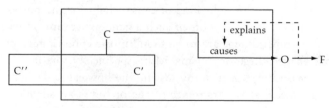

Fig. 4.1. *The causal structure of functions*

---

[24] Sober (1984*b*: 199) says, 'To call a characteristic an adaptation is to say something about its origin. It is for this reason that adaptations stand in contrast to fortuitous benefits.'

[25] See Enç 1979. For the purposes of the problem of deviance, many other naturalistic analyses of function (e.g. Millikan 1984, just to mention one out of many) will be compatible with these claims.

plant causes the fragrance (O) is explainable by the fact that the fragrance attracts the bees (F). This explanation, as mentioned above, is provided by the theory of natural selection. Natural selection has brought it about that there is a nomic dependence of the fact that the plant produces this fragrance on the fact that the fragrance attracts the bees: there are close enough possible worlds in which the bees fail to be attracted by the fragrance, and these are worlds in which the plant has gone extinct or the fragrance has atrophied.[26]

On the other hand, if on one occasion, I get offended by the fragrance and throw the flower away, thereby causing cross-pollination, the fact that the plant produces the fragrance cannot be explained by the fact that the fragrance offends me—until the time when my behaviour begins to contribute causally to the prevalence of the fragrance in the population of orchids, that is, until the fragrance becomes an adaptation for its capacity to elicit this type of behaviour from me.

THE EXPLANATORY RELATION REQUIREMENT

General

It is now easy to ground the notion of a system's executing its function on the existence of this explanatory relation. Let us take the revised minimal condition that gives a causal definition for some concept Φ:

> *Revised Minimal Condition:* Some event, structure, or state, S, is a Φ if and only if it is caused in the way it is supposed to be caused by a C-type event (or a C-type object).

And I shall say that

> C causes the structure *in the way it is supposed to* just in case:
> For any intermediate link, X, in the chain from C to S, the fact that C causes X is explained by the fact that X results in S.

---

[26] It is true that there may be equally close possible worlds in which the bees are not attracted to the fragrance, and yet the fragrance is retained because it is genetically linked to some other feature that is functional, or because, in terms of ecological economy, it is too 'expensive' for the plant to eliminate the mechanism responsible for the production of the fragrance. The fact that these worlds are possible does not affect the truth of the claim that the required explanatory relation holds.

Here the core idea is that whenever Φ is attained in the system in the way it is supposed to, we will be assured of a non-deviant chain.

Since the focus of this chapter is the problem of deviance as it arises in the causal theory of *action*, I will skip over cases of deviance that arise in the other three causal theories. I leave it to the reader to see that the explanatory relation requirement is violated in each of these cases. For example, the crack-on-the-wall scenario is deviant simply because, given the design of the gadget, the fact that the drop in the temperature caused the coil to break is not explainable by the fact that the break caused the pointer to read 30°.

Deviance in Action Theory

Adapting the general minimal condition to causal theories of action, we can formulate it as follows:

CTA: The behavioural output of an organism is an intentional action A if it is caused in the way it is supposed to be caused by an intention to do A.[27]

E_o: An intention to do A causes an event in the way it is supposed to if and only if for any intermediate link, X, from the intention to the event, the fact that the intention causes X is explained by the fact that X results in that event.

Several refinements on this version of the explanatory requirement are in order.

The intention that defines the action is a link in a long chain of events. As I shall be arguing in the next chapter, the antecedents of the event constituted by the formation of the intention are beliefs and desires that get computed in a complex process. The reasons for the action (and the formation of the intention) are to be found in a subset of the beliefs and desires. When the intention is formed, typically it is an intention to bring about some distal event. And such an intention is backed by a plan that links this distal event, through cause–effect chains anticipated by the instrumental beliefs of the agent, to some

---

[27] As we will see in Ch. 6, bringing about 'unintended' but foreseen consequences of intended actions may also count as intentional action. To allow for this possibility, I offer being non-deviantly caused by the intention to do A as only a sufficient condition for A's being an intentional action.

basic result. So the general schematic diagram of Figure 4.1 may be redrawn as Figure 4.2 to represent the causal chain involved in action.

As philosophers who have been interested in deviant causal chains in action have remarked, deviance can infect the chain from the intention to do A, I(A), to the event that constitutes the *result* of A, E_A, in either of two places. The deviance can occur either between I(A) and O, or between O and E_A. Accordingly, examples of deviance have been traditionally treated under two separate categories. Antecedential deviance, as it appears between the intention and the basic *result*, and consequential deviance as it appears between the basic *result* and the distal event that satisfies the intention.[28]

This difference between the two categories is reflected in the view I defend here. When we examine the causal pathway in the framework of the function of the system, we can distinguish cases in which the system malfunctions (the category of antecedentially deviant cases) from those in which the system functions well, but the co-operation of the environment is totally fortuitous (the category of consequentially deviant cases). Although the traditional literature on deviance treats these two categories separately, and gives different conditions of non-deviance for each, I will attempt to show that the requirement of explanatory relation provides a unified account not only for these two types of deviance, but other categories that have since been discussed.

If we look at the antecedential segment, we can see that E_o should be understood as requiring the following. The fact that the intention to perform some basic act causes an intermediate neuro-muscular event should be explainable by the fact that that neuro-muscular event will produce the basic *result*. Normally when an agent intends to

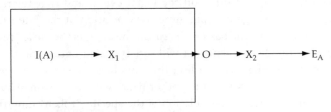

Fig. 4.2. *The causal structure of action*

---

[28] These terms, 'antecedential' and 'consequential', were introduced by Brand (1984).

perform some basic act, she activates a circuit the function of which is to produce a basic act that matches what is intended. So normally, given the 'design' of this circuit, the intermediate events that occur between the intention and the basic *result* are directed at the goal of producing that basic *result*—these intermediate events are caused to occur *because* they contribute to the production of the basic *result*. In the deviant case of the nervous actor scenario, the intention to appear nervous, I(A), causes (via the thought of appearing nervous) a state of nervousness, and the state of nervousness causes the actor to appear nervous. Here the fact that the intention to appear nervous causes nervousness has nothing to do with the fact that the nervousness results in appearing nervous. The two facts are independent of each other. Given the details of the scenario, the intention to appear nervous would have caused (via the same path) the nervousness *even if* (due to a possible self control on the part of the actor) the nervousness did not result in appearing nervous.

If we look at the consequential segment, the simplest way of applying E_o is to read X as the basic *result*, and see if the explanatory requirement is satisfied. In other words, we want to ask, 'is the fact that the intention to do A causes the basic *result* explainable by the fact that the basic *result* leads to the satisfaction of the intention?' First, we should remember that in the chain of events starting at the basic *result*, the relation is not always causal. So we should understand 'leading to the satisfaction of the intention' as allowing for any of the generative relations (causal, constitutive, augmentative, etc.) among events.

Secondly, the requirement of the explanatory relation is satisfied typically when there is, other things being equal, a lawful relation between the basic *result* and the distal event, and that relation is anticipated by the agent in planning the execution of the intention.[29] The agent performs the basic act *because* she expects the basic *result* to generate the distal event that will satisfy the intention. So the link that does the explaining is a link that involves a generative relation between *types* of events. On the other hand, what is explained by this anticipated type generative relation is the specific (token) intention's causing the (token) basic *result* in question.

---

[29] See Enç and Adams 1992, for a discussion of the affinity between purposive behavior and behavior that it is the function of a system to produce.

Putting these two remarks together, we can write E_0 as

> E: An intention to do A causes an event in the way it is supposed to
> if and only if for any intermediate link, X, from the intention to
> the event, the fact that a tokening of the intention causes a token X
> is explained by the fact that under the circumstances that type of
> X would generate that kind of event.[30]

In the non-deviant case of the nervous actor scenario, the actor
exploits the deviant causal path of the first scenario, and in doing so
transforms his appearing nervous into an intentional act. We can see
that E is satisfied. This is a case of a consequential causal chain because
the act of appearing nervous is no longer a basic act.

Using the revised version, E, of the explanatory relation requirement, we can now ask: 'Is the fact that the actor's intention (to appear
nervous according to the plan described) causes him to think of delivering his lines as if he were nervous explained by the fact that
thinking this way would cause him to be nervous?' The answer is
clearly 'yes'. The whole 'point' of the actor's intentionally generating
this thought in his mind is that he knows that the thought will make
him nervous and thus secure the event of his appearing nervous.

EXAMPLES OF DEVIANCE

It might be useful to mention here two of the most often discussed
cases of antecedential deviance.

1. Frankfurt's (1978) example of the inexperienced accomplice.
Abel, who is attending a party, wants to spill his drink because
he wants to signal to his confederates to begin the robbery, and he
believes, in virtue of their prearrangement, that spilling his drink will
accomplish that. (He forms the intention to spill his drink.) But Abel is
inexperienced in crime, and this leads him to be very anxious. His
anxiety makes his hand tremble, and so his glass spills.

2. Davidson's rock climber.[31] A climber, who intends to loosen his
hold on the rope so as to get rid of the weight and the danger of holding

---

[30] I am indebted to Greg Mougin for this wording.
[31] Davidson 1980: 79. I have changed Davidson's reference to a desire and a belief into an
intention to make the example conform to the general format of the discussion of this
chapter. Similar liberties will be taken in subsequent examples.

another man on the rope, is so unnerved by this intention as to cause him to loosen his hold. When he loosens his grip, his doing so is not an intentional action.

It should be clear that (1) and (2) are both variations of the first version of the nervous actor scenario. As diagnosed by the violation of the explanatory requirement, they both involve deviant causal chains because the system, which has the function of producing a basic act that matches the content of the intention, malfunctions, and produces a basic act in a way that it is not supposed to.[32]

Next, we can look at two examples that are offered in the literature as cases of consequential deviance.

3. Chisholm's example of the rich uncle (1966: 29–30). Carl intends to kill his uncle to inherit his fortune. While he is driving to his uncle's house, where he intends to commit the act, his thoughts agitate him and make him drive carelessly. As a result he hits and kills a pedestrian, who, as luck will have it, happens to be his uncle.

4. The lucky soccer player (Ginet 1990: 79). The player kicks the ball intending the ball to go into the goal. Instead of taking the intended direct trajectory, the ball bounces off the backs of two players and rebounds into the goal. (The players off whom the ball bounces are assumed to be inactive.)

Brand classifies (3) explicitly as consequential, and offers his requirement of a close enough match between the act plan and the actual unfolding of events as a diagnostic device for detecting deviance. Searle, in discussing a similar example also appeals to a version of Brand's requirement: 'we assume that the [agent] had a complex intention involving a specific series of by-means of relations…and these conditions were not satisfied' (1983: 109). But I tend to think that they each share a common feature with the two examples cited as

---

[32] In a sense, Brand's (1984) requirement for antecedential chains, that the intention *proximately* cause the action, or Searle's (1983) requirement that there be an *intention in action* that interfaces with the action, are both roughly in agreement by my requirement. The system is 'designed' so that when the intention causes the basic *result* non-deviantly, it causes it by triggering the module (the molar unit) that corresponds to the basic *result* directly. So the design does not leave any room for any intermediary between the causal role of the intention and the triggering of the unit that constitutes the basic *result*. And if we think of the direct triggering action of the intention as Searle's intention in action (or as a complete package of Bach's (1978) feedback loops of 'executive representations'), it becomes possible to see why the three requirements should roughly be coextensional. The reason I prefer my requirement is that, apart from being general, it has the richness to explain why the other two work to the extent that they do.

cases of antecedential deviance. The feature is that the basic act in every one of them, if considered in all its causally effective properties (that is, the properties in virtue of which it causes the intended final event) is non-intentional. Carl's act of holding the steering wheel and pressing on the accelerator at the time of the accident (call this act 'Carl's driving'), assuming this was a basic act of Carl's, may have been intentional, but his driving *carelessly* was *not* intentional. This is borne out by the same sort of reasoning that reveals that the climber's release of the rope and the accomplice's spilling his drink were non-intentional. So the deviance infects the part of the chain that connects the intention to the basic act. In addition there is an element of chance that enters into the chain leading from the basic act to the final event: it was by chance that the pedestrian was the uncle, and it was by chance that the two soccer players were positioned in exactly that way. It is perhaps this element of chance that distinguishes these two from the earlier cases of antecedential deviance.

However, this classificatory problem need not detain us, for I intend my explanatory requirement to work for both categories of deviance. To see how it does, we can ask of each of the four cases: 'Does the fact that the basic act would have the intended result explain the fact that the intention caused the particular basic act (with its salient features) in question?' And the question receives a negative answer in each case.

Is the fact that Carl, the nephew, was driving carelessly at the time of the accident explainable by the fact that his driving carelessly was to cause his uncle's death? The answer should be 'no'. The two facts are independent of each other. The fact that Carl's driving carelessly would cause the death made no contribution to the fact that his intention made him drive carelessly.

Again, when we look at the case of the soccer player, we can conclude that the intention causing the kick to be directed at the back of the first player, instead of the goal, is not explainable by the fact that the ball's bouncing off that player's back would result in a goal. The kick's being directed away from the goal had nothing to do with the fact that being so directed would be causally sufficient for the ball's ending up between the goal posts. In other words, it is *false* that the features of the basic act in question that was causally relevant to the bringing about of the intended final event were caused by the intention *because* those features would bring about the intended final event. The reason for the basic act's having those features lay in the degree of ineptitude of the agent. We might say that those features were not the intended features of the basic act.

It may be instructive here to contrast the case of the soccer player with a case where a man intends to kill his victim by shooting him in the heart. He takes aim at the heart, and kills his victim by shooting him in the head. The intuition is that whereas the player's goal was not intentional, the man in this example killed his victim intentionally.[33] I think that the judgement depends on how the intention is fleshed out.[34] In the normal case in which one aims at the chest to kill someone, one realizes that aiming at the chest might result in hitting him in the head, and thus killing the person. Therefore, a case can be made that part of the reason why the man's intention resulted in his aiming at the chest is that aiming at the chest would result (given certain other factors, which might obtain) in hitting him in the head, thereby causing his death. For instance, it might be true that he aimed at the chest, *rather than lower*, because aiming at the chest gives him a better chance at hitting him in the head, which is very likely lethal.

However, changing these details might make the example deviant. And the account of deviance I propose would explain why. Suppose that the man believes the victim is coated in armour save one hole over his heart. Unbeknownst to him, there is also a hole in the armour covering his head. If he aims at the heart, thinking this is the only way to kill him, but if again the wind blows the bullet with the result that it hits him in the head, then it seems that the fact that (given the characteristics of the wind) aiming at the heart would result in the victim's death (by hitting him in the head) does *not* explain why his intention resulted in his aiming at the heart. What explains why his intention resulted in aiming at the heart is the fact that in normal conditions (when there is no such wind) aiming at the heart would result in killing him by hitting him in the heart. But in the example, this latter law is not the operative law that explains why in this token case aiming at the heart killed the victim. So we do not have the right explanatory relationship between the two segments of the causal

---

[33] Both Ginet 1990: 87 and Brand 1984: 28–30 attempt to capture this contrast by trying to see how close the execution was to the complex intention. Ginet's second soccer player example, in which the ball bounces off the goal post and goes in (1990: 79), is the intentional version of (4).

[34] I am indebted to Greg Mougin's help here.

chain. This supports the intuition that the man killed his victim non-intentionally.[35]

These considerations should not lead us to conclude that whether the chain is deviant or not depends on whether the agent's beliefs about how his action will result in the desired effect are true or not. Suppose I hire an assassin to kill Hermann, and I give him poison to accomplish this. The assassin's job is to give the poison to Hermann. I tell him falsely that the poison is a heavy dose of morphine (it will make him stop breathing), when it is in fact a rat poison (it will cause him to haemorrhage), with the result that he plans to kill Hermann by causing him to stop breathing. It will still be true that the assassin's intention caused the haemorrhage *because* haemorrhage would cause death, provided that the fact that haemorrhage would cause death is the reason why I gave him the rat poison to use. The assassin would administer whatever substance I had given him. So his intention results in the haemorrhage because the substance I gave him would induce haemorrhage and haemorrhage would result in death. The chain is not deviant, even though the assassin's plan for killing Hermann contains false beliefs.[36]

A more far-fetched example may further illustrate that the presence of a false belief is not sufficient for deviance.[37] Suppose Stan has a neighbour. Stan wants to damage his neighbour's house, and thinks

[35] Mele and Moser (1994) offer one of the most extensive recent examinations of deviance. One pair of examples they use parallels very closely the pair of shooting cases discussed here. One minor difference is that, in their first example, the killer hits his victim in the head because he errs slightly in his aim, rather than aiming correctly at the heart and having his bullet be deflected by the wind. They, too, would seem to agree with my judgement that in the first example the killing is intentional, whereas in the second example the killing is unintentional. (In their second example, Arnold, the killer, has the false belief that bullets can kill only by penetrating the heart, and his bullet, owing to a slight inaccuracy of his aim, hits the victim in the head, and to Arnold's astonishment, the victim dies (p. 51).) Mele and Moser conclude that the agents' evidential conditions are what separate the two cases. I tend to think this is right. There was an important difference between what the two agents had reason to expect. My explanatory condition clarifies why that difference is important to deviance. The fact that Arnold's aim was directed at the head cannot be explained by the fact that such an act would kill the victim. And the reason such an explanation is not forthcoming is to be found in Arnold's expectations.

[36] Intuitions may get strained in these improbable examples involving false beliefs leading to false expectations. The reader may find the judgements generated by the explanatory relevance requirement, as formulated by E, counterintuitive. If so, I have nothing to say in defence of E, except to point out that in discussing these cases with colleagues, students, and friends, I have discovered so many divergent intuitions that I have come to trust E more than the array of pre-theoretic intuitions that are designed to test E.

[37] I owe this scenario to Noel Hendrickson, who offered it to me as a counter-example to my account. I prefer to bite the bullet here.

that the best way of achieving this is to fell the tree in his yard, making sure it falls in the direction of his neighbour's house. A demon who knows Stan's mind, without letting Stan know about it, empowers him with a psycho-kinetic capacity: when Stan intends to damage his neighbour's house (by knocking the tree down towards the neighbour's house) his intention will directly cause the tree to fall in that direction. One day Stan, finding the desire to damage his neighbour's house irresistible, forms the intention to damage the house by chopping the tree with his axe, but before he can go and get his axe, thanks to the powers the demon had given him, his intention causes the tree to fall in the direction he had intended. And the roof of the neighbour's house caves in. Here the fact that the fall of the tree would cause damage to the house explains why the demon rigged things so that the intention to damage the house caused the tree to fall. Consequently Stan damaged his neighbour's house intentionally. If this judgement appears counter-intuitive, it may help to see that what the demon did was just make felling the tree a basic act for Stan. That Stan did not know at the time that he had added an unusual basic act to his repertoire is not a reason to judge his act of damaging the house to be non-intentional.[38]

The next set of cases involves a different kind of luck—luck that depends on a mistake.

5. Lucky Catherine.[39] Catherine intends to enter the room after the queen enters. The queen has already entered when Catherine sees Anne enter the room; she mistakes Anne for the queen and enters after Anne. It was just luck that the queen had entered before Anne, so Catherine does not intentionally enter the room after the queen.

6. Clueless Kate (Ginet 1990: 80). Kate intends to enter the room after the queen enters. Kate believes correctly that the queen has already entered. This belief is not based on any false belief, but it is totally unjustified. She had no reason at all for holding it.[40]

[38] If the reader finds the verdict not too implausible, then the case is a clear counter-example to the requirement (proposed in various forms by Brand, Harman, Searle, Ginet, Thalberg, Mele) that if the act is to be non-deviant then it should approximate the act plan. Another counter-example to such a requirement is to be found in Moya 1990: 121–2.

[39] Ginet 1990: 78. Mele (1987), who introduces a similar example. His example involves two mistakes that cancel each other. He argues that such cases are different from ante-cedential and consequential cases of deviance. He calls them tertiary.

[40] Ginet offers the intuition that Kate's entering the room after the queen was unintentional. I think this is right. The case of Clueless Kate prompts Ginet to formulate a justified belief requirement for an act's being intentional. A more effective version of the relevance of the epistemic state of the agent is to be found in Mele and Moser 1994.

In (5), it was just fortuitous that Anne had entered the room after the queen. So it is *false* that the fact that Catherine's intention caused her to enter after Anne is explainable by the fact that her entering after Anne would constitute her entering after the queen (would make it the case that she entered after the queen). The connection between Catherine's entering after Anne and her entering after the queen is due to chance so the fact that her entering after Anne *was* an act of entering after the queen cannot explain why Catherine's intention caused her to enter after Anne. (The fact that Catherine *believed* that entering after Anne was an act of entering after the queen would explain this, but that is not what the requirement demands.) So the explanatory requirement is violated, and we do not have an intentional act. In determining whether the explanatory requirement is satisfied or not, it is important to be sensitive to the causally relevant properties of the events that are being considered. The property of Catherine's basic act that was relevant to that act's being an act of entering after the queen was its being an entering after Anne. Her intention's causing a basic act with that property had nothing to do with the fact that the basic act would lead to the satisfaction of her intention to enter after the queen. The explanatory relation is severed when the intention's causing some event is independent of that event's bringing about the satisfaction of the intention.

Similar comments can be made for the case of Clueless Kate. Given that there were no grounds whatsoever for Kate's belief that the queen had entered, the fact that the queen entered at time t could not have any relevance to the explanation of why Kate's intention caused her to enter *after* t.

The case of lucky Catherine is reminiscent of the Gettier-type examples against simple justified-true-belief accounts of knowledge. And this, in turn, may prompt some to apply to the problem of deviance a version of a reliabilist approach to knowledge.[41] Indeed, it may appear that my explanatory requirement derives from this type of approach.

John Gibbons makes an explicit case for requiring knowing (from an externalist point of view) that performing a basic act will lead to the

---

[41] As is clear from the context, Ginet's appeal to a justified belief is purely internalist. Mele and Moser (1994), on the other hand, by their appeal both to evidential base and to 'suitably reliable skill', 'suitably reliable means', and 'reliable control' most likely have a hybrid internalist–externalist account of justification in mind.

intended result, R, as a necessary condition for bringing about R intentionally.[42] He says,

Bobby intends to kill his uncle by planting a bomb in his house and then, after moving a safe distance away, pressing the large red button on the remote control device. He doesn't know much about how these things work. He thinks that pressing the button will cause the bomb to detonate but has no idea about the details of this process. His belief is true and, we can suppose, justified. But here's what happens. A satellite, launched by the National Security Agency and designed to prevent bombings of just this kind, intercepts Bobby's transmission; this causes the satellite to send a warning to the intended victim; but, because of an unfortunate choice of frequency, this causes the bomb to detonate. Bobby killed his uncle and caused to bomb to detonate, but he did not do either of these things intentionally....

In the case as described, Bobby's ignorance about the details means that his plan is quite simple: press the button and blow up the house. In this respect, Bobby is like many of us who call people on the phone, play CDs, and stop cars without having any idea about how these things work....What Bobby lacks is knowledge....One thing makes him justified—information about the reliability of the device—while something very different makes his belief true. This is like the original Gettier examples.[43]

It is clear how the two cases involving Catherine and Kate violate the knowledge condition. Indeed, I am sure Gibbons would also argue that cases (3) and (4) fail to be intentional because they again violate the knowledge condition. Close as Gibbons's condition is to my explanatory requirement, the two are not coextensional. There are cases of intentional action where the explanatory requirement is satisfied but where there fails to be knowledge. And there are also cases where there is knowledge (understood in terms of a reliability theory) but in which the act is non-intentional. To see the first type of case, it is sufficient to remember the contrast mentioned earlier between causal theories of knowledge and causal theories of action.[44] (I take up the second type of

---

[42] Gibbons 2001: 590. Gibbon's thesis is much subtler than what I suggest above. He does not talk of necessary conditions and denies he is giving an analysis. But my formulating his thesis in this way will help me highlight the close affinity of his approach to mine, as well as an important difference between them.

[43] Bobby's justified true belief that is not a case of knowledge shows that mere justified belief is not enough to eliminate cases of non-intentional action. It is also easy to see that my explanatory requirement gives the right answer here: the fact that pressing the button would alert the Agency and thus accidentally cause the bomb to detonate was not why Bobby pressed the button.

[44] To make this point I do not need to confine the knowledge condition to a causal theory of knowledge. Any adequate reliability theory of knowledge will do.

case at the end of this chapter.) For me to know that my basic act, B, will result in R, it is not enough that under the circumstances B would cause R; it is also required that there be a reliable connection between B and R. But in certain cases, even when the reliable connection between B and R is lacking, one's bringing about R may constitute an intentional act.

Suppose Rob, just like Bobby, wants to kill his uncle with a bomb. Rob's remote control device, unbeknownst to him, has a faulty connection. The odds are 1 in 100 that the connection will be made when the button is pressed. Although Rob has a justified belief, he does not know that pressing the button will detonate the bomb. When he presses the button, as luck will have it, what is improbable happens, and the bomb detonates. Rob kills his uncle intentionally. And given the circumstances, the fact that pressing the button would detonate the bomb does explain why Rob's intention to detonate the bomb (hence to kill his uncle) caused him to press the button.[45]

It might be tempting to think of Rob's case in the same category as a class of cases widely discussed in the literature. These cases include that of a lab technician who, intending to enter a code into a computer and thus shut down a nuclear reactor about to explode, punches ten digits at random, and by incredible luck, succeeds in averting the disaster (Mele and Moser 1994: 40), that of Sally, who wants to win the lottery and buys a ticket, which happens to be the winning ticket (see below[46]), or that of a man who needs to toss 66 on a 100-sided die in order to activate a camera, and who gets lucky (Mele and Sverdlik 1996). In all such cases the unanimous intuition seems to be that the agents were too lucky to have acted intentionally. I agree that the acts in these three

[45] The similarity between this case and the case of the lucky soccer player (or any other case involving luck in the scenarios illustrating deviant chains) is deceptive. The difference is best brought out by either of the following two considerations. (1) The feature of the soccer's basic act that resulted in a goal (e.g. its being a kick aimed at one of the players) was not a consequence of the fact that a kick aimed at one of the players would lead to a goal. (Also, Catherine's basic act of entering the room had the property of being an entering after Anne. This was the property that was relevant to the action's being an entering after the queen. That feature was not caused by the fact that Catherine's entering after Anne would constitute her entering after the queen.) But all aspects of Rob's pressing the button that were causally relevant to exploding the bomb were caused by the fact that pressing the button would explode the bomb. (2) If the soccer player were watching the event's unfold and saw the ball hit the player, he would regard his plan to have failed. But this is not true of Rob. (Also if lucky Catherine identified Anne before she saw the queen in the room, she would judge her plan to have been thwarted.) It is this difference between the agents' epistemic conditions that explains the difference described under (1).

[46] Also used by Mele and Moser (1994: 55).

scenarios were not intentional, but not because the agents were 'too lucky'. Although the probability of success may be exactly the same, Rob's action is significantly different from them. As I shall argue in the next section, the difference consists in the fact that Rob's luck involved his being hooked up to a system that luckily was functioning at the time as it was supposed to, whereas in cases of luck that resulted in deviance no such system was involved. To see that the momentary well-functioning of an unreliable gadget is sufficient to yield intentional action, we again exploit a version of Frankfurt's counterfactual contravener. Suppose unbeknownst to Rob, the contravener has arranged it so that the detonator functions only between 2.00 and 2.30 p.m. And as luck will have it Rob forms the intention to detonate the bomb at 2.10 p.m. It seems clear that the fact that the detonator would not have worked if Rob had formed his intention fifteen minutes earlier is irrelevant to the question whether he intentionally killed his uncle.

CASES INVOLVING TWO AGENTS

Perhaps this exhausts the discussion of deviance in causal chains as deviance has been conceived traditionally. But there is a family of unusual causal pathways leading from the intention of an agent, via the action of a mediating second agent, to an action of the first, some of which count against the act's being intentional.[47]

The best of way of approaching this family of cases is first to look at prosthetic devices.

Prosthetic Devices

1. It is, I think, absolutely clear that whether one has a prosthetic arm or a real arm makes no difference to our judgements about the intentionality of an act that involves the basic act of an arm movement. And

---

[47] Ginet confronts some of these cases and designs his conditions of an act's being intentional with them in mind. But it is John Bishop (1989) who gives a systematic treatment of them. (He calls them heteromesial cases.) I am indebted to him for alerting me to the fact that the adequacy of a general account of deviance requires attending to these cases. Bishop's solution to heteromesy is to require that whenever there is a feedback loop in the causal mechanism, the feedback be routed to the first agent's central mental process if to anyone's. The progression of examples below is also inspired by his treatment.

even when the prosthetic device has a loose wire that makes contact only some of the time, when it does make contact and the arm moves as intended, the movement would be intentional.

2. Suppose the prosthesis is further upstream in the causal pathway. Suppose, for example, that when the intention to raise the arm is formed, a brain state, B, results, and electrodes in the brain transmit by radio signals the information about B to a satellite computer, which in turn signals the electric motor of an artificial arm that moves the arm in the way intended. Again, the intuition is that the agent raised her arm intentionally. This is borne out by the fact that, given the design, the system that includes the agent and the elaborate prosthesis was functioning in the way it was supposed to. And the explanatory requirement that tests for this gives the right answer: the fact that the radio signal causes the arm to rise explains why the intention causes the radio signal. The engineers who designed the prosthesis would not have incorporated a circuit in which the intention causes the signal if the signal could not get to produce the intended arm movement.

3. If the prosthetic setup in (2) is functioning only intermittently, then when it does work, the arm raising should be judged as intentional. This judgement parallels the case where a person is struck by paralysis 90 per cent of the time she intends to move a limb, and yet when she does move the limb as intended, the movement is judged intentional. When the prosthesis works, the system is functioning as it is supposed to and there is no room for deviance. As I argued above, the lack of reliability in the workings of the prosthetic device is not enough to produce deviance.[48]

In cases (1)–(3), we have been assuming that the agent is not aware of the existence of the prosthetic device. This is realistic enough because most persons are not aware of the neuro-physiological causal pathways that lead from their intention to their basic acts. So I have not been implicitly relying on a belief condition involving how the arm moves. If we give the agent the knowledge of the working of the device, the only thing we change *might* be that the arm movement is no longer a basic act.

---

[48] The fact that the function of such devices is to enable the agent to move the relevant limb is what satisfies the explanatory requirement as formulated by E. It was exactly this fact that was exploited in the example of Rob, who detonated the bomb intentionally by using an unreliable gadget that was designed for the purpose of detonating the bomb.

4. Suppose, however, that there is no design, no 'device', no system to function or malfunction. Bishop and Peacocke mention an example of David Pears (1975). In the example a gunman's nerve to his finger is severed, but his brain event caused by the intention to pull the trigger attracts a lightning bolt which provides the required impulse to the finger. The consensus is that the gunman pulls the trigger intentionally.[49] I have to disagree. There is no system that was performing its function at the time of the action in the way it was supposed to. And hence the explanatory requirement cannot be satisfied.[50] I admit that some readers may regard this case as a serious counter-example to the solution I have defending here. But the intuitions, whatever they may be worth in such fantastic science-fiction cases, may be challenged by the following three-step reasoning:

(a) Sally buys a lottery ticket with the intention to win. When the improbable happens, and she does win, the intuition seems to be clear that it is *false* to say that she won the lottery intentionally.

(b) In a game of darts, I aim at the bull's eye, and throw the dart. When the improbable happens (let us say that, due to my ineptness at the game, the probabilities are comparable to those of Sally's ticket being the winner), and I do hit the bull's eye, it seems equally clear that I hit it intentionally.[51]

---

[49] Bishop (1989: 174 n. 14) and Peacocke (1979: 89–93) share this intuition. Pears originally disagreed on the grounds that the process is not reliable, but he is reported by Peacocke to have changed his mind later. As should be clear, I do not hold reliability of the process to be a necessary condition for non-deviance. Nonetheless, I am committed to judging this to be a deviant path.

[50] The case is similar to Gibbons's example of Bobby, the bomb detonator, which was presented as a case of deviance. It is hard to see how one would be consistent in having the intuition that Pears's gunman pulled the trigger intentionally, *and* that Bobby exploded his bomb non-intentionally. The only difference is that in the example of Pears's gunman the action is a basic act, and the indeterminacy is between the intention and the basic act, whereas in Bobby's case the indeterminacy infects the path to the distal event. It is hard to see why that difference should be significant. Indeed since my explanatory requirement is designed to work equally well for antecedential and consequential chains, I am committed to denying that such a difference makes a difference.

[51] Mele and Moser (1994) would seem to disagree. They discuss a basketball player, B.J., who has a 50% success rate of sinking his free-throws. They admit that when B.J. sinks a shot from the free-throw line, he does so intentionally. But they go on to say 'drop B.J.'s free-throw percentage .001%—while everything else in the case remains the same. The case then approaches a lottery case in certain respects' (1994: 62). Intuitions are hard to budge. And there may be scenarios in which I would agree that B.J., with a 0.001% rate of success, would sink his shot non-intentionally. One such scenario is where B.J. closes his eyes and throws the ball any which way, without using any cues, without trying to achieve eye–arm co-ordination, without aiming, etc. But I am assuming that when I throw the dart, with an equally low rate of success, I am aiming, or at least trying to aim.

What is the difference between (*a*) and (*b*)? One conjecture I can offer is that, in the dart example, my success depended on the fact that at that moment my basic act of throwing the dart had the features it did *because* those features would result in a hit. Although it was a 'one in a million' affair, *at that moment* my system functioned the way it was supposed to. But Sally's method of picking the ticket made no contribution to the fact that the ticket was a winner.

Even at this point intuitions may vary. One may wonder why, for example, the lucky soccer player's scoring a goal (by having the errant ball bounce off the backs of two players) is non-intentional, and yet my hitting the bull's eye is intentional.[52] The key lies in the fact that in the token dart throw in which the intention brings about the relevant features of the basic act, the token causal connection between the intention and the basic act is forged just because a basic act with those features would result in a bull's eye. When I make the successful throw, I by luck tap into a system that for once functions the way it was supposed to. On the other hand, the soccer player, who perhaps stumbles and kicks the ball off the direction of the goal, does not do so because a ball kicked in that direction would score a goal. In neither the lottery nor the soccer player's errant kick is there a system that is such that if it functions the way it is supposed to, the intended result would ensue.

(*c*) Fred shoots an electron gun. There are 100 locations the electron can randomly land in. One of the locations is rigged to a device that will execute a cat. In the remaining 99 positions the cat will survive. Fred intends the cat to die. And he is lucky; the electron lands in the one slot that results in the cat's death. It is true that he killed the cat.[53] But did he kill it intentionally?

The intuitions may urge us to say 'yes'. But if my conjecture about the difference between (*a*) and (*b*) is right, then (*c*) is clearly of the same kind as winning the lottery, as throwing a 66 with a 100-faced die. It resembles these more than the dart throw because we cannot say that,

---

[52] In another version of the lucky soccer player, the player kicks the ball, intending to score a goal. The ball bounces off the goal post and goes in. In this version the player is said to score a goal intentionally (Ginet 1990). Authors who treat cases like these decide whether the act is intentional or not by looking to see if there is close enough of a match between the way the act was performed and the way it was planned to be performed. As I have mentioned above, on my account, the determining factor is not the closeness of the match, but whether the system is functioning the way it was supposed to.

[53] The example is borrowed from Dretske and Snyder 1972.

when the electron lands in the lucky slot, the system functioned the way it was supposed to. In this respect the electron gun is very different from Rob's remote control device with the faulty connection. Even though the odds of Rob's detonating the bomb are exactly the same as those of Fred's killing the cat, when Rob succeeds, he detonates the bomb intentionally because for once his device worked the way it was supposed to.[54] So if our intuitions do lean us towards finding Fred's killing the cat as an intentional act, I suggest we are being misled by the fact that it involves a 'gun', we mistakenly subsume it under acts of 'aiming'. We ignore the fact that there is no system that is functioning the way it is supposed to. Admittedly, these are all examples involving non-basic acts. But they illustrate how intuitions may be shaped by mistaken assumptions. My defence in the Pears example is that we arrive at the wrong intuition that the act is intentional because we subsume the random atmospheric occurrence under designed prosthetic aids.

Second Agents

1. Suppose that some connection in a prosthetic device is severed. And a second agent holds the wires together. Clearly, this addition to the scenario does not affect our original judgements.

2. If the second agent had a shaky hand and the connection is secured only some of the time, still the agent equipped with the prosthesis acts intentionally whenever the connection happens to be made. This case is no different than that of the intermittent prosthetic device (point (3) in the previous section).

3. Suppose, again, that an agent is equipped with a prosthetic device, and also that a second agent has some way of telling (for example, by means of some advanced use of f-MRI) what the first agent intends to do. The prosthetic device is disconnected from the first agent's brain, but the second agent sends a signal through his computer to the prosthetic device that enacts the first agent's intention. Suppose that

---

[54] The difference between Fred and Rob may be illustrated by another pair of examples. Suppose we strap Clive to a chair, secure the chair on a rotating platform, blindfold him, and give him a ball. We tell him that if he can hit a stationary target with the ball while the platform is rotating, he will win a prize. Without any clue as to the location of the target, at some point Clive throws the ball, and hits the target. He did not hit it intentionally. In contrast, in a revised scenario, the target is a fragrant rose bush, and Clive uses the scent as a cue. And as unreliable as his cue was, he gets it right. When he does, regardless of the low probabilities, we should say that he hit it intentionally.

the first agent intends to raise his arm. Thanks to the second agent's intervention, his arm goes up. Does the first agent perform an intentional act? Indeed, does *he* raise his arm, or does the second agent raise it?

I think, we need to consider two distinct scenarios:

(*a*) Suppose the second agent is committed to sending the appropriate signals to the device that will guarantee the execution of the first agent's intention—suppose the second agent is a technician who is assigned the job of satisfying the intentions of the first agent without questioning. Under this description, a case can be made for the claim that the first agent raised his arm intentionally. The case is perhaps clearest if we replace the second agent with a robot, which is programmed to press the appropriate buttons when it identifies the intention of the first agent. This will be so even if the robot is prone to losing power and, as a result, sometimes becoming inactive (or if the committed second agent sometimes falls asleep on the job).

(*b*) Suppose the second agent is capable of evaluating the intentions of the first agent, and is empowered to censure the first agent when she judges the act to be impermissible. Now when the first agent intends to raise his arm, and she sees nothing wrong with the act and presses the right buttons and the first agent's arm goes up, the first agent did not act intentionally. In fact, I am inclined to say that she (the second agent) raised his arm for him.

The difference between the two scenarios, (*a*) and (*b*), can be captured by considering the two systems from the perspective of their respective functions. In (*a*) the second agent is a mere extension of the prosthetic device and the way she acts merely replaces a circuit in the system. Her role is no different from the role of the second agent in cases (1) and (2). The system incorporating the two agents and the prosthetic device is functioning exactly the way the first agent plus the prosthetic device were supposed to. That explains why we judge the acts produced in scenario (*a*) as intentional. But in scenario (*b*), the function of the whole system is no longer that of satisfying the intentions of the first agent. As I shall argue in the next chapter, intentions are formed in causal consequence of a process of deliberation. (I shall take pains to describe this process as one that invokes only event-causation.) The deliberative system receives as inputs information concerning the circumstances, consults a series of instrumental beliefs, as well as a preference ordering of outcomes, and chooses a course of action that involves the most preferred consequences. The system comprised of the first agent, plus any prosthetic devices he may be plugged into, can be said to have the function of satisfying whatever intention is reached through the process of deliberation by executing the basic act that is part of the content of the intention. Only when the system executes this function (in the way it is supposed to), is the action intentional. When we couple this system to a second system that introduces a second deliberative process, we no longer retain the functional integrity of the first system.[55]

As a result, when the first agent's arm goes up in response to his intention to raise his arm, this rising of the arm is the result of the intentions of the second agent, too. This is a real case of 'shared intentions'. Both agents must have reached through a deliberative process an intention with the same content (i.e. the intention to raise the first agent's arm), and the basic act is actually 'in response' to both intentions. That explains why it is false to say that it was an intentional act of the first agent. There *was* no *agent* of whom it was an intentional act.

I finally return to my claim about Gibbons's thesis that a reliabilist account of knowledge would provide the key to deviance in action. I claimed above that knowledge that one would be performing an action is neither necessary not sufficient for an act's being intentional. I gave an argument there to show that it is not necessary. Here is a brief remark designed to show it is not sufficient. Suppose we have a scenario as in (3*b*). And the first agent knows (by satisfying some reliability condition) that whenever he intends to greet someone by raising his arm, the second agent is guaranteed to approve the act, and press the right button. So the first agent knows that intending to raise his arm at this time will result in his arm's rising. If my diagnosis above is right, then his arm's going up as predicted will not be an intentional act of his.

---

[55] Consider the case when a demon out of the blue induces an intention in me—an intention that given my beliefs and desires I myself would not have formed—and the intention causes a bodily movement. Since the intention was not formed out of a process of deliberation that computed *my* beliefs and desires, my action was not intentional. Similarly if a process of deliberation uses a second agent's beliefs and desires, as it does in (3*b*), and the outcome forces the first agent's action, then we should judge that action to be non-intentional, too.

SUMMARY

This chapter was devoted to defending the causal theory of action against the charge that the possibility of deviant causal chains is a serious threat to the success of such a theory. As I see it, the threat is supposed to come from the alleged fact that when a deviant chain occurs, we use our pre-theoretic intuitions to recognize that the chain is deviant and that the ensuing behaviour is non-intentional, and yet no account of what constitutes a non-deviant chain in terms of mere event-causation has been, and is likely to be successful. Hence our pre-theoretic intuitions must be based on a notion of action, of agency, that cannot be analysed away in favour of causal relations among events.

My strategy has been to grant the proponents of this charge that accounts of non-deviance that look for the necessary and sufficient conditions in the *structure* of causal chains are bound to fail. I have instead claimed that conceiving the agent as a well-functioning system and locating cases of deviance in those instances when the system does what 'it is supposed to do', but 'not in the way it is supposed to do it' gives a better chance of confronting the charge.

It is true that appeal to functions in addressing problems in the philosophy of mind has a controversial history. It has been claimed by many that naturalized teleology is full of pitfalls, and it often runs the risk of begging the question.[56]

But the explanatory relation requirement I have extracted from the notion of functions seems to me to be free of the alleged shortcomings of the use of functions in naturalizing the mind: it does not presuppose a unique and determinate function assignment to systems. All it requires is that we know how things are supposed to unfold. And I have suggested that we can know this either by studying the mechanism whereby the intention causes the basic act, or by looking to see whether the reasons the agent has for performing the basic act are explained by how the basic act would result in the satisfaction of the agent's ultimate intention. The former study presupposes that the psychological state of intending can be naturalized and the causal

---

[56] Fodor (1990: 106) expresses his pessimism for the determination of content for representational systems by using naturalized teleology eloquently: 'Teleology goes soft just when you need it most; you get indeterminacies of function in just the cases where you would like to appeal to function to resolve indeterminacies of content.'

loop can be analysed in terms of events. The latter identification requires our understanding reasons (in the forms of beliefs and desires) to be again naturalized by reference to mere events.

Readers who have doubts about the success of these two types of naturalization will be sceptical of the viability of the causal theory from the start. They need not base their scepticism on the possibility of deviant causal chains. This chapter was not addressed to such sceptics. In arguing that the possibility of causal chains is not a problem for the causal theory of action, I have assumed that beliefs, desires, intentions are part and parcel of the causal order of nature and that the attempts of naturalizing them will eventually be successful.

5

A Causal Model of Deliberation

INTRODUCTION

All philosophical causal theories, especially the causal theory of action, are supposed to be defeated by the problem of deviance. The thesis of Chapter 4 has been that deviance is really not a serious problem. I argued there that general conditions can be formulated that make no reference to agency, agent causation, or agent control. These conditions will specify what counts as a 'normal' causal chain leading from the intention of an agent to her behaviour.

I tend to think that the harder problem for a causal theorist of action is to persuade the sceptics that a coherent concept of *agency* or of *control* can be located in mere event causation. If the reader will recall the negative arguments of Chapter 1, all of the mental episodes that are invoked by the causal theorist to analyse the origin of action, like beliefs, intentions, and 'pro attitudes' (i.e volitional factors such as desires, motives, and evaluations) must be assumed to be *mere events or states*—they cannot be irreducible mental *acts*.[1]

Given these constraints, one can easily be sceptical of the claim that what we take to be acts of an agent consist merely of a sequence of events that are just causally connected with each other.

There are at least two angles from which a critic of the causal theory of action can legitimately express this criticism. The first type of criticism involves the notion of agent-control. If an agent's action is the causal consequence of a series of events, then what sense can one give to the notion of the action's being under the agent's control?

---

[1] In all this there has been an unstated assumption that these events or states are supervenient on the physical states of the agent, plus perhaps on the past and present facts about the relevant segments of the agent's environment. This latter assumption is nothing less than faith in the ultimate success of the attempts at naturalizing the mind, and it will not be discharged in this book. I will take myself to have achieved what I have set out to achieve if I can persuade the reader that the following conditional is true: if the mind can be naturalized, then the causal theory of action that I describe in these chapters is capable of solving the First Problem of Action Theory, *and* show how concepts of agency and control can be derived from it.

D. Velleman (1992: 461) puts this worry about the causal theory succinctly: 'reasons cause an intention, and an intention causes bodily movements, but nobody—that is no person—does anything'.

It is important, though, to disassociate this sort of scepticism from a different type of scepticism, one that accuses the causal theory for being committed to determinism, and maintains that control is incompatible with determinism.[2] Actually, the truth or falsehood of determinism is really not relevant to whether a coherent case can be made for the causal theory of action.[3] Thinking of any position that is not libertarian as one that affirms *determinism* is something that we have inherited from the nineteenth century, and does not have much to do with the essence of the libertarian versus the anti-libertarian debate.

The anti-libertarian position I wish to develop is fully compatible with indeterminism. As we saw in the previous chapter, even if the system that executes intentions is not reliable, when it does execute them in the way it is supposed to, the behavioural output is an intentional action. And when it misfires, we do not have an action at all. In the same way, the system that generates intentions in response to beliefs and pro attitudes does not need to be fully reliable either. People may sometimes form intentions contrary to what they want and perceive to be in their best interest, or they may not form any intention whatsoever when they clearly see a course of action to be one that they value most. So whether the process that links beliefs and desires of an agent through her intentions to her behaviour is deterministic or indeterministic is of no concern for the causal theorist. As long as the causal theorist does not allow for the existence of an 'agent', who has the power to step in and 'take advantage' of the gaps created by the indeterminacy of the process, he can allow any degree of indeterminacy, short of pure randomness.

It is a trivial consequence of this indeterministic framework that when an agent acts—when her behaviour is caused by the sum total of her beliefs, desires, and intentions *in the right way*—it was possible for

---

[2] The well-known consequence argument found in Van Inwagen 1983, and Ginet 1990, among others, has as its conclusion that determinism precludes control. The argument has been discussed extensively in the last two decades. An excellent treatment, with references to reformulations, criticisms, and defenses of the argument is to be found in Kane 1996: 44–52. Also see Hendrickson 2002.

[3] John Bishop (1989: ch. 2) provides an extensive discussion showing why the critics of the causal theory of action need not use determinism as a premise in their arguments against the causal theory.

her not to have acted that way. The causal theory I defend here is opposed to the libertarian view because it rejects their thesis that the freedom of the act (or the control that the agent has over her action) *consists in* the mere existence of this possibility.

By the same line of reasoning, the question of determinacy ought to be irrelevant to the critics of the causal theory, too. To be more forceful, the scepticism ought to be expressed in terms that are neutral to the issue of determinism. And it is not hard to see how this can be done. It can be said, for example, that according to the story told by a causal theorist, an action consists of a bodily movement, caused (deterministically or indeterministically) by certain events or states in the person, and these, in turn, are caused ultimately by either the genetically encoded 'hard-wired' states, or by events that have happened to the person in the past. What room is there in the story for the agent? Where do the boundaries of the agent begin and end? And more importantly, even if we can draw such boundaries by tracing the outlines of the person's skin, where is the point in this causal chain at which the causal theorist is going to locate *control*?[4]

An alternative and more colourful formulation of the same criticism can be given by using an example of Van Inwagen's (1983: 109–12). Suppose that, thanks to a device implanted in us, all our intentions, beliefs, and desires that are the causes (deterministic or indeterministic) of our behaviour are being generated by Martians. Would we be acting as agents in such a scenario? If the answer is 'no', what relevant difference can possibly exist between the normal human agent as depicted by the causal theorist and the victim of Martian manipulation? In each case, the mental states that cause the behaviour are being caused by external events, and the person is just an inert box. This is a powerful criticism, and I hope to return to it at the end of the chapter.

For a second perspective from which the causal theory of action may be criticized, consider the behaviour of the moth. When the auditory system of the moth registers a sound wave of high frequency, the moth takes a dive. The mechanism that produces this behaviour is an adaptation for escaping predation by bats. (The sonar mechanisms of bats operate at high frequencies.) The behaviour of the moth is caused (*a*) by the disposition the moth has for diving when the requisite sound wave

---

[4] Again Velleman (1992: 463) states the problem clearly: '[The agent's] role is to intervene between reasons and intention, and between intention and bodily movements. …And intervening between these items is not something that the items themselves can do.'

is registered as input, and (*b*) by the input's being registered. The wiring that has emerged thanks to natural selection is what constitutes the moth's disposition to dive under these conditions. But it is absolutely clear that if we were to impute agency to the moth, it will only be a *façon de parler*. Certainly, the moth does not have the proper kind of *choice* or *control* over its dives. So the causal theorist ought to be able to say what it is that separates rational agents from the moth. And apart from pointing to the complexity of the mechanism in rational agents, which is just a quantitative difference, not a qualitative one, the causal theorist cannot in principle have any resources with which to do this. So the causal theorist cannot in principle explain the source of choice or control.[5]

I shall take this second version of the criticism of the causal theory seriously. The account I propose to develop will aim at showing a qualitative difference between hard-wired behaviour and rational behaviour. I shall first examine the motivational states of simpler organisms. Starting from dispositions, as those in the moth, developed through natural selection, and moving to capacities acquired by operant conditioning, I shall admit to the sceptic that the causal connections between such motivational states and behaviour are not the right kind to yield rational action—that these states are not candidates for *reasons*. The argument will take its force from one central thought: the instrumental beliefs that make up part of one's *reasons* for one's actions have conditional content. The causal role that is played by the representation of this conditional relationship is what makes the resultant behaviour rational. In contrast, the cognitive representations of simpler organisms, even if they can be assigned conditional content, do not play a causal role. Two claims will be defended. (1) The essential element in rational action is a computation that involves deliberation, the weighing of pros and cons of the consequences of one's prospective actions. (2) This process of deliberation can be explained by reference only to events, states, and the causal relations among them, *provided* that some of these states are representational, and the causal role played by these representational states is in virtue of their conditional

---

[5] John Bishop, referring to Dennett's example of the tropistic behavior of the wasp *Sphex*, puts this criticism succinctly. He says, 'It is not so much that we fear *Sphexishness*; rather, we find difficulty in understanding *how it could be possible* for a physical system to count as an agent, given that we don't help ourselves to something like emergent agent causation.'

content.[6] The following pages will be devoted to preparing the stage for a full statement of this thesis. I shall then address the first type of criticism of the causal theory of action—a criticism that maintains that a causal theory cannot capture the active role of agency—and argue that the criticism is misplaced.

HARD-WIRED BEHAVIOUR

I propose to spend some care in discussing the behaviour of the moth because in some sense of the word, it is 'purposive'. But as I mentioned above in making a concession to the sceptic, it is different *in kind* from the purposive behaviour of rational agents. I am hoping that discovering the mark that distinguishes this difference in kind will provide the key for a successful defence against the sceptic. Is the behaviour of the moth a mere enactment of a disposition that the moth has to take a dive when it registers a high-pitched sound? If it were, it certainly would not count as purposive in any sense of the word. This point has been observed very eloquently by Stampe (1986) and Millikan (1990). Millikan speaks of unexpressed biological purposes as determining the 'proximal' and 'distal' rules that a male hoverfly follows when he darts after a female, launching himself on a course that is determined by the angular velocity of the image of the female across his retina. 'To say that a given male hoverfly has a biological purpose to conform to the proximal hoverfly rule is very different from saying that he has a disposition to conform to it. The normal hoverfly has...a disposition to squash when stepped on, but [this] disposition [does] not correspond to biological purposes or to competences' (1990: 220). Stampe, too, points out that when I want to eat the peach in my hand, I am disposed to take a bite out of it. But my desire, in addition, gives me a reason to take a bite out of it, whereas a mere disposition to do something, like the disposition I have to fall when tripped, or to blush when embarrassed cannot constitute *a reason for* doing those things. Stampe's answer to the question, 'why *should* the desire cause the behaviour?' takes him to the ideal causes of desire, and to the observation that the state of the body that under ideal conditions causes the desire is the state in which the organism benefits from the behaviour that is the effect of the

---

[6] Some of the material for this chapter comes from my 'How Causes Can Rationalize: Belief-Desire Explanations of Action' (forthcoming).

desire. The two authors have different objectives: Millikan seeking to bring determinate content to the rules which rational agents follow, and Stampe seeking to understand why desires should have the functional role they are seen to have. But both turn to the same form of teleological consideration involving normal functional explanations, or what, in my view amounts to the same thing, to a notion involving what would happen if the state in question were produced under a set of conditions of well-functioning.

Both Stampe and Millikan are right in pointing out that a mere dispositional conception of beliefs and desires, a conception that forms the fundamental insight of the functionalist characterization of mental states, is inadequate to answer their respective questions.[7]

If we ask, why *should* the moth (or why is the moth *supposed to*) take a dive when it hears a high-pitched sound, a good answer would be, because under ideal conditions, the state in which the moth's receptors are registering such a sound wave is caused by the sonar mechanisms of the predator bats, who will momentarily descend on the present location of the moth, and under those conditions taking a dive benefits the moth. Such an answer appeals to teleology in locating the origin of whatever normativity is implied by the question.

Adapting the conditions that were offered in Chapter 4 to ground teleological function attributions, we can notice in cases like the diving behaviour of the moth that the inner state, S, of the moth that causes its diving behaviour has the function of enabling the moth to escape predation because the following general conditions are satisfied:

(i) When a set of specifiable well-functioning conditions, C, obtain, S is triggered by an input, I (the high-pitched sound, in the case of the moth), and S triggers B (the dive).

(ii) When a set of specifiable 'normal' conditions, C', obtain, I, the input, is caused by environmental (or internal physiological) facts, F (the presence of the bat).

(iii) When a set of specifiable 'normal' conditions, C' obtain, B has the consequence Q (escaping the predator).

---

[7] By 'a functionalist characterization', I have in mind the view that gives the identity conditions of mental states in terms of the causal role they play in the economy of mental occurrences. Their causal role consists in their capacity to give rise to other states or behavioural outputs in response to inputs from perceptual systems or other states.

(iv) The fact that S causes B (when F) is explainable by the fact that B (normally) causes Q.[8]

This schema makes clear the type of explanation we seek in order to answer the preliminary question, why the state we have labelled S *should* cause the relevant behaviour. We understand why the moth's inner state *should* cause its behavioural output. This understanding is brought to us by first finding out what the far-reaching goals of these systems are—its unexpressed distal purposes, as Millikan puts it—and then by noticing that, under normal conditions, the proximal effects of these states best serve these goals provided that the normal cause of the state obtains.

As I have granted, if this were offered by the causal theorist as a model of rational action, the sceptical critic of the causal theory would be justified in being incredulous. If the best the causal theory can do in explaining what acting for a reason consists in is to rely on such explanations of why agents should be doing what they do, then perhaps the mysteries of agent causation ought not to look so repulsive after all. The first question to ask therefore is: what exactly is missing in the causal pathways that constitute the diving behaviour of the moth that disqualifies it from being a piece of rational behaviour?

The Causal Structure of Hard-Wired Behaviour

In order to appreciate the proper answer to this question, I shall try to give a best case for the argument that the behaviour of simple organisms contains a proto model for rational action. Some of the steps towards the best case may go against common sense, but when we see why the best case fails, we might be closer to our proper answer.

Let us say that we may attribute to the moth the built-in goal M(Q) of escaping predation. And the state, S, it acquires when it registers a high-pitched sound may, again without too much of a stretch, be assigned a representational content, F—that of the presence of a predator. The moth is also equipped with a means, the basic behaviour B, of achieving the goal. Figure 5.1 provides a simple characterization of the causal structure. Here I is the input which causes the auditory perceptual state S, and S represents F, the presence of a predator, and Q is the

---

[8] In Ch. 4 the first three clauses were telescoped into just one. I have separated out the three sets of conditions here to make the relevant parts of the causal chain more perspicuous.

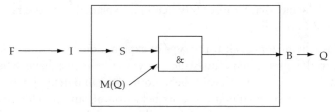

Fig. 5.1. *The moth's dive*

content of the omnipresent motivational state: avoid predation. In this setup, F causes S, which, in turn, thanks to the &-gate, causes B, and B results in Q. Furthermore, S causes B *because,* under the conditions, B *typically* results in Q. This latter fact, which satisfies condition (iv) above, is derived from the past history of the moth species by the forces of natural selection. Dretske (1988) makes elegant use of this fact. He calls the causal role attributed to the fact that, in the past when predators were present, the dive was correlated with successful escape, 'a structuring cause': it causes the structure of the network wherein S has been recruited to be a cause of B. The structuring cause explains why the &-gate is the way it is. This is in contrast to the causal role attributed to S, which Dretske calls 'a triggering cause'. The wiring of the &-gate acts as what we might call a standing causal condition, one that (causally) explains, as Dretske will have it, why S causes B.[9]

We can take a further step here and ask whether the internal wiring that contains the &-gate represents anything. It might be thought that a teleosemantic approach to the content of representations based on an aetiological account of functions (one that is consistent with the conditions (i)–(iv) above) may lead us to an affirmative answer here. On this kind of approach, a structure will be said to represent the conditions

---

[9] It is important to note that when Dretske introduces the explanation by structuring causes in the context of classical conditioning, he locates the explanans in the *past* experience of the organism. 'So what causes the dog to salivate? This clearly is a request, not for the triggering cause of the dog's behavior, but for the structuring cause…The causal explanation [of the behaviour—which for Drestke is not the salivation, but *the bell's causing the salivation*] resides not in the stimulus that elicits the behavior, but in the dog's *past experience*.' (1988: 44; my emphasis) But later, when he begins to introduce his theory of the explanatory force of representational (semantic) content, he speaks of a *general* causal relation between the basic behaviour and the goal. He says (I have changed the lettering to conform to the above): 'What the theory of evolution has to tell us about these cases [he actually has in mind the moth, here]…is that S's production of [B] is at least in part the result of its indication of F. [B] is produced by an indicator of F because such an arrangement *confers* [my emphasis] a competitive advantage on its possessor' (1988: 92).

that underwrite the function attribution to the structure. Arguably, the function of the wiring that contains the &-gate is to help the moth escape predation. And the wiring serves this function by eliciting diving behaviour when a bat is present. So the fact responsible for the formation of the wiring that realizes this function, that is, the fact that in the past, when bats were present, diving resulted in escaping predation, is a plausible source for assigning the representational content to the wiring. On this line of reasoning, one might maintain that the wiring *means*: 'If diving action is taken when a high-pitched sound is registered, predation is avoided.'

Following this line of reasoning, one can then press on and suggest that the drive $M(Q)$, together with the conditional representation (if B when I, then Q), which is the analogue of a proto-instrumental belief, are among the causal antecedents of the behaviour. One can further maintain that these causal antecedents (*unlike* the causal antecedents of the realization of a simple dispositional property, like that, say, of sugar's dissolving in water) explain why the moth *should* take a dive when it hears the sound.

It is true that this line of reasoning does give us a difference between purely causal systems and teleological systems, but the mark of distinction, the mark that allows us to identify the output of a system as the sort of thing it *should* be producing under the conditions, is too weak to yield the mark of acting for a reason. In other words, the mark in question, that is, the function assigned to the internal wiring of the moth, does tell us the difference between stumbling when tripped or blushing when embarrassed on the one hand, and pulling one's hand away by reflex when one touches a hot surface, on the other. It succeeds in showing us this difference because there is a feature common both to mere motives that, when triggered by incoming information, produce behaviour *and* to desires which, when coupled with beliefs, give rise to rational action. This feature tells us why one should in general act in ways that one believes will satisfy one's desires. There is a sense of 'should' in which it is literally true that, given that I want a peach, I *should* do whatever it is that I think will satisfy that want, *and* that the moth, when it registers the tell-tale high-pitched sound, *should* take a dive. Both of these uses of 'should' take their force from the fact that if these systems were to fail to do what they *should* do, they would not be fulfilling that which it is their natural function to fulfil. The systems are natural teleological systems, and as such, they are expected to conform to certain norms that are dictated by their function *and* their *design*. It is these norms that legitimize the application of 'should' to both of these systems. The moth's system is 'designed' to make it dive when certain conditions are present because doing so under those conditions is 'good' for the organism. The rational agent's system is 'designed' to make her do whatever she thinks will satisfy her desires under the circumstances because doing so is in the long run 'good' for her.[10]

On the other hand, what constitutes *reasons* is not confined to the fact that one is designed to act so as to satisfy one's objectives. The difference between the moth's system and the system that governs rational behaviour is as important as the difference between the rational behaviour of an agent and her conditioned or unconditioned reflexes. When one reflexively pulls away one's hand from a hot surface, one is doing what one 'should' do, but the fact that the surface is hot is hardly the *reason one has* for doing it.

We could see this even more clearly if we look at the internal wiring of a thermostat that has been set to 68°. When the room temperature falls below 68°, the radius of the curvature of the bimetallic strip decreases, and the bending results in the closing of a circuit that turns the furnace on. We can represent the gadget schematically as in Figure 5.2. Here F is the room temperature; I is the temperature of the air in contact with the bimetallic strip. C is the bent state of the strip, and M is the setting of the thermostat, which in physical terms consists of the distance between the tip of the strip and a fixed contact point. B, of course, is the closing of the circuit and turning the furnace

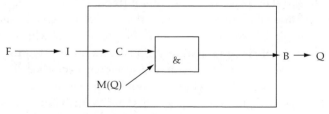

Fig. 5.2. *The thermostat*

<hr />

[10] The idea that satisfying one's desires is in the long run good for the organism is premised on assumptions that take desires to be representations (or misrepresentations) of what would be good for the organism, *cf.* Stampe 1986. See also Papineau 1988 for a different approach to a similar idea.

on (by the tip of the strip touching the contact) and Q is the bringing of the room to the set temperature.

The wiring that includes the &-gate, for reasons that parallel those used for the moth, may be assigned the representational content 'If the circuit is closed when the room temperature is below 68°, then the room temperature will go up'. But it is clear that, even if this is a reasonable assignment of representational content to the wiring, the *content* of the representation, the *conditional*, plays no causal role whatsoever. The causal roles come only from I and M, and the &-gate—and of course, following Dretske, from the engineer who designed the wiring. And if an alleged representation is causally inert, then I think it is a mistake to reify it.[11]

Since the only difference between the moth and the thermostat lies in the forces that led to their design, and since that difference could not be the basis for a difference in the representational capacities of their respective circuitry, I submit that we should reject the suggestion that the moth's wiring contains the representation of *any* conditional relation.[12] I may seem to be belabouring the obvious here, but some literature in computer science is in disagreement.

Von Neumann Machines

For obvious reasons, philosophers interested in artificial intelligence would like to revive the traditional distinction between systems that are merely rule *conforming* and systems the behaviour of which can be described as *following* a rule. Presumably, the windshield wipers in my car merely *conform* to the rule, 'If the switch is on, the wipers move'. They do not *follow* that rule. D. Lloyd writes,

A system is a Rule Conforming System if ['If X then Y' describes the system such that when the system is in state X, it tends to move into state Y]. A system is a Rule Following System when 'If X then Y' causes (as well as describes) [the system to be such that when the system is in state X it tends to move into state Y]...A computer exemplifies a Rule Following

---

[11] It is important to note that the structuring explanation, the explanation of why I and M cause B, does not need to assign any efficacy to a *conditional representation*, and Dretske is careful in avoiding this mistake.

[12] By this I mean to deny also that the wiring of the thermostat has the representational content, 'If the temperature is below 68°, then close the circuit'. Similarly it would be a mistake to say that the moth's wiring represents 'If high-pitched sound, then dive'.

System. Somewhere in the computer…is an explicit rule, a representation, or a set of representations, which can be interpreted (by programmers) as meaning that when Control-N is typed, execute a line feed on the screen. Because that rule is there, inside the computer, the computer has the disposition to respond to Control-N with a line feed. Given a different program, the behaviour of the computer would have been different. In contrast, the planets are familiar examples of a Rule Conforming System. The laws of gravity describe their behavior, but they do not move because those laws are inscribed somewhere. (Lloyd 1989: 123–4)

What Lloyd describes here is very much like what classical AI envisaged. In a Von Neumann machine, the central processing unit is presented with two types of inputs, first, the rule that it accesses, that is, the rule that determines what function is to be performed, and second, the input that constitutes the argument for that function. Presumably, in Lloyd's example, the rule, 'If Control-N, then line feed' is called in, and the rule operates on some previously recorded parameter that determines the value of the line feed. Suppose that we are willing to admit here that the rule, the conditional, 'If Control-N, then line feed' is functioning as a cause of the output. What is important to realize though is that the causal role of this conditional can be captured by an &-gate similar to that of Figure 5.1 or 5.2.

The only difference between these figures is that in Figure 5.3 we attribute to some state of the system a representational content, and the content is the conditional, 'If Control-N, then Q'. But in this system, the input is the *antecedent* of the conditional rule. This is what enables us to represent the wiring as an &-gate. The inner structure is similar to the 'rule' embodied in the wiring of the moth:

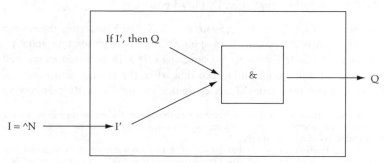

Fig. 5.3. *Internal wiring of a Von Neumann machine*

if high-pitched sound, then dive. The conditional rule in the central processing unit does no more causal work than the 'rule' by which the moth acts does causal work in the moth.[13] I shall argue that this is in contrast to what takes place when an agent acts for a reason. In agents, the instrumental belief has a conditional content of the form, 'if under such and such conditions (C), such and such is done (A), such and such will result (Q)', and the input provided by the object of the desire is the *consequent* of the conditional. And if the conditional and its consequent are to act as causes, the wiring should not be represented as an &-gate. The causal pathway realized by the wiring should confer independent efficacy to the consequent and allow it to enter into the computation as a separate unit. My argument will rest on the conjecture that it is this kind of detachability of the consequent that constitutes the normative force of reasons.

Before I can develop my argument, I need to discuss one other possible candidate for the origin of reasons and do some ground work in preparation for the argument.

LEARNT BEHAVIOUR

It might be maintained that the key difference between the wiring of the moth and the instrumental beliefs that guide the rational behaviour of an agent is the fact that the agent acquires these beliefs during her lifetime. The key here rests on the following question: what can natural selection explain about the belief of individual organisms? It has been maintained, for example, that there is an important difference between the structuring causes that arise in natural selection and the structuring causes that operate on individual organisms during their lifetime.[14] Taking the &-gate of the moth, depicted in Figure 5.1, the difference may be expressed in the following way. The &-gate that has been shaped by natural selection fails to explain why the *individual*

---

[13] It is instructive to note that Lloyd's examples for rule-conforming systems are all cases that can be subsumed under *mere dispositions*. As we saw above, although the moth's behaviour is distinct from the realization of a mere disposition, it is short of a system that operates in response to the normative force of reasons. Even if it may be classified as a rule-following system, it should not be described as a system in which the conditional rule plays any causal role.

[14] This difference was originally introduced by Sober (1984*b*), and since has become a source of controversy. See e.g. Neander 1988; Sober 1995; Walsh 1998. It was used to good effect by Dretske.

moth dives, rather than gets into a holding pattern, because all that can be explained by natural selection is why this type of behaviour is prevalent among moths, not why individual moths act the way they do. The most natural selection can help us explain is why one should act in ways one believes will satisfy one's desires. The explanation would point to the plausible conjecture that acting in ways one 'thinks' would satisfy one's 'desires' has contributed to the fitness of past individuals, and that this trait has become prevalent in the species. However, in order to explain the behaviour of an individual organism now, one has to find causes that have been shaped during the lifetime of the individual. Such causes are best located in learning histories—it is only in organisms with such histories that we can hope to find the first emergence of anything that comes close to beliefs and desires.

Correct as the observation of the difference between the scope and the respective explananda of selectionist explanations and explanations due to learning may be, I am sceptical that the difference captures what is essential to reasons for action. There is a type of learning that is actually said to hold in the case of rats and some birds. When these creatures eat something that smells or tastes a certain way and thereupon get sick, they learn not to eat food that smells or tastes that way ever again. Certainly *the reason* why the rat is not eating soap now is that the previous time it ate it, it got sick. But that is not sufficient to render the rat's behaviour explainable by imputing *reasons* to the rat. When the individual rat learnt to avoid eating soap, we may presume that the conditioning established a neural connection in the rat that transforms the input of a certain taste or smell into the output of not eating. If we ignore its aetiology, the structure involved here is the same as that involved in Figures 5.1 and 5.2. And my claim has been that the causal pathway that that kind of structure can support is not the pathway proper to reason-based behaviour. The pattern of learning that gets the rats to avoid poisonous foods is typical of all types of operant conditioning. (Compare here the pecking behaviour of the pigeons described in Chapter 2.) Even if the beliefs and preferences of a rational agent were acquired through operant conditioning, the functional role they play in intentional action is quite different from the role played by the internal states of these rats, or so I will argue.

UNCONSCIOUS BEHAVIOUR

In order to make the main premise of my argument as plausible as I can, I would like to look briefly at a different type of phenomenon, where, intuitively, it also seems correct to deny that the agent's action is based on the reasons the agent has.

Psychologists have recently been studying cases where, due to localized brain damages, the patients manifest behavioural deficiencies. A type of case reported by Penfield involves epileptics who can be struck with seizure while they are walking, driving, or playing the piano, and who are able to continue their activities while they are in seizure. But these *petit mal* patients, as they are called, perform these activities, during their seizure, mechanically, without the flexibility, adaptability, and creativity they are capable of when they are normal. Penfield uses the label 'mindless automata' for them. The descriptions of the behaviour of these patients remind one of the egg-rolling behaviour of the greylag goose, made famous by Lorenz and Tinbergen (see Gould 1982). When the goose observes an object of roughly the size and shape of an egg near its nest, it initiates the fixed-action pattern of rolling the egg up to the nest, and it continues the motions in air even if the object is moved out of its path. There seems to be an important difference between a normal piano player who has reasons for continuing to play the tune she has started and the *petit mal* patient who continues to play the tune during an epileptic seizure. It seems literally correct to say of the normal person that, given her reasons and her perceptions, she *should* continue to play, whereas the *petit mal* patient seems clearly to lack any reasons to continue to play—at least, he lacks the kinds of reasons that render his action of continuing to play that of a rational agent. I do not mean to deny here that, in so far as the action of *playing* the tune is concerned, the *petit mal* patient may be doing something as a fully rational agent. The action I mean to focus on by the description 'continuing to play' is one that is in contrast to stopping in the middle of the tune.

One can argue for the same point from a different perspective. We have seen in our discussion of basic act tokens how, for an accomplished pianist, playing a whole tune may become such a routine that in some tokenings it may be produced as a basic act. Now, in the basic act token of my raising my arm, although I will have reasons for raising it, I will not have *reasons* for sending nerve signals to my arm muscles, or for bringing about any of the *component* events of that basic *act* token. The orchestration of these events is taken care of by a subsystem, which, once triggered, is not, for the purposes of that token, under the control of my cognitive centres. And if the description of the *petit mal* patient's behaviour is correct, the playing of the whole tune for him is as 'simple' a basic act as my raising my arm. And just as my sending nerve signals is not something that I do because I have a reason for doing it, the *petit mal* patient's *continuing* to play the tune is not something he does because he has a reason for doing it.

I admit that, even if the diagnosis I have offered for why aspects (component parts) of the *petit mal* patient's piano playing are not things he does for a reason is correct, it does not immediately yield for us the causal structure that underlies rational behaviour. But it helps to form an initial conjecture: in the normal piano player, inputs are being routinely monitored and checked against a set of beliefs and desires, so that if altering the course of action in some way is preferable to going on in the same way, the action is altered. In other words, there is always a potential for making a decision, and the decision, when it occurs, is based on comparing alternatives with each other to see which is preferable. In the *petit mal* patient, on the other hand, for the duration of the seizure, no alternatives can be considered, no comparisons can be made.[15]

A related contrast can be made between the way we normally allow incoming information to influence our behaviour and the way information that is sometimes described as being *unconsciously* processed influences the behaviour of certain types of patients. People who report having no sight in one half of their field of vision apparently have some unconscious awareness of the objects in their blind half (Weiskrantz 1988). In one experiment, patients who are shown a river in their blind half, tend to disambiguate the word 'bank' shown in their sighted half as 'river bank' (Weiskrantz 1986). It seems again that it would be a mistake to ask for the *reasons* the blind-sighted people have for their choice of meaning in such experiments. If this is right, it can support the above conjecture further. The behaviour of the blind-sighted subjects is shaped (their 'guesses' are formed) without

[15] To continue the analogy with arm raising, sending nerve signals to my arm muscles is not something I do for a reason just because typically when I am set on raising my arm, I am not in a position to consider alternative signals I can send and to figure out which is preferable.

deliberation, without comparing alternatives. They are formed in direct response to latent information.[16]

Some philosophers take the results of these experiments very seriously, and they judge categorically that the decisions subjects reach are not based on the reason the subjects have. And based on this judgement, they defend the view that the function of consciousness is that of enabling the information represented in our brains to be used, among other things, in rationally guiding action.[17]

ACTING IN RESPONSE TO IRREPRESSIBLE INNER FORCES

To contrast acting for a reason with acting in response to an irrepressible inner force, we might look at Hume's theory of motivation. Hume thought, for example, that kindness to children, together with hunger, lust, love of life, was one of the primary passions we are possessed of. When an agent acts in a way that constitutes acting kindly towards children, and the propensity towards being kind to children is an overriding character trait for the agent, it seems wrong to say that the reason she had for her action was that she was kind to children. Here I do not want to imply that one cannot have a genuine desire to be kind to some child. It is just that when one acts *out of kindness*, where being kind is a built-in trait, as opposed to acting *because one wants to be kind*, one does not have the burden of considering alternatives and evaluating their costs and benefits and comparing them to those of acting kindly. The model I have in mind here for Hume's primary passions is one where the motive to action is an irresistible pressure, and this pressure has the net effect of shunting out the process of evaluating the consequences of the action by comparing them to the consequences of acting otherwise (or of not acting at all). I shall later suggest that Hume's theory of passions promotes this peculiar model

---

[16] The contrast conscious/unconscious plays no important role in my arguments in this chapter. That is why I am deliberately ignoring the controversy that exists both about the details of the methodology used in the set up of the experiments, and as to what exactly these findings show about consciousness. So I allow the possibility that some cognitive deliberation may be going on at some level in these subjects. If so, I am prepared to say that they are acting for a reason.

[17] Umiltà (1988) cites several experimental results all of which suggest that there is a central conscious process that exercises 'strategic control over lower order mental operations'.

of motivation just because, for Hume, passions do not have representational content—they have only an object they are directed at and a degree of strength with which they compete with other passions.

Of course, this does not mean that one cannot thereby *choose* one's *way* of being kind to a child. 'S did A because S had a reason for doing A' is an intensional context: not all referring expressions to the act token A retain the truth of the sentence. So when one performs an act of kindness to a child out of a Humean primary passion, that act, in so far as it is an act of kindness to a child, cannot be rationally explained. But if the act of kindness *was* one's giving the child a doll to play with as opposed to letting her pet the cat because one saw the possibility that the cat might scratch the child, there certainly is an explanation based on the agent's reasons. And the availability of such an explanation is contingent on the agent's having considered the alternatives. Approaching the same theme from the opposite end, we should consider those actions discussed by Hursthouse (1991).[18] Some of Hursthouse's examples are actions that are correctly explained by the agent by saying, 'I did it because I just wanted to, or I felt I had to'. Among the cases she cites are behaviour explained by joy: running, jumping, leaping up reaching for the leaves on trees; behaviour explained by horror: covering one's eyes when they are already shut; explained by fear: hiding one's face, burrowing under the bed clothes. In each of these cases I would maintain, and Hursthouse would mostly agree, that it is hard to find *reasons for which* the agent does these things. To reiterate my diagnosis for the last time, the judgement on these arational acts is based on the fact that consideration of alternatives is not part of their causal ancestry. (I will suggest in the next chapter that some of these arational actions may be intentional, but they will not be intended.)

A CAUSAL MODEL FOR DELIBERATION

So far, I have been belabouring the conjecture that, in acting for a reason, the agent typically considers alternatives, and chooses among them. To put this conjecture first in ways that a sceptic of a causal theory of action would not object to, we can describe it as follows.

---

[18] I say 'approach it from the opposite end' because in contrast with the very distal enactments of primary passions, these actions are very proximal.

When an agent finds herself in a situation where she wants something and decides on the means of satisfying that want, she typically will have evaluated the different routes that seemed to be available to her. The evaluation will have included estimating the consequences of the different means and ordering them according to some 'desirability quotient'. The decision, the choice of the means, then, is the result of this process of evaluation. In other words, the choice is determined, and the intention to act a certain way is formed, (i) by what the agent thinks is available to her in terms of proximal behaviour, (ii) by how likely she takes these behaviours to yield the object of her desire, and (iii) by how 'costly' each of these available behaviours seem to be. Furthermore, acting for a reason also presupposes that these choices, once made, are revisable after the project of pursuing the object of the desire is launched: discovering unforeseen obstacles, or finding better or easier means to the goal, or stumbling on competing projects that appear overall more desirable than the one in progress might make the agent change course. Not all of these factors need to be operative in everything one does do for a reason, but most of the time, most of them seem to be. This process requires a particular type of interaction between the different things that are desired and the contents of instrumental beliefs. Figure 5.4 schematically represents such a process.

Here the instrumental belief has as its content a conditional of the form 'if under conditions C, A is done, then Q will obtain'. And Q is the object of one's considered desire. Notice that the operation performed by the box marked X cannot be that of a simple &-gate because A is not contingent on the joint action of the two inputs C and D(Q).

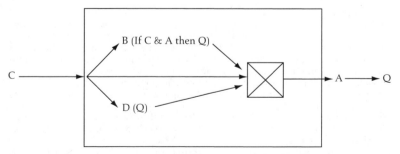

Fig. 5.4. *Acting for a reason*

Practical Syllogism

The challenge that faces the causal theorist is that of showing how the process can be represented in terms of causal pathways that connect mere events or states, without relying on idioms like choosing, deciding, forming an intention—idioms that can be read as implying irreducible mental acts. The foregoing should have made it clear that this challenge cannot be met by the logic of simple &-gates that represent the wiring of thermostats or of moths. Perhaps the traditional conception of Aristotelian practical syllogism comes close to capturing the force of the deliberative process. Suppose I want to eat suitable food. Given the expression of the content of my desire as a premise, I reason, 'If I eat dry food, I will have eaten suitable food'. So I form the intention to eat this dry food.[19] (Or, as Anscombe prefers to put it, I thereby eat this.) It is true that this process cannot be represented by the flow chart of Figure 5.1. The reasoning involved is not deductive.[20] Anscombe (1957: 60), criticizing attempts to convert the syllogism into an argument from premises to a conclusion, recommends thinking of practical reasoning as a way of calculating what to do, recognizing that it is 'essentially concerned with "what is capable of turning out variously"'. She says:

There are…three types of cases. There is the theoretical syllogism, and also the idle practical syllogism, which is just a classroom example. In both of these the conclusion is 'said' by the mind which infers it. And then there is the practical syllogism proper. Here the conclusion is an action whose point is shewn by the premises, which are now, so to speak, on active service.

There are two strands to Anscombe's view here. The first is the reasoning the agent performs prior to acting with an aim to figure out

---

[19] Anscombe (1957) maintains that my wanting to eat suitable food should not be *part* of the practical reasoning. According to her, practical reasoning takes place from the belief that if this is dry food then it is suitable to eat to the act of eating *in people who want to eat suitable food* ('Dry food suits anyone, etc., so I'll have some of this' (1957: 66)). This cannot be right. If it were, then the propositional content of the want would play no role in the reasoning. P. Clark (1997) argues convincingly that practical syllogism is a two-step reasoning. According to Clark, the second step starts from the object of the want and concludes with the basic act (i.e. the content of the intention). Clark rightly points out that in causally *explaining* the action one needs to advert to wants and beliefs, but in rationalizing the act, only the intentional objects of these states are relevant. In what follows, I shall think of the process of deliberation as providing the rationale for the action, and speak only of the representational contents of beliefs and desires.

[20] In fact some philosophers (e.g. Kenny 1966) have suggested that practical syllogism should be viewed as a piece of abductive reasoning.

what to do, and the second, the task of explaining (showing the point of) the action *after* the agent acts. I will attend to this second strand at some length in the next chapter. If, however, we turn to the reasoning that helps the agent who is faced with 'what is capable of turning out variously', as Aristotle is quoted as having said, it would be best if we supplemented the simple structure of the practical syllogism with additional 'premises'. For the situation to be genuinely one which *may turn out variously*, it would be reasonable to assume that alternative courses of action are available. For example, dry food need not be the *only* suitable food that there is, or *this* dry food may not be the only dry food that there is. The reasoning that is involved is best thought of as one that forces a choice, say, between the cornflakes in the cupboard and the granola obtainable from the store a short walk away, each alternative presenting an array of pluses and minuses—cornflakes not as healthy as granola but closer and more immediately available, etc. And the agent will weigh them one against the other and presumably arrive at a choice of the least undesirable path. Watson (1987: 168–9) summarizes the point I have been developing in this chapter very well when he says:

[The spider] has no choice whether and wither to guide [the movements of its limbs]. Having such a choice requires being a chooser, and that requires certain cognitive capacities at a minimum, the capacity to entertain, and be presented with alternatives for selection....The distinctive libertarian thought is that I must have the power to determine which, among the alternatives I have the capacity to entertain, I shall will (undertake, try for,...). All that is clear about this power is that it cannot be secured merely by the indeterministic interpretation of alternative possibilities.

I propose to show that 'the distinct libertarian thought' can be easily captured by the causal theory of action without resorting to concepts of willing, undertaking, or a special sense of trying, even without having to appeal to the necessity of indeterminism.

Alternatives and Choice

Let us review that materials that would be needed for the process that is capable of leading to such a choice. First, the agent should be aware of the circumstances. Second, the agent should possess a repertoire of basic act types. Third, she should have some objective, some goal, some object she desires. Fourth, combining the first three, she should have some idea of what sorts of basic acts, performed under the circumstances that obtain, are likely to result in getting the object desired. These constitute the various alternative courses of action 'open'. In limiting cases, the alternatives may be as simple as performing the basic act that is likely to lead to the object of desire, or, under the circumstances, abandoning the quest for that object and not doing anything. Fifth, she should be capable of computing some of the consequences of each of the alternatives. Sixth, she should be able to evaluate the arrays of consequences and identify the course of action that generates one of them as the best (or at least no worse than the rest).

An important disclaimer is in order here. I do not mean to require of each piece of rational behaviour that it be preceded by a consideration of a large number of alternatives, a computation of the consequences of each alternative, and an evaluation of the consequences. In most of our activities as rational agents, we decide what to do so quickly that it does not seem that any deliberation has taken place. Two types of cases stand out. (1) There are habits that one has formed, and one enacts them without any deliberation. (For example, Herman always removes the key from the ignition before he opens the door of his car.) Although, typically, no weighing of the pros and cons takes place before a habit kicks in, habits are usually the result of an earlier stage of deliberation. And in so far as the circumstances are perceived to conform to those in which the habitual action was adopted through deliberation as the best means of reaching some goal, and the goal is still a relevant concern, enacting the habit is a piece of rational behaviour. But if the circumstances are inappropriate for the act, or the goal is no longer desirable, the act will be unreasonable, maybe even non-rational. (If Herman's wife is listening to her favourite song on the car radio, and Herman, having intended to leave the ignition on for his wife, removes the key before stepping out of the car to drop the letter into the mail box, then what Herman does is a piece of non-rational behaviour. His reason for originally acquiring the habit was that he wanted to make sure not to lock the key in the car. But that reason was not operative in the circumstances.) (2) There are limiting cases where the choice between taking the only course of action available and not doing anything may be so obvious as to not merit the vocabulary of computing and evaluating. Consider finding oneself alone near the front door of a house that is on fire. One would immediately leave. This does not mean that the alternative of staying in the house is not available. It is just that the computation is very simple and the evaluation is obvious. Other examples are easy to find. One sees the picture frame crooked, gets up and straightens it. One feels thirsty, goes, gets a glass, fills it with water, and drinks it. One hears Schönberg playing on the radio while having supper, picks up the remote control and turns it off. Similarly, when one says, 'Here I stand; I can do no other', one does not necessarily mean that there are no alternatives available. It is just the result of recognizing that the consequences of the alternatives are so unacceptable that they make where one 'stands' the only viable choice. In summary, the appearance of lack of deliberation is not always a sign that no deliberation has taken place.

It is important, of course, to set these cases apart from those that, by all outward appearances, may *seem* identical. What I have in mind are behaviours that one is driven to by sheer emotion. For example, I may leave the house that is on fire by the nearest door impulsively, without any awareness of any alternatives: I may be in the grip of fear, running for my life. Only counterfactual considerations would reveal the difference. In those situations in which my behaviour is not intentional, even if I knew that the door leads to a corridor the roof of which is caving in, and the firemen are to enter through the window to try to rescue me, I would probably still run out through the door.[21] More mundane examples can be found: consider the case where the person one is talking to has a pierced tongue with a ring, and as much as one tries not to look, one finds to one's embarrassment and distress one's eyes being irrepressibly drawn to it; or the case in which the dipsomaniac, having had enough nightcaps, decides to go to bed, and yet finds himself pouring 'one last one' for himself. The phenomenology of these cases is typically different from those in which one acts intentionally without seeming to deliberate. Although it is possible to mistake one for the other, in the intentional ones one characteristically feels that there is a choice, and on the view of deliberation I am proposing here, the choice is between letting the picture hang crooked

---

[21] In the second act of Puccini's *Turandot*, Calaf's behaviour is a perfect example of such a non-rational act. He is being told by all concerned that the likely consequences of attempting to solve the princess's puzzle are terrible, and he is being given all sorts of incentives for not attempting this act. But his passion (one prefers to think of it as his instant infinite love for the princess, but the chances are that much baser passions are at work) blinds him to all alternatives.

and getting up and straightening it; or between suffering the atonal dry exercise while trying to enjoy the anchovies and reaching for the remote control to press the button. These are the alternatives that are available, and the reason the choice does not seem to amount to much is just that one alternative is a lot more attractive than the other, and the relevant side-effects and consequences of each are too minimal to be worth considering. The computation is there to be made, and it is done quickly, efficiently, without taxing the capacities of the circuitry.

To illustrate how each of the six elements above—(i) circumstances, (ii) available relevant basic acts, (iii) a goal (or a set of competing goals), (iv) instrumental beliefs, (v) the computed consequences of the basic acts, and (vi) the evaluation—may be realized in an agent let me take a simple example in which the alternatives are limited to two. I shall run the example without involving a power to *initiate* causal chains, or the need to perform emergent acts of agency.

Suppose I hear the phone ring, and get up to answer it. Here the six elements in question might be:

1. I hear the phone ringing. I am sitting in my armchair by the fire and reading a book.
2. I do nothing and let the answering machine pick up the call, or I can get up and answer it.
3. I want to talk to my doctor who might be calling me; I don't want to disturb my comfort.
4. I know that if I get up and pick up the phone, I will be able to talk to the caller; if I do nothing, I will remain comfortable.
5. I think that if I get up and answer the phone, it is more likely than not that I will have responded to a phone solicitation and disturbed my comfort for nothing, but I might talk to my doctor. If I do nothing, I will be comfortable, but there is a chance that I will not get to talk to my doctor until tomorrow.
6. Disturbing my comfort for a probable phone solicitation does not seem nearly as bad as missing the call from my doctor.

Items in (4) are simple belief states, brought to the forefront of my mind by the perceptual state in (1) and by the basic acts (items in (2)) that are the two relevant responses to the perceptual state. Items in (3) are standing desires. So no *act* of agency is involved in (1)–(4). To arrive at the items in (5), there needs to be a computation. But the computation is nothing other than an inference from my empirical beliefs. This too may be a purely causal process. The key factor here is the evaluation in (6).

How do I arrive at the preference ordering of the two alternatives? If I have a built-in strong preference that places talking to my doctor much higher than my discomfort, then this elaborate set up would be a Rube Goldberg version of the simple &-gate circuit of Figure 5.1. The syntactic elements of such a built-in preference would immediately place a mark on the conditional in (5) that contains the basic act of getting up to answer the phone. And that basic act would be called up without any process that deserves the label of deliberation.

For there to be genuine deliberation, the semantic contents of the consequents of the conditionals in (5) need to contribute to the generation of the preference ordering of (6). The only way this can happen is for the computational system to run a series of 'what-if' scenarios. The system first supposes that the basic act of getting up to answer the phone is undertaken. This supposition detaches the consequent of the first conditional of (5), and brings up the representation of my discomfort, a probable conversation with a solicitor, and a low probability of talking to my doctor. Then the system supposes that nothing is done. This supposition in turn detaches the consequent of the second conditional of (5), and sets up a representation of a different state of affairs. Each representation, together with the circumstances (e.g. I am expecting the doctor to tell me about the results of a some crucial labwork), is combined with a higher order of priorities, which are not necessarily reflected in my current desires (e.g. information concerning my health is more valuable to me than a great amount of comfort, and a lot more valuable than being able to avoid irritating conversations), and an inference as to which consequent matches my higher order priorities is carried out. The result of this inference is the preference ordering of (6).

Clearly all these steps in such a simple decision are carried out at lightning speed. One does not feel the agony of deliberating and deciding. However, if these steps are bypassed, and as soon as I hear the phone, I jump up to answer it like a mechanical toy, my behaviour would not be a reason-based one.[22]

---

[22] Paul Grice gives as an example of an akratic behaviour that of a man who having resolved not to be disturbed by anything, gets into a hammock with a long drink and a good book, and upon hearing the phone ring, jumps up to answer it. This, just like Herman's behaviour of removing the ignition key against his 'better judgement', is a case of non-rational behaviour.

Causal Pathways Involved in Choice

All that needs to be done here is to show that the computation needed to get me to answer the phone when the phone rings and I think it might be my doctor calling can be implemented by causal pathways. A slightly more elaborate example is described in the Appendix at the end of this chapter. There I also discuss some of the issues involved in generating computer programmes to model these deliberative processes. The interested reader is urged to look at it at this point.

Figure 5.5 charts a general picture of these pathways. Let us assume that the agent already possesses a representation of the present conditions, F. Let us also suppose that under the conditions F, there are n alternative courses of action, B_1, B_2,...B_n, available to the agent. These alternatives would generate n conditionals of the form, 'Under F, if B_i, then Q_i'. Here Q_i refers to all of the anticipated distal outcomes and side-effects of doing B_i under the conditions, F. The What-If Generator produces as outputs these Qs, which are individually fed to the Evaluator. The Evaluator compares these individual anticipated consequences (Qs) to a standing higher order of preferences and, by using an inferential process involving other beliefs, computes an ordering for them. The Q that appears highest in the ordering is fed

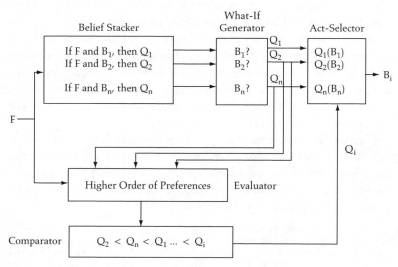

Fig. 5.5. *Deliberation*

into the Act Selector, which matches that Q to its corresponding behaviour. So there are three elements in one's acting for a reason:

(i) the presence of alternatives represented as conditionals, the consequents of which are the estimated outcomes of the actions referred to in the antecedents,

(ii) a process of deliberation which consists in the selection of one of these alternatives by computing which alternative has the consequent that represents the most attractive outcome as determined by a set of higher order priorities of the agent, and

(iii) the actual course of action that is chosen as a direct causal result of (ii).

The operations involved in analysing the conditionals with an aim to find the one with the Q that matches best the standing preferences of the agent, and identifying its antecedent, though, presuppose representational structures which are so articulated as to embody a complex representational content, where the individual elements of the content, F, Bs, and Qs are themselves represented in the structure. Only if the neural wiring that represents 'Under F, if B_i, then Q_i will occur' is such that distinct parts of the wiring contain representations of B_i and Q_i, can the system make the computations it needs to make. That is the only way it can 'choose' the course of action which, under the circumstances, and given what is wanted and what is not, it *should* choose. The essential role played by the semantic representations I examine in the example of the Appendix. I argue there that the mere syntax of a programme will not satisfy the requirements for the process of deliberation because it would be incapable of explaining why the Qs are ordered the way they are by the higher order priorities of the agent.

In this model there is no presumption that the agent is the 'ideally rational agent' sometimes assumed in decision theory. In other words, not all the possible courses of action need to be considered, nor is it assumed that all the foreseeable consequences of the actions actually considered are anticipated. So I am willing to admit that, in the simplest case where the only alternatives considered are merely doing something and not doing it, if some of the consequences of each alternative are taken into account and the Evaluator identifies a preference as existing between these two sets of consequences, then the agent is acting as a rational agent—albeit perhaps not a very wise or an effective one.

Fine-Tuning the Model

Indeed Figure 5.5 simplifies the process involved in deliberative action perhaps too severely to capture the full force of action rationalization in folk psychology, which typically takes the following form: 'S did B_k because she wanted Q^*, and she thought B_k would be a "good" way (the "best" way) of getting Q^*'. In the schema depicted in Figure 5.5, there is no explicit reference to Q^*, the object of one's desire, and as such the conditionals represented do not explicitly mention the conative force that initiates and fuels the deliberative process. Suppose I want to get food. Here my goal, food, (Q^*) is the principle which the Belief-Stacker uses in selecting the conditionals. The consequents of the conditionals that are made available to the Evaluator, the Qs, share Q^* among them—each Q is the anticipated consequence of a specific way of getting food, each 'way' corresponding to a different B, for example, stuffing the doughnut on the counter in my mouth; or making an omelette with the eggs in the refrigerator and eating it; or going to the store, buying a chicken breast, lighting the charcoal, grilling the chicken, and eating it; and so on. As long as at least two alternatives are available, and there is some preference ordering for the consequences of these alternatives, and that ordering is implicated in the selection of the proximal behaviour B_k, I am judged to have reasons for doing B_k, as opposed to any of the other Bs.

So, for example, my preference ordering might require a reasonable balance between convenience and health so that making an omelette is computed as being the least effortful way of getting least harmful food. But did I have a reason for *getting food, simpliciter*? The answer to that question depends on whether I considered during my deliberation any other current desires, which generated alternatives to eating, and on whether the set of conditionals selected for comparison to the Evaluator included conditionals with consequents that represented those alternatives. For example, if my desire to lose weight made me consider not eating and taking a pill to stop the hunger pangs, as opposed to eating something, and the anticipated consequences of the former were less favourable than those of making and eating an omelette, then not only did I have a reason for making and eating an omelette, as opposed to, say, eating the doughnut, I also had a reason for eating, as opposed to not eating. However, if my 'desire' for food has a built-in strength that always overrides every other alternative and blocks them from consideration, like Hume's overriding passion of kindness to children, then I did not have a reason for eating, versus not eating—not eating was not something that was presented to me as an option.

Naturally there are intermediate cases. For example, I may have a standing desire to lose weight, and at some time in the past, I may have examined and (foolishly) found all the alternatives that would satisfy that desire less favourable than eating something high in calories whenever I feel hungry. The memory of this deliberation in the distant past may not even be accessible to me now. But still, it is arguably correct to say that in choosing the omelette now, even though I do not consider not eating as an alternative, I had a reason for eating.

I will resist the temptation to incorporate further complications into the simple model of Figure 5.5. I would be happy if one feature of that model gives us a sufficient condition for having reasons in the form of desires (i.e. the requirement that alternative courses of action exist, the consequences of which contribute to the choice of action), and a second aspect of that model provides a necessary condition for the same thing (i.e. the existence of representations of conditionals that have compositional complexity so that their consequents can play a causal role). I do not have the more ambitious intention of giving a necessary and sufficient condition for having reasons for acting.

The key element in this model is that, in order for the consequences of the different acts to be evaluated with reference to the higher order priorities of the agent, they must be articulately represented. If the preference ordering with reference to which the comparison will be made is to have its items correspond roughly to the desires of folk psychology, these items have to be themselves representational; they cannot be the non-representational passions that Hume spoke of.[23] For if they are non-representational, then their strength will be sufficient to force the choice of action by an &-gate like that depicted in Figure 5.1.[24] If they are non-representational, then, they will lack

---

[23] 'A passion is an original existence, or, if you will, modification of existence, and contains not any representative quality, which renders it a copy of any other existence or modification. When I am angry, I am actually possest with the passion, and in that emotion have no more a reference to any other object, than when I am thirsty, or sick, or more than five foot high' (Hume 1740: 415).

[24] In the Appendix at the end of the chapter I discuss how merely assigning ordinals to the consequents of the conditionals (instead of giving them representational complexity) collapses the computational algorithm to one that codes for non-rational behaviour. Thinking of the items in the preference ordering purely as forces with a certain strength (i.e. as Humean passions) will have just this effect.

contents (at best they will only have intentional *objects*), and consequently the Qs would not be separately represented in the representations of the conditionals and hence will not be able to enter into the
computations required by the model I propose for rational action.[25]

Deliberation and Compatibilism

The model of deliberation presented above is compatibilist in spirit
because the question as to whether the complex causal relations that
connect the reasons of the agent to her action are governed by deterministic or indeterministic laws is irrelevant to the judgement that
the action was done for the reasons the agent had.[26] As long as in a
given token case the proper set of reasons causes 'in the right way' the
behavioural output through pathways schematized in Figure 5.5,
the behaviour is to be judged as rational. And this judgement will
not be affected by whether the system that processes the current
desires, the long-term priorities, and the instrumental beliefs of the
agent to generate the behavioural output is deterministic or indeterministic in its operation.

A note of clarification is in order here. Most debates over compati-
bilism are carried out with reference to questions of freedom, control,
or autonomy. I do not mean to identify free acts with actions done for
reasons.[27] I shall briefly discuss notions of free and voluntary acts in
Chapter 7, but it is important to note here that acting for a reason is a
(strong) necessary condition for acting freely, or so I shall maintain. In
my view, if one's capacity for deliberation is blocked in a given case, if,
for example, one kicks at the car tyre out of frustration or anger, or if
one takes one's shirt off in a post-hypnotic trance, one's action would
not be free. I admit that the act's being reason-based is not *sufficient* for
the act's being free. However, that having been said, one might still be
sceptical about the viability of my attempt to show that the source of

---

[25] It is interesting that Hume's theory of action renders all acts of agency into behaviour
that is modelled on acting out of love for children, not acting for the reasons one has. This
point was brought home to me by Terry Penner during discussions we had on Socratic
egoism.

[26] As Mele (1995a: 170) puts it, in the context of questions concerning autonomy, 'an
account of autonomy that is presented as being neutral on this question [i.e. the question of
the truth or falsity of determinism] is presented as being a compatibilist account'.

[27] Instead of talking of 'actions done for reasons', I could say 'rational acts', but that term
suggests not just acts done for the reasons the agent had, but also acts done for good
(reasonable) reasons. So if I use 'rational' in this chapter, I mean to exclude this suggestion.

reason-based actions is derived from a process of deliberation that is purely causal *because* one was convinced that no coherent sense of freedom or autonomy would be applicable to such a causal account of reason-based actions. The conviction would be based on the charge that a necessary condition for free action is being violated in my causal model of deliberation. So either being a reason-based action is not necessary for that action's being free, which is implausible, or my causal account of deliberation does not capture the essence of rational action.

The discussion of this issue in the literature of the last two decades concentrates on one candidate for such a necessary condition: indeterminism, that is, the thesis that starts from the formation of the beliefs and desires of an agent, through a decision, an intention, to the execution of the action must essentially contain an indeterministic element; and by 'an indeterministic element' we are to understand that there must be some moment in the course of this process when there are alternative ways the process can unfold, and it is undetermined by anything that has happened up to that moment as to how it will actually unfold. The literature that takes up this issue is vast and subtle. In the context of defending my model of deliberation, I can only give a rough presentation of the issues involved.[28]

On the face of it, if this is the necessary condition that the model of deliberation is accused of betraying, it is unclear how justified the accusation is. After all, as I have remarked several times in the course of presenting the model, no assumption is being made in the model about determinism. An easy way of fending off the accusation would be to admit that the indeterminacy of the subatomic world is bound to manifest itself in the events that involve the neurons and the synapses of the brain, which ultimately underlie the causal processes of deliberation, and to grant that any deterministic talk about reasons causing action is a simplification. The real nature of mental activity *is* indeterministic.

To think that such an admission will appease the sceptic and bring the causal theory into the good graces of the incompatibilist is to misconstrue the real source of discontent. It should be clear to the

---

[28] The reader interested in the depth and sophistication with which these issues are discussed is encouraged to look at, among others, Van Inwagen 1983; O'Connor 2000; Kane 1996; Ekstrom 2001*a*; Watson 1987; Velleman 1992; Clarke 2000; McIntyre 1994; Finch and T. Warfield 1998.

reader by now that the sceptical worries are due to deep libertarian sensibilities. These worries stem from a concern that *agency, determinative power, control* over one's actions cannot be derived from mere events caused to occur by other events in the agent. And the concern will be there regardless of whether the causation is deterministic or indeterministic—unless something else is added to the picture.

The sceptics disagree as to what that something else should be. And we can divide the proposals as to what it should be into two rough camps. In the first camp are those libertarians who require that the agents, either through causal powers that are inherent in them or through some capacity essential to agency, intervene between reasons and intentions and between intentions and bodily movements. This intervention is possible only if there are gaps in the causal sequence of events at which the agent can exercise her potency, and such gaps can exist only if indeterminism is true of the physical world.[29] I have given expression to my concerns about agents' capacity to intervene in this manner in Chapter 1. Even many libertarians find the invocation of such a power to explain autonomy and control too mysterious to do any theoretical work.[30]

The proposals that fall into the second camp are closer to the spirit of the causal theory in that they eschew adding irreducible agency to indeterminism in order to capture the incompatibilist sense of freedom. R. Clarke (2000: 160–6) has recently argued that libertarians need not endorse an agent-causation view. For Clarke, a libertarian requires only two conditions to be met for an agent's to be morally responsible for her action: (*a*) that it be open to the agent to perform some other action, and (*b*) that it be shown that this openness is not due to mere indeterminacy; that it be because the agent has control over which of the alternatives comes about.[31] According to Clarke, libertar-

---

[29] Among defenders of agent causation, one can cite Reid 1969; Taylor 1966; Chisholm 1966. More recent and subtler versions may be found in Velleman 1992; Clarke 1993, 1996; O'Connor 2000. Examples of views that require agents to have the capacity to initiate action without invoking the notion of agent causation can be found in O'Shaughnessy 1973; Hornsby 1980; Ginet 1990.

[30] As Van Inwagen remarks, any attempt to render agent causation less mysterious does no more than mark the problem for which the libertarian seeks a solution (1983: 151–2).

[31] Many authors acknowledge the fact that merely showing that freedom (or moral responsibility) is incompatible with determinism does not further the libertarian cause unless one can also show how free action is possible in an indeterministic framework. See O'Connor 2000 and Kane 1996 for elegant statements of this challenge.

ians will be able to satisfy these conditions without having to appeal to a notion of irreducible acts of volition in a scenario of the following kind.

An agent has decided earlier to do something. At some point she notices that it is time for her to do that thing, and as a result acquires the intention to do it. And she then straightaway does it. All of this is consistent with a purely event-causation account. Suppose, however, that there is an indeterminacy between her intending to do this thing and her actually doing it. It is, say, given all the laws of nature, (equally) possible that right after she acquires the intention, she might worry that doing this thing may be in conflict with some prior commitment, and as a result decide to reopen her earlier decision. And if this were to happen, she may not act at all. Clarke says, 'a libertarian might propose that an agent acts with direct libertarian control if: following the acquisition of her intention to act now, it is causally open to her to act as she intends, and causally open to her that she perform no action at all right then' (2000: 162).

As Clarke is fully aware, this second part of the picture is also fully consistent with a purely event-causation account of action. It is a picture in which an agent finds herself at some juncture with a reason-based intention to do something and, because of indeterminism at that juncture, it is possible for her to act on that intention and to do that thing, and it is also possible for her to be struck with doubt and do nothing. ('Between the intention and the action there falls the shadow.') Let us call this the Hamlet syndrome. If she does the thing intended then, provided that the additional relevant conditions are satisfied, she is responsible for doing it. But if she freezes in her tracks and does nothing, then, since she has not actively refrained from doing that thing, she will not be responsible for not doing anything. (This is Clarke's judgement, too: 2000: 163.) A causal theorist would have nothing to object to in these judgements. In fact the judgements would be directly derivable from the account of deliberation presented above. But what is hard to see is why the fact that the agent is responsible for acting as she intends is *to be derived from* the possibility that, given the same circumstances, she may not act at all. Why, in other words, is someone who has the Hamlet syndrome (more) responsible for her action than someone, who, like Luther, finds he 'can do no other'?[32]

R. Kane, who develops a subtle version of libertarianism that a causal theorist can accommodate, is also concerned to locate the source of freedom in something in addition to chance indeterminism. He points out, quite rightly, that the sniper's 'ability' to miss his target cannot be what makes his act of killing his victim a free act (1996: 110).

Kane's solution, which he calls *plural voluntarism*, consists in requiring that the agent, thanks to the indeterministic causal processes that underlie the connection between reasons and action, could have done something other than what he did, and this something else would also have been under his control. And the picture in which this requirement is satisfied is one where there are two sets of reasons (say, moral considerations versus considerations of self-interest) that are in conflict with each other, and which set gets to produce the action is due to the failure or success of the effort of the will. And what are identified as efforts of the will need be nothing other than the indeterministic processes in the brain, which a chaos theory might make sense of. This is certainly a scenario that is consistent with the causal theory. But my puzzlement, which I expressed in connection with Clarke's view, persists here as well. Granted that the result of my 'effort of will' might be undetermined, why think that this indeterminacy is what renders my actions free? Kane himself may be sensitive to this puzzlement because he talks about 'an agent's trying to overcome temptation' (1996: 133) or about how an agent can make 'the reasons she wanted to act on more than any other *by* choosing for them' (135).

Mele (1995a) criticizes Kane, I think rightly, for limiting free choice just to cases of internal conflict. Mele identifies several links in the causal chain leading from deliberation to action as possible locations for indeterminacy: (*a*) between the intention and the action, (*b*) between a judgement and the intention, and (c) between a deliberation and the judgement. He argues that indeterminacy in the first two links constrains, rather than enhances, control. But unlike Kane, instead of

---

[32] My puzzlement may alternatively be expressed by asking what in this picture satisfies the second of Clarke's conditions for libertarianism, i.e. what makes it the case that the openness as to what an agent does is *because* the agent has control over which of the alternatives comes about.

locating the freedom-generating indeterminism in the third link, Mele suggests that a more coherent libertarian sense of freedom can be derived from a picture in which it is undetermined as to what reasons occur to an agent that are to be used for the process of deliberation.

Ekstrom (2001a), who rightly finds fault with locating the source of libertarian freedom in the chance affair of which reasons occur to an agent, suggests, instead, that the freedom-enhancing indeterminism should be placed just before the formation of the preferences as to what to desire and what to do. (This would be the formation of what I called long-standing higher order priorities of the agent.) In this manner, an account of the *self* can be brought to bear on the question of what one does freely.

None of the libertarian positions that attempt to derive freedom from the indeterminism residing in the causes of the deliberative process have any bearing on the causal theory of action. The causal theory, as I have presented it, is silent on how an agent's beliefs and desires or long-term priorities are shaped. These libertarian positions are neutral as to whether the pathway from the deliberation to the action (the pathway in which a causal theorist is interested) is deterministic or not. As far as I know, they will have no reason to reject the distinction that was drawn in Chapter 4 between two types of chance, one which preserves agency and one which yields a deviant causal chain. And none of them needs to reject the causal theory I have offered on the grounds that such a theory has to violate some key requirement of a libertarian sense of freedom.

On the other hand, the puzzlement that I have expressed in connection with Clarke's and Kane's ways of rescuing libertarianism from an indeterministic causal theory extends over to libertarian positions like Mele's and Ekstrom's.[33] And the puzzlement is just that, without introducing irreducible agency, causal indeterminacy seems to be the wrong source with which to explain how one could have done otherwise. I will recommend in Chapter 8 a notion of a voluntary act that is more compatibilist in spirit, and suggest that such a notion is in better harmony with a causal theory of action that I have been developing here.

---

[33] I do not intend to represent Mele as a libertarian here. The view I described above is his diagnosis, without endorsement, of how a libertarian *can* account for autonomy in a world of causes.

THE PHENOMENAL FEEL OF FREE CHOICE

As I suggested above, the feeling that one has when one takes oneself to be making a free choice or to be acting in conformity with intentions formed through deliberation is recognizably different from the feeling of 'being driven' to a choice or to an action. Both the compatibilist and the indeterminist who takes freedom to be consistent with a (naturalist) causal account of action face the task of explaining the source of this difference. (This task is of no concern to libertarians who subscribe to agent causation or to theorists who, like Ginet, posit powers essential to agency because for them this phenomenal difference is the given that provides conclusive evidence for their theory.) For example, Kane attempts to discharge this task by suggesting that an agent may be phenomenologically experiencing the chaotic process in the brain as resisting one consideration in favour of another. I would like to suggest, on the other hand, that the model of deliberation I have proposed is capable of showing how the phenomenological difference can be accounted for.

The particular feeling that needs to be explained may be described as follows: when we take ourselves to be making a rational decision, we typically think that the future is open, that we can do this *or* we can do that, and that it is *up to us* which we do. It is clear that the explanation of this feeling cannot lie in the mere fact that the indeterminacy of nature renders my future open. That, by itself, will not show the origin of the feeling that it is up to *me*.

The model of deliberation I offer above contains a solution to this puzzle. It shows in what way it is true that it is up to us what we do in the future, and at the same time, it shows how this is compatible with my reasons determining what I will do.

If it is true that an essential element in deliberation is the need to run what-if scenarios (in order to find out which course of action involves the most desirable consequences and side-effects), then the deliberator must put herself into a frame of mind in which she *knows* that she *can* initiate each of the courses of action represented in the antecedents of the conditionals. Without this, the model of deliberation I propose could not be implemented.

For example, if I want to get into my house, I may be able to deliberate between going through the back door (closer, but requires walking on a muddy path) or the front door. It will turn out that, since getting my shoes muddy that day is a lot worse for me than walking a few additional steps, I will *not* go through the back door. But for me to find this out, I need to reason through and predict the consequences of my doing some of the things I know I have the causal power to do; I try to see what will happen when I go through the back door. Going through the back door is something I know I can do. It is 'up to me' whether I do it or not. Of course, in contrast, I do not run the what-if scenario with the conditional, 'If I walk through the wall of the house, it will be quicker and cleaner'. I do not run this because it is *irrational* for me to think I *can*. Similarly, if a committed vegetarian is faced with a menu on which the *only* vegetarian item is Fettucine Alfredo, the deliberation will be confined to either ordering it or walking out.

These examples show that, if the agent may not assume that under the circumstances she *can* take a certain course of action, then she should not include that course of action in her deliberation. So they support the claim that, if it is reasonable to include a course of action in one's deliberation, then one must assume that one is free to take that course of action. This means that, in so far as it involves the running of what-if scenarios, the act of deliberation makes it very *natural* for us to place ourselves in a framework in which we try to see how we are going to determine the future. And we can do this even if we believe deep down that, whatever one chooses, that choice has already been determined by one's beliefs, desires, and preferences.

I submit that the source of our conviction that at the moment of decision, the future is open to us comes from our ability to assume that we actually can perform the actions described in the antecedents of the conditionals, and detach the consequents by modus ponens. This conviction is what makes it possible to deliberate (along the lines of the causal model presented above) which future to take—the deliberation enables us to discover which future we will take.

INTENTIONS

Returning to the flow chart of Figure 5.5, which was proposed as one way of modelling the computations involved in deliberation (in a way that is consistent with the causal theory), I should admit that a decision to pursue one course of action among several alternatives does not always lead to action—at least, it does not always lead to action right away. This indicates the need to introduce one last complication to the flow chart. The complication consists in recognizing the role of intention in a causal account of action. This chapter has concentrated on the causal role of reasons in action, but as several authors have convincingly argued, and as I shall discuss at some length in the next chapter, intentions need to be recognized as irreducible causal intermediaries between reasons and actions. Intentions play two types of roles. In one capacity, they impose certain rationality constraints on the deliberative process. If some intention that is already present in the agent presents a conflict with any of the alternative courses of action that are being considered in the process of deliberation, then either these alternatives are going to be eliminated from the what-if scenarios, or the earlier intention will need to be evaluated. If Carl has already formed the intention to let his son drive the car that evening, then Carl cannot include killing his uncle by running him over that evening *without* reopening the deliberation that resulted in the decision to let his son take the car. Just as instrumental beliefs involving things one knows one cannot do (like walking through solid walls) are not allowed into the Belief-Stacker, instrumental beliefs involving things that are inconsistent with one's prior intentions (like the intention to keep a vegetarian diet) are also out of bounds, *unless* the prior intentions in question are reconsidered and the cost of revising them is included in the current deliberation.

In a second capacity, intentions trigger the basic acts at the right time and guide the agent in the execution of the plan (the course of action) that was chosen. This guiding role is carried out (i) by calling in further basic acts as anticipated by the plan, and (ii) by filling in or revising the details of the plan as needed. These two capacities may be represented by revising Figure 5.5 as shown in Figure 5.6.

In so far as intentions trigger the basic acts from which a whole complex action may unfold, intentions are the obvious candidates to use in a causal theory of action. It was in this spirit that in Chapter 2, roughly, an (intentional) action was defined as behaviour that is caused by an (appropriate) intention. And it was in the context of such a causal theory that the problem of deviant causal chains was taken up in Chapter 4.

But it should be clear from the discussion of this chapter that, unless the triggering event of a basic output is the result of a deliberative process, that is, unless the output is a distal effect of the reasons the

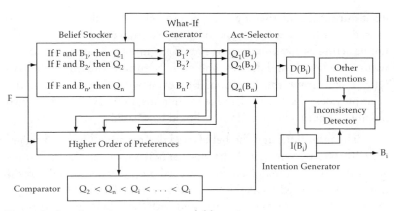

Fig. 5.6. *Consistency constraints in deliberation*

agent has, the output will not be an intentional act.[34] Indeed, I would like to suggest that a necessary condition on *intending* is that it be the causal consequence of such deliberation. What is crucial for the purposes of a causal theory, though, is that an adequate causal theory must include the role of reasons among the causal antecedents of actions. Failing to do so will open the gates to counter-examples where intentions are induced in a person by external manipulation, and where such intentions cause the behaviour of the person. Only an inadequate causal theory, a theory which identifies acts of agency simply with what intentions cause, needs to be embarrassed by such examples. On the causal theory defended here, one can either accept the suggestion above, and declare these artificially induced states not to be intentions at all, or point to the lack of proper causal ancestry for these 'intentions' and judge the behaviour they cause not to be acts of agency.

THE SCEPTIC REVISITED

I should close this chapter with a discussion of Van Inwagen's example that was introduced at the beginning. The example was designed to

---

[34] In Ch. 6, three types of apparent exceptions to this claim will be noted and discussed: (1) arational actions, (2) simple acts, like crossing one's legs, or catching a ball coming towards one's face 'almost by reflex', (3) things done 'as if on automatic pilot', like the things one does in driving.

elicit our intuitions that a person whose beliefs and desires are being caused by Martians by means of a device implanted in him would not be acting as a *rational agent* even if his intentions were consistent with those beliefs and desires, and such intentions caused the behaviour. I will grant the intuition. But even with that intuition, the example does not do any damage to the causal theory. There are two possible scenarios here, and they should be treated separately.

1. The intentions and the beliefs and desires are all induced separately by the Martians. The Martians just make sure that the intentions are of the sort that may have been caused by the beliefs and desires if things were allowed to take their natural course. (This is what it might mean for the intentions to be consistent with the beliefs and desires.) In this scenario, the intentions lack their proper ancestry, and hence the casual theory gives us no reason to judge the behaviours they cause to be acts of rational agency. These behaviours are not good candidates for acts of agency for the same reason that an externally induced intention that is *inconsistent with the beliefs and desires* does not give rise to an act of agency. For the purposes of the causal theory in question, a necessary condition for an act of agency is that the intention that causes it be caused (through the process of deliberation) by the agent's reasons. If this condition is violated, it is irrelevant whether the intention is consistent with the reasons or not. (Compare, for example, my having a perceptual experience as of seeing a vase. Suppose the experience is being induced in me by a Martian who has momentarily blinded me so that the vase in front of me cannot cause in me an experience which would have been qualitatively identical to the one I am now having. No reasonable causal theory of perception would have the verdict that I am seeing the vase.)

2. The Martians just induce the beliefs and desires, and then let the natural course of events evolve, wherein the person, through a process of deliberation, arrives at an intention, and the intention causes the behaviour. In this scenario, it is not up to the causal theory of action to generate the ultimate verdict as to whether the behaviour is an act of agency. As far as the causal theory of action is concerned, provided that the Martians have succeeded in inducing in this person *genuine* beliefs and desires, the behaviour satisfies all the conditions of intentional action. The ultimate judgement would depend on one's theory of mental states—the theory which tells us

how mental states like beliefs and desires acquire their content. On one version, these states are strictly supervenient on the physiological states of a person, that is, if two persons are 'cell-by-cell identical', then they must be psychologically indistinguishable. On this version, there would be no problem for some technologically advanced Martian to fiddle with the person's neural connections and thereby induce in him a whole belief–desire network as genuine as yours or mine. As a result, this person's behaviour would be intentional action. However, there is another version of the theory of mental states on which, for a state to count as a genuine belief, it must have the proper aetiology. If my belief 'X is liquid' has a causal history that connects the referent of 'X' to water on Earth, then it is a belief that *water* is liquid. If its causal history connects it to the substance XYZ on Twin-earth, then it is a belief that *XYZ* is liquid. And if a creature is formed in a swamp due to some bizarre radioactive atmospheric phenomenon, and the creature is, by some improbable chance, cell-by-cell identical to me, the creature has *no* beliefs. So on this version, none of the states caused by the Martians in the person would be genuine beliefs or desires. And as a result, on this version, the person would not be acting intentionally.

I submit that our intuitions in the second scenario are going to be shaped by the version of the theory of mental states we are inclined to accept. I do not think the second scenario has anything to teach us about the causal theory of *action*.

Appendix
Can the Deliberative Process be Programmed?

Consider a simple decision problem. Suppose Sam expects the outdoor temperature to rise to 90°. The increase in temperature may be gradual, or the temperature may rise very fast. Sam has access to an air conditioner and to a fan. And Sam's priorities include a reasonable balance between comfort and economic use of energy sources.

It might be instructive to ask if the problem can be represented by a computer programme.

We may set up the parameters of the example as follows.

> A: The temperature increases fast (by more than 0.2° per minute in the last half-hour) to above 76°.
>
> B: The temperature increases slowly (not by more than 0.2° per minute in the last half-hour) to above 76°.
>
> X: The temperature does not increase to above 76°.

The three alternative actions are:

> AC: Turn on the air conditioner.
>
> FAN: Turn on the fan.
>
> NO: Do nothing.

(*a*) If A and AC, then maximal energy consumption and 73° within one hour (comfort).

(*b*) If A and FAN, then minimal energy consumption and > 80° (heavy discomfort).

(*c*) If B and AC, then maximal energy consumption and 73° within half-hour (comfort).

(*d*) If B and FAN, then minimal energy consumption and < 80° (slight discomfort).

(*e*) If X and NO, then no energy consumption and no discomfort.

And the preference ordering is: $b < c < a < d < e$, where the letters *a*–*e* refer to the consequents of the conditionals in (*a*)–(*e*), and '$x < y$' stands for '*y* is preferred to *x*'.

If an engineer were given the task of designing an 'intelligent' thermostat to implement this decision procedure, the simplest logic she would employ would consist in first recognizing that there are three possible inputs, A, B, and X, and then noticing that to conform to the preference ordering, it would be sufficient to channel these inputs to one of the three possible outputs: AC, FAN, or NO. More specifically, the engineer needs to find a circuit the behaviour of which is described by the following:

> If X, then NO.
>
> If A, then AC.
>
> If B, then FAN.

A circuit that implements the flow chart in Figure 5.7 would do the trick. But this circuit falls short of modelling the deliberative process that was an essential element of the way the example was set up. It is clear that the circuit is not significantly different from the thermostat of Figure 5.2. Can we improve on the algorithm to get it to match the what-if reasoning of the deliberative process? As a first shot, we might try to assign some numbers to

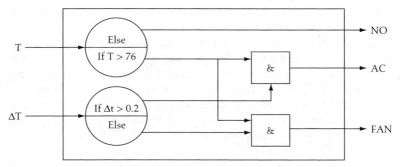

Fig. 5.7. *A decision problem*

the preferences (1 to 5, with 5 the highest) and instruct the system to run through the conditionals, and to perform the operation specified in the second conjunct of the antecedent of the conditional that yields the higher consequent. Thus:

> If X and NO, then 5
> If A, and AC, then 3
> If A, and FAN, then 1
> If B, and AC, then 2
> If B, and FAN, then 4

But the computation involved in this algorithm is extensionally equivalent to that of the simpler algorithm.[35] And as such, it is equally incapable of capturing what is essential to acting for a reason. The pattern that was proposed as the model for deliberative choice had a feature that the second algorithm lacks. The feature *explained* why the preferences were ordered the way they are. On the causal theory of action, any model of acting for a reason must satisfy two criteria: (1) it must show the pathway through which reasons cause the act, and (2) it must explain the action by rationalizing it. It is this second criterion that is not met by the second algorithm. The circuit that will implement the second set of instructions itself does not contain any information as to why, for example, I prefer the fan over the air conditioning under certain circumstances. And the only way such an explanation can be achieved is to give *representational content* to the consequents of the conditionals. Their content will be the anticipated consequences and side-effects of the acts cited in the corresponding antecedents. And the what-if computation will detach each of the representations that corresponds to the various acts

---

[35] I am grateful to Martin Barrett for pointing this out to me and for helping me in general with the technical aspects of this argument.

available under the circumstances, and compute a preference ordering with reference to the particular circumstances and to a standing ordering of general utilities. This latter ordering, we must assume, is generated *naturally*, in the way evaluative beliefs and desires of a person are typically induced.[36] In other words, it is not surprising that the mere syntax of the computational algorithms fails to capture the rationalizing role of reasons. We need to have the representational element, and we need to have this element occurring in the consequent so that it can be separated out and evaluated against other alternatives. Any attempt to collapse the two steps of the computation (separating out the consequent *and* evaluating it with reference to a higher ordering of utilities) into one will deprive the model of its explanatory role, because it will not exploit the causal role of genuine beliefs and desires.

To appreciate this point better, we need to note that the example we have been considering was an artificial one. It was artificial because it examined a restricted segment of an agent's deliberation, abstracted from all other contexts. The preference ordering that is referred to in the ranking of the different alternative actions should give us a general profile of the agent's way of weighing environmental considerations against his own comfort. And we should expect this profile to be reflected in choices he will be making in other contexts.[37] It is this fact that makes it imperative for the computational procedure to be able to separate out the consequences of anticipated actions in different contexts and relate them to the same general utility ordering. Acts of an agent are sometimes rationalized by showing how they cohere with other acts of the agent. And this would not be possible if the last steps of the computation were made to collapse into one.

I am hoping that the lengthy discussion of this simplistic example of deliberation has helped establish the following points:

1. Reading representational complexity into the syntactic structure of computational algorithms is a mistake.

2. Reasons explain an action only if it can be shown that the agent's choice of the action was in response to the fact that the expected consequences of the action were evaluated as being higher in the agent's preference ordering than consequences of other acts available to the agent at the time. (Here by 'in response to', I mean 'a causal consequence of'.)

---

[36] It is the job of the naturalistic account of beliefs and desires to describe what this 'typical induction' consists of. As I said earlier, I take my job to be to argue that, *if* such a naturalistic account is successful, then nothing stands in the way of deriving agency from a causal theory of action. If I do my job well, then the sceptic will have to redirect the criticism to the prospects of a naturalistic account of beliefs and desires, and stop badgering the causal theorist of action.

[37] No presumption of strong consistency is being made here. But the demands of rationality will certainly impose some constraints on the agent's utilities.

3. Such an evaluation is affected by having the representation of the consequences of the available actions occur in the consequents of the conditionals. These representations will be detached by running the what-if computations and compared with each other with reference to a standing utility ordering.

4. The model I am proposing is not just a more complex version of the model that corresponds to the second set of instructions. Even when we take a sophisticated chess-playing programme that examines and evaluates a branching tree of possible moves, we would be considering a programme that is a vastly complicated version of that model—a programme that has a 'look-ahead' function, one that calculates probable future outcomes contingent on a present choice of action, and evaluates the outcomes according to the values given to it by the programmer.[38] This is short of the *representational* complexity of the model I propose because the values of the outcomes in the chess programme are not determined by a computation based on a utility ordering that reflects genuine beliefs and desires of the agent.

---

[38] I owe this point to Zachary Ernst.

6

Intentions

INTRODUCTION

Is intending to do something a psychological state that is distinct from the states of believing and desiring? If not, what sort of analysis of intending in terms of other basic psychological states is the one that best conforms to ordinary uses of 'intend' and explains its role in agency? If, on the other hand, it is distinct, what sort of a state is it (what is its functional role), what is its content, and what facts about intentions explain the various constraints they are subject to? These are the questions this chapter will be devoted to. My first objective is to propose a theory about the nature of intention and its content. I will then try to show how this view explains many of the features of intentions discussed in the literature better than most other views I am familiar with. This second objective is complicated by the fact that there is surprising diversity of opinion as to what features intentions really have. Some of the more frequently asked questions about intentions concern (i) the reducibility of intentions to other mental states, (ii) the relation between intending to do A and believing that one will (can) do A, for example, whether the former entails the latter, (iii) the relation between intending to do A and doing A intentionally, and (iv) the constraint that intentions be (*a*) consistent with each other, and (*b*) consistent with one's beliefs. Ideally, a theory is best defended by showing how well it explains a set of basic facts about its subject. Given the disagreements that exist over issues (i)–(iv), a straightforward defence of the view I shall propose seems to be unavailable here because the 'basic facts' one would like to appeal to are themselves in dispute. One needs to argue for one's judgement as to the nature of these facts as well. And these arguments are unavoidably influenced by one's theory about intending. The only defence I can give against such a charge of circularity here is twofold: one, that the more uncontroversial features of intentions turn out to be unsurprising consequences of my view about intending, and two, that the existence of some of the controversy itself can be made intelligible in the framework of my view.

THEORY OF INTENTION

Holistic Content of the State of Intending

I argued at the end of Chapter 5 that actions are typically preceded by a deliberative process. This process consists in identifying one course of action among available alternatives as the most preferred means of achieving some goal. The process may be represented in terms of the following algorithmic model. The agent considers some alternatives she believes to be available to her. She takes into account some of the consequences and side-effects of the alternatives and, consulting a set of higher order priorities, she computes a preference ordering for them. This model was depicted in greater detail in Chapter 5 as containing the following stages: the instrumental beliefs of the agent are represented by a set of conditionals; the antecedents of these conditionals describe the basic acts the agent believes she can perform under the circumstances, and their consequents are descriptions of the goal together with some of the relevant consequences and side-effects the action is expected to give rise to; these consequences and side-effects are run through the agent's desire profile and her higher order evaluative judgements; each is assigned a desirability quotient; the cumulative value of these quotients, computed according to some algorithm, is then compared to the value computed for alternative actions; and the result is the choice of one of the basic acts, as well as its anticipated consequences, as representing the 'most preferable means' of achieving the goal. The model is derivative of decision theoretic models. It differs from them in that the means are only skeletally represented, and only a fragment of the non-goal-directed consequences and side-effects anticipated by the agent are taken into account (only the ones that have negative or positive value for the agent); furthermore, it is not assumed that an explicit computation of the expected utilities of each alternative is carried out—the probabilities are at best comparatively considered.[1]

[1] Harman (1986a: 104–5) points to the difficulties of using the model of rational gambling policies in practical reasoning. What is offered here is much weaker than a quantifiable decision procedure.

When the choice is made, a command is issued to execute the basic act described in the antecedent of the conditional picked out by the process. And if the instrumental beliefs are true, the goal is achieved. Furthermore, if the evaluations have been realistic, the goal is achieved roughly in a way that seemed to the agent to be least objectionable.

George wants to get a book from the library. This is his goal. (Here let us ignore whether this goal is itself a means towards a further goal.) He believes he can bicycle there, take the bus, or drive his car. He deliberates as follows: 'If I bicycle, I will get some exercise and save money, but since it might rain, I might get soaked. 'If I take the bus, it will cost me $1.50, and I will walk two blocks; since it might rain, I might get wet. If I drive, then it will cost me $5.00 to park under the library building. I would rather not risk getting soaked. I don't want to pay $5.00. So I will take the bus and carry an umbrella just in case it rains.' (In another scenario, he could find spending $1.50 also unacceptable, and then the deliberation might lead him to abandon his goal.) Thus the deliberation has resulted in a course of action: George has settled on one of the three 'act plans' he has considered, and he can begin executing it at the appropriate time.[2]

This model of deliberation, which has so far made use only of desires and of evaluative and instrumental beliefs, will enable us to locate intentions in the economy of action. I will argue below that the model will enable us to identify a mental state as the state of *intending*.

In such a deliberative process, we can see that the *decision* involves (1) a goal (the purpose with which the action is to be launched), and (2) a chosen *plan* that (*a*) strings together means to intermediate ends until the string connects some basic act that is in the basic act repertoire of the agent with the goal, and (*b*) takes into account the desirability quotient of the anticipated side-effects and consequences of the means.

More often than not, such a string is incomplete, and in many cases, even very skeletal. Usually the details are filled in, or the project is scuttled as new circumstances present themselves. If act plans were not

---

[2] *Taking the bus to the library* is not a good candidate for a basic act. To be more accurate, I should break the plan into a sequence of actions strung together to form what some philosophers (e.g. Goldman, Ginet) have called aggregate acts. But for the purposes of this example, I will ignore the interesting differences between plans that contain only one basic act (like flipping the switch) and those that have several basic acts structured in some temporal order (like baking a soufflé or taking a bus).

relatively indeterminate in this way, very few act plans would be executed.[3]

However, on the view of intending I wish to defend, for a state to be the psychological state of intending to do something, that state *must* include an acknowledgement of some means of achieving that thing, as well as an assessment of the effects of those means. Without such a minimal plan, one can hope to do that thing, wish to do that thing, but one cannot be intending to do it.

Once the decision is reached, the plan for the act is represented in the intention of the agent. In other words, the state of intention has as its content not just the goal, but also all the intermediate ends and the side-effects that have been anticipated in the decision.

This intention state ultimately causes the basic act at the appropriate time. Thus the intention is what eventually triggers the basic act.[4] And as the circumstances unfold, the plan is made more determinate, details are revised, and, if needed, new intermediate goals are set. These alterations are conducted with an eye to the goal as the ultimate focal point. But even the goal is not immutable. If, on the way, some side-effects or some of the consequences turn out to be a lot more undesirable than expected, the goal itself may be scuttled.

One more example may make these points clearer. My goal is to eat a peach. I plan to get up from my chair, walk to the fridge, open its door, feel the peaches in the fridge, pick out a ripe one, go over to the sink, peel the peach, and eat it in several bites. In the process, I expect I may stain my shirt.

The intention I formed, the intention that includes all of the items in the above list, was formed in response to a desire I had, the desire to have some refreshing thing to eat. Notice that some of the anticipated side-effects, such as my displacing air molecules, or my expending energy as I walk to the kitchen, are not part of the content of my intention because they have no relevance to the deliberation that resulted in the choice of that act plan. The search for the refreshing

---

[3] Searle (1983: 93) makes a similar point when he says that prior intentions need to be indeterminate, or else they would be rarely satisfied.

[4] It is possible to assign the function of triggering the basic act to a separate module. Searle (1983), for example, names the state that triggers the action 'intention in action'. For Searle, intention in action takes on the further role of presenting a number of subsidiary actions that are not represented in prior intentions (in Searle's account, 'prior intention' is comparable to my notion of intention). The way I have characterized basic acts, many of these subsidiary actions (such as changing gears in driving a car) turn out to be components of the basic acts themselves.

thing was restricted to the things I knew I could eat without having to go out of the house. Of the fruits at home, the apples were not as attractive, and the pears were not ripe yet. So the decision to eat a peach, even if it was reached quickly, without a great deal of consciously agonizing over the alternatives, was reached after a deliberative process. And the decision also involved some outline of *how* I would get at the peach. (I knew where to walk when I got out of my chair), and *how* I would eat it (I knew I would not stop at the cupboard and take a plate because I knew I would not be eating the peach at the table). Furthermore, although I anticipated staining my shirt, I preferred that consequence to taking the trouble of placing a napkin over the front of my shirt. So the whole sequence of basic acts I performed was directed at the goal of eating the peach. And I could have revised any of these if unexpected obstacles came up. The force that unified these several basic acts and made them all stages of the means of achieving the goal was guided by the deliberative process that resulted in the final decision. The final decision was not just the decision to eat a peach but one that included some (maybe tentative) answers to where, when, and how. Without some mental state, the content of which represented such an act plan and which persisted through the execution of the act plan, the separate basic acts may not have been performed in the right sequence, may not have been co-ordinated, or even may have been replaced by other irrelevant ones. In the process of executing my decision to eat a peach, if the chosen act plan were not acting as a guide for me, what would get me to the fridge door, as opposed to the pencil sharpener on the way out of my study? And the act plan would not be able to act as a guide and move me in the right direction unless it contained some representation that causally constrained my actions and ensured that I produce the right string of basic acts.[5] So when I am in a state in which I intend to eat a peach, that state typically represents more than just my eating a peach. It represents, rather, the whole act-tree that includes the act plan as well as the side-effects that were considered in the deliberative process. A similar view is to be found in Mele 1992*b*. He says, 'The content of an agent's intention to A is simply the plan component of his intention

[5] Mele (1992*b*: ch. 8), in agreement with Bratman, includes the following items among the functions of intention: prompting practical reasoning, co-ordinating all of one's plans, and initiating, sustaining, guiding, and monitoring action. It would be hard to imagine how all these functions can be performed by a state whose representational content is confined to one single act.

to A' (1992b: 218), where the plan component may be 'one that specifies a goal and a particular route to that goal' (216). Gustafson (1985: 108), too, has sympathy with this view: 'Expressions of intentions include descriptions of the means to be employed for further purposes or intentions as well as descriptions of further purposes and goals themselves.' But neither author places any weight on the deliberative process that, as I see it, plays a crucial role in the determination of the content of intentions, and as a result, neither is inclined to see the anticipated side-effects as belonging to the content of an intention.

It might be objected here that the content of an intention need not include all the elements that are used in arriving at the decision. The anticipated side-effects and the consequences belong to the decision, but their representation does not serve any function that can be reasonably attributed to intentions. Their function (say, that of co-ordinating and guiding action) can be achieved by merely keeping an eye on the means–end relations.[6]

But the objection ignores the essential revisability of intentions. Revisability requires not only that the means–end planning must be supervised to see if the goal is likely to be reached as planned, but also that the side-effects be kept in survey to make sure that nothing worse than what has been anticipated is about to happen. If the content of the intention does not include the side-effects, then the intention cannot fully co-ordinate and guide action.

Such a conception of intending has been called the 'holistic view of intentions'. I propose to argue for it by showing that, if one adopts this conception, then one can make sense of some of the disagreements among philosophers concerning intentions.

The Rationalizing Role of Intentions

The holistic view of intentions is a view about the psychological state that persists in the agent, which sometimes changes in its details prior to and throughout the course of the agent's action. The state is formed as a causal consequence of a process that operates on the beliefs and desires of the agent, and it is distinct from any of those beliefs and desires. It is the state that initiates the action, and then co-ordinates and guides its components.

---

[6] I owe this objection to Richard Teng.

But intentions have a second role that has not yet been mentioned. As Bratman so aptly puts it, our intentions are, like Janus, double-faced. On the one hand, they guide our actions. On the other hand, they are involved in our explaining actions by rationalizing them. When we ask George why he is going to the library, or why he is taking the downtown bus, one answer is 'because he intends to borrow a book'. The answer simultaneously achieves several things: (i) it informs us that George has made a decision that makes borrowing a book from the library a goal of his; (ii) it explains some action of George's (e.g. his taking the downtown bus) by implying that George took that action because he believed that that action would be a reasonable means for his goal; (iii) it tells us that George took that action intentionally. So the primary force of the claims of the form, 'S did B because S intended to do A', or alternatively, 'S did B with the intention of doing A', is that of rationally explaining S's doing B. Here the surface grammar in which these claims are formulated suggests that the intended act is an *act type*, and that the relation in which the act token B stands to the act type A is one in which B, under the circumstances, is conceived by the agent as a means to a generic end.

Actually there are two uses for the explanatory role of such singular intention attributions. In the first, as illustrated by the example about George's intention to borrow a book from the library, the attribution of intending to do A explains an action, B, of the agent that contributed to the satisfaction of his intention. In the second, the attribution of the intention to do A explains an action, B, of the agent that was contrary to the intended A, by implying that the agent (falsely) believed that B would result in A, or that doing B *would be* doing A. 'Why did George turn left into the dead-end street?' 'He intended to go to the library and thought that he could get there by turning left.' 'Why did Hal add a quarter cup of salt to the pie filling?' 'He intended to add a quarter cup of sugar...' In each case, the explained act is an act which the agent believes (truly or falsely) to be instrumental to the fulfilment of the attributed intention.

What is the relation, then, between these two roles—the initiating, co-ordinating, and guiding role, on the one hand, and the explanatory role, on the other? The question forces a decision. The decision is between (*a*) maintaining that 'intending' is ambiguous, each of the two meanings given by the different roles intention plays, and (*b*) trying to show that the explanatory role is derivative of the co-ordinating role.[7] I am of the opinion that the second of these options, if it can be successfully carried out, is the preferable one. It is preferable because claims of discovering ambiguity should be a philosopher's last resort. As Davidson (1980: 88) says,

> it is not likely that if a man has the intention of trapping a tiger, his intention is not a state, a disposition or an attitude of some sort. Yet if it is so, it is quite incredible that this state or attitude (and the connected event or act of *forming an intention*) should play no role in acting with an intention.

(It is clear from the context that the function of the expression 'acting with an intention to do A' is to explain some action of the agent.) So it is hard to maintain that *intending* 'in one sense' is as unrelated to *intending* 'in the other sense' as the two meanings of 'bank' are unrelated to each other.

In addition, it is not difficult to show that the rationalizing role of intentions can be derived from the structure of the psychologically real intentions that co-ordinate action. We can relate the 'two senses' of 'intention' if we notice the central feature of rationalizing explanations of action. These explanations succeed by attributing to the agent the intention to perform a token of some act type. And this attribution is derived from the actual full-fledged intention involved. Here is the way I would like to flesh out this suggestion.

We can represent the general structure of the act plan that has been settled upon as an outcome of the deliberative process by the schema in Figure 6.1. Here B is the first basic act, G is the goal, A_1, A_2, and B',... are the intermediate means for the goal; Es are the anticipated side-effects and K is an expected consequence of the goal. The arrows are doing double duty: (*a*) they may indicate merely the generative relations that obtain between different descriptions of an act, or (*b*) they may string together different acts as means to ends that

---

[7] Moya (1990: 192–3) explicitly argues for the ambiguity of 'intend'. For Moya, 'intention' means, in one sense, 'intention with which', which implies mere purposive behaviour. In the other sense, it means 'future intention', which requires plans, imposes commitments, and obeys strong consistency constraints. Bratman (1987: 132–3), too, maintains that there is a weak sense of *acting with an intention to do A*, in which all that is implied is that the agent has some pro attitude towards doing A, without having a distinct attitude of *intending* to do A; and a strong sense of the same expression in which one actually has formed the intention of doing A, with all the commitments which intentions generate and the constraints to which they are subject. Meiland (1970: 7–11), too, speaks of two types of intentions: purposive and non-purposive. His purposive intention matches neatly with Moya's intention-with-which, but his non-purposive one spreads to each item in the act plan and generates an extensional context.

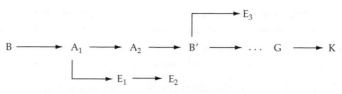

Fig. 6.1. *An act plan*

occupy different stages in the accomplishment of G. (For example, B may be my flipping the switch, A_1 turning the light on, A_2 illuminating the room, B' walking to the book shelf, G reading Bratman, E_1 waking up the dog, E_3 suffering the pain in my knee joint that my walking causes, K staying awake all night.)

I said above, in passing, that in this schema the act (or the complex set of acts) is a token act (or a set of token acts), as represented by the agent in terms of what he believes to be true of the very act he is about to perform, and what he takes to be relevant to the deliberation. It has to be a token because if he were to discover some new fact about the act, he may re-evaluate his decision. (For example, if I were to know that in reading the book I would grunt and groan, and as a result wake up my wife in the next room, I might postpone the reading to a later time.) If the deliberation merely consisted in considering the relations between act types, newly discovered features of the present situation would not have any bearing on the deliberation. It is only because the deliberation is about a specific act (or a cluster of specific acts) that one revises or abandons one's decision about what to do on discovering new facts about the circumstances.

However, act types play an important part in constructing an act plan like the one represented in Figure 6.1. The conditionals of the form 'If under C, I do B, then A_1, and E_1...' are expressions of the agent's empirical beliefs concerning what generalizations hold under conditions C. The principle by which these conditionals were chosen and considered was that some of the conjuncts in the consequent are the intermediate means that lead to the goal. So part of what justifies doing B is the fact that it is a sufficient means for doing A_1, which in turn is a necessary means for doing G.[8] So when one says, the agent intended to do A_1 (or intended to do G) in order to explain why he did B, one

---

[8] Actually in such a complex act the conditional to be considered would be 'If under C, I do B, B' (in some specified order), ..., then A_1, A_2, ..., E_1, ..., E_3, G, and K.'

highlights this means–end relation. But what is important to realize is that this relation exists in virtue of the fact that a deliberative process has taken place and one of several alternative act plans has been computed to be preferable to the others. In other words, citing, say, my reading Bratman as the object of my intention succeeds in explaining why I flipped the switch, or why I illuminated the room, only because the act plan has the total structure that has been anticipated by the agent. The act cited (e.g. G) is only a component of the holistic content of the intention the agent has formed, as are all the other items that appear on the act plan. The psychologically real attitude is the intention to act as represented by the act plan. However, the acts cited in rational explanations of action are privileged items on the diagram (in a way that Es and Ks are not) because their presence explains why the conditional was selected in the first place. (In considering whether to read Bratman this evening, my deliberative mechanism selected conditionals by scanning through the different means of achieving this, not by scanning through the conditionals that invoke acts that lead to my waking the dog, or staying awake tonight.) It is this privileged status that enables us to use them as rationalizers of our actions. And in this use the logic of explanation forces us to consider only one property of the act in question (that is, to consider the act as an act type) because it is that property that is relevant to considering the different means, and to displaying the means–end relations that form the basis of rationalizing exlanantions.

DISAGREEMENTS OVER FEATURES OF INTENTIONS

Reduction

The first disagreement is over the issue of reduction. Some have offered analyses of intending to do something in terms of judgements, beliefs, desires, willings of the agent; others insist that intending is a distinct psychological state, not implicit in other attitudes.[9] The view I propose places me firmly in the second camp. But I do not think that

---

[9] Audi (1973), Beardsley (1978), Davidson (1980), Grice (1971), each have proposed reductive analyses. The dissenters include Bratman (1987), Harman (1986b), Mele (1992b), Tuomela (1977).

the inclination to seek for a reductive schema is a gross misconception of the concept of intending. The explanatory role of intentions provides a reason that could at least make sense of such an inclination.

The key feature of all the reductive accounts of intention that I am familiar with is that they all focus on the rationalizing role of intentions. And in so doing, they single out wants (or some positive judgements about an act) and beliefs about one's prospective actions as the elements in the analysis. For example, Beardsley (1978) maintains that intending to do A consists mainly of consciously wanting to do A and consciously believing that one will do A. Other more sophisticated analyses may also be appreciated from this stand-point. As a second example, Davidson identifies intending with an all-out judgement, which is conceived as an attitude towards a proposition.[10] Davidson's account, too, presents the intended act as one that is consciously chosen as a goal which renders intelligible other actions that the agent takes to be means towards that goal. Grice's (1971) analysis in terms of willing that one should do A and simultaneously believing that one will do A as a result of this willing is also in this vein.[11] In all these approaches the intention to be reduced is an intention to do one particular thing, where the act type in question is individuated in terms of a property. And it is true that folk psychology favours this conception of intentions, that is, when we ordinarily speak of intentions, we use them to provide rationalizing explanations of our actions.

In summary, there are three issues that are interdependent: (1) the daily discourse of intentions exploits their explanatory role; (2) this discourse attributes intentions to agents action by action; and (3) reductive analyses of intentions focus on the daily discourse of intentions and hence on their explanatory role. In so far as the reductive accounts

---

[10] Here Harman is right in pointing out that some restriction should be imposed on the types of events that the all-out judgements are about if all-out judgements are to be identified with intentions. For my all-out judgement that there be peace in the world is not sufficient for my having the corresponding intention. Harman suggests adding that the judgements be restricted to those events one conceives of as the upshot of one's making the all-out judgement in question (Harman 1986b: 81).

[11] More accurately Grice's analysis is as follows: S now intends to bring about R at t if and only if: (1) S wills now that R occur at t, and (2) S believes that his present will that R occur at t will result in his bringing about R at t. Grice's original target is to explain how one can believe that one will do what one intends to do without that belief resting on independent evidence for the truth of the proposition so believed. Introducing willing here allows for a special type of evidence: one knows from experience that bringing about R is a matter within one's control, provided that there are no interfering factors, and one's having reason to suppose that, on this occasion, there will be no interfering factors (Grice 1971: 18–19).

concentrate on intentions in their rationalizing capacity, it is reasonable to expect that the rationalizing capacity of intentions may be reduced to some epistemic state combined with some evaluative judgement (or some desire state).

However, if what I have proposed above is in the right direction, then intentions, in so far as they explain action, are not distinct psychological states. The rationalization is derived from the specific features of the psychological state of intending, which comprises all the elements (desirable and undesirable) that enter into the deliberation. This state of intending possesses a degree of plasticity and revisability, and it guides and controls action. It is not to be expected that a state that has all these features can be analysed just in terms of desires and beliefs. On the other hand, the narrow focus of the reductive attempts explains why it seems so natural to look for intentions among beliefs and desires. But it also makes these attempts vulnerable to criticisms. These criticisms find counter-examples that tend to suggest that our concept of intending is not fully captured by the proposed reductions.[12] The counter-examples are generated by looking to the whole picture in which the privileged means–end relations among anticipated actions are represented. The reductive attempts, which look so attractive when some means–end relation is considered in isolation from the whole picture, seem pointless in the context of the general account of intentions.

The Strong View

A second source of disagreement in the literature concerns the relation between intending to do A and some belief involving one's doing A. Two versions of the view (sometimes called the *Strong View*) that makes belief a necessary condition for intention are often discussed. The first version, which I will call the *Strong Version*, states:

An agent intends to do A only if she believes she will do A.[13]

---

[12] I will not rehearse the criticisms here. The reader is referred to to Bratman 1985 (criticizing Davidson); to Davidson 1980 (criticizing Grice); to Harman 1986*b* (criticizing Beardsley, Davidson, Grice); and to Moya 1990 (criticizing Davidson and Audi).

[13] Here the careful formulation of the belief condition given by Brand (1984) is welcome: S intends at t_1 to do A at t_2 only if S believes at t_1 that she *herself* will do A at t_2. In other words, there is an irreducible indexicality in such beliefs.

The second version (the *Weak Version*), on the other hand, gives a negative requirement for intentions:

> An agent intends to do A only if she does not believe that she will not do A.

Both versions employ intention attributions, the object of which are single acts, not whole act plans. And as such it might again be more illuminating to evaluate these versions by focusing on the rationalizing role of intentions. However, in so doing we must not lose sight of the fact that the rationalizing role of intentions is derived from their status as real psychological states.

The Weak Version

The version of the Strong View that imposes the absence of the belief that one will not do what one intends to do as a necessary condition on intending is not very controversial.[14] It is easy to show why it should be so widely accepted by looking at the way intention attribution rationalizes (explains) behaviour. Suppose S's B-ing is explained by saying that S intended to do A. For example, my reading Bratman is rationalized by my having intended to get clear on the reasons for holding the Strong View. It seems clear that if S believed that he was not going to A, then the attribution of the intention to A would fail to explain S's act of B-ing. For example, if I believed, in this context, that I was not going to get clear on the reasons for holding the Strong View, then it would be impossible for my intention to get clear on this topic to explain why I was reading Bratman.

In discussing the rationalizing role of intention attributions above, I maintained that to say that an agent intended to do A and to expect this attribution to explain why she did B, one would be representing the agent as having the belief (at the time she did B) that B was a (possible) means to achieving A. That the agent has this belief is a necessary condition for the success of the explanatory task. If the belief is absent, then the intention to do A will not explain why she did B. But if the agent believes that she will not do A, then she cannot have the belief that something she is currently doing (specifically B) is a possible

---

[14] For one thing, the Weak Version is entailed by the Strong Version; hence anyone who endorses the Strong Version is committed to the Weak Version. Bratman (1985) argues convincingly that Davidson accepts the weaker version that requires that intentions merely be consistent with one's beliefs. Bratman himself (1987) does not want to include the stronger version in his theory, but it is clear that he endorses the weaker one.

means to doing A.[15] Hence if the claim that the agent intended to do A is to succeed in explaining her behaviour, B, it is necessary that the agent did not believe that she would not do A.[16] In other words, it is a logical consequence of the rationalizing role of intention attribution that one must not believe that one will not do what one intends to do.

This perhaps explains why the Strong View has sometimes been offered as a necessary condition on *holding* intentions. If rationalization were the only role of intentions, it would be reasonable to maintain that, if one had the belief that one would not do what one intends to do, one could not (logically could not) hold the intention. However, the rationalizing and explaining role of intentions is just one aspect of the holistic view of intentions. It is certainly logically possible for an agent to be so irrational as to have committed to an act plan that strings together a whole bunch of actions, which she somehow believes will not lead to her goal. Her having this goal will not explain why she performs any of the actions she does perform. (Her brand of irrationality will make it impossible to 'rationalize' any of her actions.) But her state will not violate any law of logic. So although the Strong View is a logical constraint on explanation by intention attribution, it is derivative of a rationality constraint on an agent.[17]

The rationality constraint, as we have been examining it, operates *within* the act plan that forms the content of an intention. It requires that the agent lack the belief that she will not do any of the things that are marked as the intermediate goals (or the final goal) in the act plan.

---

[15] The force of this 'cannot' is derived from the assumption that the agent's beliefs are minimally consistent. Any rationalization of action clearly operates with such an assumption. I owe this point, as well as parts of the subsequent discussion to Joey Baltimore.

[16] Two types of exceptions may be thought of here. Consider the example of the warrior who with his sword single-handedly attacks fifty enemy soldiers. In one scenario, the warrior believes he could escape death by surrendering or running away, but attacks the enemy all the same, knowing there is no way he can win, because dying as a hero means more to him than living branded as a coward. (I owe this example to Alan Sidelle.) In this scenario, I suggest, it would be false to attribute to the warrior the intention to survive the fight in explaining his act of attacking the enemy. His intention was to be a hero, and it is this intention that explains his behaviour. We can imagine a second scenario in which the warrior does not have survival as a choice: he can either die submissively or try to fight his way out, believing that he will not succeed. (See Mele 1992b for a discussion of cases similar to this.) Again, I would maintain that the warrior cannot *intend* to survive the fight. He can be said to be trying to survive because there is no similar belief requirement on trying. I discuss the notion of *trying* below.

[17] Bratman (1987: 30–2), who endorses the Weak Version of the Strong View, offers it as a condition of rationality. (See his discussion of the constraints on intentions, i.e. that they be strongly consistent with one's beliefs.) I have been urging that we recognize the logical aspect of the view.

But there is an additional rationality requirement that should be mentioned at this point. Rationality would seem to demand that all the intentions that the agent concurrently has be subject to the belief requirement. Suppose I intend to do A, and I also intend to do B. The rationality constraint we have been considering would require that I do not believe that I will not do A, and that I do not believe that I will not do B. *That* constraint would be satisfied even if I believe that I cannot do both A and B. But if I do believe I cannot do both, then it would be irrational for me to intend to do A *and* at the same time to intend to do B.[18] Thus we need an additional inter-intentional rationality constraint as well. Such an extension of the rationality constraint is also reflected in the explanatory role of intentions. If I can explain why James made a hotel reservation in Chicago for next Saturday by saying that he intended to visit his uncle in Evanston, my attempt to explain why James bought a plane ticket to New York for next Saturday by saying he intended to see his son sing at the Met next Saturday will certainly fall short of its target—unless I implied that he believed he could be in both places at the same time.

The Strong Version

However, the case is more complicated for the Strong Version, which requires that one believe that one will do what one intends to do. And the complications make the existence of the controversy over this version of the Strong View intelligible. In what follows, I hope to use my thesis about intentions to explain both sides of this controversy. The thesis again is that intentions have holistic content, and the rationalizing role of intentions is achieved by picking certain specific, privileged components of the whole content (components that stand as ends to other components that are the means) and explaining some of the agent's actions by attributing to them singular intentions to perform those specific component actions.

There are two types of cases that are given as reasons for rejecting this stronger condition. I take up each of these cases separately.

1. Doubt. When I get up in the morning, remembering that it is the garbage day, I intend to take the garbage out on my way out. I form the intention with the full knowledge that when I am on my way to the office I tend to act on automatic pilot, and as a result recognize that

---

[18] The fact that the Weak Version is too weak to fully express the rationality constraint on intentions was brought to my attention by Joey Baltimore.

there is a chance that I will forget to fulfil my intention, and realize that I have some doubt that I will take the garbage out.[19] It seems arguable that the fact that I have some doubt here should not be incompatible with my intending to take the garbage out. Certainly such an intention does explain why I go to the kitchen before I leave. But we can deal with cases of this type by following Wayne Davis (1984). Davis points out that, although believing that p is inconsistent with doubting that p, it is not inconsistent with having *some doubts* that p, that is, with *not being certain* that p. In fact anyone who appreciates Hume's view on the issue can allow that one's psychology makes it quite possible to believe that p even when one has certain sceptical doubts concerning p.[20]

I can believe that I will play tennis this afternoon although I know that there is some chance of rain which will make me cancel the game (Davis's example). Hence one can intend to do something when one is not *certain* that one *will* do it, without contradicting the view that believing is necessary for intending. This simply means that when one intends to do A, even if one does have some doubts in the back of one's mind, one can still rationally believe that one will do A, and be justified in so believing.[21]

2. Disbelief. But more interesting are those cases where the agent clearly does not believe that he will do A, when it seems quite proper to attribute to him the intention to do A. I am pretty bad at darts. I am told by my team I must hit the bull's eye. Thinking silently that it would take a miracle for me to succeed in this, I aim, throw the dart, and surprise myself by hitting the bull's eye. Since I did not believe I would, this version of the Strong View seems to require that I deny that, in these circumstances I intended to hit the bull's eye. One might think that the denial of such an intention flies in the face of common

---

[19] Bratman (1997: 186) gives a similar example of his intending to stop at a bookstore on his way home from the office while believing that he may not do so, because he tends to be absent-minded on such occasions.

[20] Grice (1971: 6), on the other hand, maintains that the belief in question 'requires the notion of having no doubt that p'. As against Grice, I tend to agree with Davis on this.

[21] When Davidson (1980: 92–4) discusses the dialogue in Grice between two characters named X and Y, he maintains against Grice that it is quite proper for X to say that he *intends* to go to the concert on Tuesday even though X thinks that since the police are going to be asking awkward questions on Tuesday, he *may* be in prison by Tuesday evening. What I am suggesting is that X's thoughts about the police investigation may not make his believing that he will be at the concert Tuesday evening irrational, and that Grice need not have insisted that X put his intention conditionally: 'I intend to go to the concert on Tuesday *if* I am not in prison'.

sense. One reason one may have for thinking this way may stem from a commitment to an alleged relation between an act's being intentional and its having been intended. When unexpectedly I hit the bull's eye, it seems clear that I do so intentionally. And if the relation in question is one wherein an act's being intentional entails its having been intended (the so-called Simple View), then we can see why it must be wrong to deny that I intended to hit the bull's eye.[22] But leaving aside the Simple View for the moment, the common-sense judgement can be defended by pointing to the rationalizing role of intending. Does not attributing to me the intention to hit the bull's eye explain why I clenched my teeth, squinted, mumbled my mantra, and threw the dart that way? If I did not have the intention to hit the bull's eye why would I go through those antics? Notice that if, instead, overcome with the responsibility placed on my shoulders, I throw the dart up in the air in disgust, what I do cannot be explained by attributing to me the intention to hit the bull's eye. So one thing that is undeniably true of the agent in cases of this type is that the agent *tried* to hit the bull's eye.[23] But what is it that I do when I *try* to A that is different from what I do when I A? In terms of the performance that takes place in a token case of trying to A, and succeeding, the sequence of actions may very well be identical to those that are performed in the token case where the agent intends to A and A-s forthwith. One essential difference between (intentionally) A-ing without trying to A on the one hand, and A-ing as a result of having tried to A on the other is cognitive. When I do A without trying, I think I know how to A and set out to do it (successfully as it turns out). When I try to do A, I think I know how to do B and I think there is some chance (remote as it may be) that in B-ing I would do A. They both involve similar act plans. Both act plans set A as the goal. (Whether A is an intermediate or an ultimate goal is irrelevant for this discussion.) They both involve B as an intermediate means for reaching A.[24] In the one I believe that B will result in A, in the other, I hope it will.[25]

---

[22] I intend to discuss the Simple View below.

[23] Mele (1992b: 132), who has a sensitive discussion of cases of this type, introduces the notion of *intending to try* to do something. I tend to think that it would be better if we could avoid using this rather technical notion.

[24] Mele (1992b: 132) is in full agreement with this. He says of two basketball players, one who believes she will miss the shot, and the other who believes she will sink it, that they 'both have the same *plan* for sinking the shot'.

[25] There may be some exceptions to the claim that the act plans are identical. (1) If A-ing is a basic act for an agent, then he need not do anything as a means to doing A, whereas a

In order to see what specific cognitive difference separates intend-ings from tryings, we need to return to the holistic view of intending. On this view what one really intends is the whole package that is represented by the act-tree. But, as I mentioned above, there are rationality constraints on the sorts of packages a rational agent can adopt. If George believes that nothing he can do will impress his wife, it is irrational for him to plan to impress his wife by doing the tango, by building a squirrel house, or by reciting 'to be or not to be' backwards. And as a concomitant of this rationality constraint, we saw that there is a constraint on the explanatory force of intention attributions. As we said, attributing the intention to impress his wife to George has zero explanatory force because, by hypothesis, there is nothing that George plans to do that could be explained by such an intention. At the other extreme, if George thinks he knows that he will impress her if he does the tango, and he thinks he knows how to do the tango, and as a result of deliberating, he decides on an act plan that contains his doing the tango and culminates with his impressing his wife, he not only intends to impress her but, rationally enough, he also intends all those things that are believed by him to be the effective means to the fulfilment of that intention. In these cases attributing to George the intention to impress his wife explains fully why George does any of the things he takes to be in (partial) fulfilment of that intention of his. In between these two extremes are cases in which the link from one intermediate stage to the next, where the first stage is conceived as a means to the second, is weakened by doubt and improbability. These are the cases where it sounds better to say, 'In trying to A, I did B with the hope that B might lead to A'. The closer these cases are to the extreme where I believe B is very unlikely to lead to A, the less happy it gets to say 'I intended to A'. 'I was trying to A' becomes a better candidate. Compare, for example, 'I want to wire a three-way switch

second agent may have to do B when he tries to A. (Compare Horowitz's playing the first few bars of the Moonlight Sonata, as against my playing a string of notes one by one, hoping against hope that the emerging tune will be recognizably Beethoven.) (2) The belief that B is unlikely to result in doing A may prompt the agent to include in the act plan either repeating the B when it does not result in A (the way one flips the switch one believes to be faulty on and off many times in trying to turn on the light), or planning some alternatives to B when B fails. (In trying to kill the mosquito, I may plan on resorting to insecticide if the slap on my ear doesn't work.) This is again a case where there may be a difference between how I perform A when I believe I will A, and how I perform A when I think it is unlikely that I will A. But such exceptions do not tell against the main claim that the difference between intending to do A and trying to do A does not *derive* from a difference in what the agent *does*; it is rather constituted by a difference in the cognitive states of the agent.

during the next hour. I used to know how to do it. I am pretty sure I will not remember and there is no source available to me now that contains a circuit diagram. But I intend to wire it in the next hour anyway' with 'I want to bake a soufflé. I know how to do all that is necessary for a good soufflé. In the past, for no reason that I could fathom a few of my attempts have resulted in fallen soufflés. But all the same, I now intend to bake a good soufflé.' The first declaration of intention sounds very strained—at least a lot more strained than the second. It is much more informative to say in the first case that I will *try* to wire it in the next hour.

In discussing the Weak Version of the Strong View (the version that places the condition that the agent *not* believe that she will not do what she intends), I maintained that the violation of that condition undermines the explanatory force of intentions. And I supported this by pointing out that the condition is derived from a rationality constraint on intending with holistic content. Now, when we turn to the Strong Version, we notice that the explanatory force of attributing an intention to do A becomes weakened if the agent does not believe that she will do A (that is, if the condition imposed by the Strong Version is violated). However, this weakening of the explanatory role (or the strain we were feeling in saying 'She is doing B with the intention of doing A' of someone who does not believe that she will do A because she does not think that it is likely that the means, B, she has adopted for A will succeed) is not reflected by the violation of any rationality constraint on intention formation. The fact that, given the circumstances, one is forced to adopt means that have little chance of achieving the end does not render the act plan irrational. If the end is important, and if there does not seem to be better candidates for the means, the plan is to be commended. In other words, the intention with holistic content in which the means–end relations are riddled with low probabilities may be as healthy and as rational as one in which the relations involve certainty. The question, then, that faces us is why it is strained to say, 'She did B because she intended to A', when we know that she did not believe she would actually do A by doing B. In other words, why is the Strong Version ever considered as a contender for the Strong View?

The answer is to be found in the contrast between the explanatory role of intentions versus that of tryings. As I said, part of the explanation achieved by saying, 'she did B because she intended to A' was to point to the agent's conception of what purpose doing B was to serve. But, as the examples in which the condition as formulated by the Strong Version is violated illustrate, a second part of the explanation consists in implying that the agent had a high degree of confidence in B's success in serving the purpose for which it was conscripted. When the degree of confidence is low, the explanation takes the form 'She did B because she was trying to A'. So when Pat is straining to lift the car so as to save the person pinned under it, she certainly does not believe that she will be able to lift it. She might even believe that she most likely will not lift it. But hope against hope, she persists. The explanation that will convey this information about Pat's cognitive state is clearly one which says of her that she is straining like that because she is *trying* to lift the car (or to save the person). To say, 'because she *intends* to save that person' would misinform. So in many contexts the information about the agent's cognitive state contributes to our understanding of the way the explanandum action is conceived by the agent. In such contexts the explanation has the responsibility of distinguishing between, on the one hand, cases in which the agent's degree of confidence was too low to justify a belief that the goal would be achieved by the selected means and, on the other hand, those cases in which there was full confidence.[26] Accordingly, when the belief is absent, we say of the agent that she was *trying* to do such and such.[27] Conversely, the presence of the belief is implied by attributing to the agent the

[26] When the agent does not have a sufficient degree of confidence about her success in achieving A by her projected course of action, to say 'She intends to A' does not give a satisfactory rationalizing explanation of why she has undertaken that action. But if other courses of action are going to be available to her after she fails doing A by doing B, then 'She intends to do A' *would* explain why she is trying to do B. Suppose I try to lift a 200 lb stone to move it to a different spot in my backyard. If when I fail (as I expect I will), I will give up, then saying 'I intend to move the stone' does not give a satisfactory explanation of why I am doing what I am doing. But, if upon failure, I expect I will think of other ways of moving the stone (e.g. use a lever, call the neighbors for help, etc.), then 'I intend to move the stone' *is* an acceptable explanation—to accept it is to read into it the implication of such plasticity. Again, the belief constraint makes sense of this: even though my confidence in being able to lift the stone is low, the combined chances of the different courses of action leading to the goal of moving the stone are high enough to make me believe that I will somehow get the stone moved.

[27] The typical cases are illustrated by the dart-throwing example. In these cases, saying of the agent that in doing B she was trying to A explains that, under the circumstances, she thought of B as the best (or the only available) means to A, while fully recognizing that, given what she knew, the 'best' was very unlikely to lead her to success in A-ing. But perhaps more significant are those cases in which the way A is carried out is different from what it would be if the agent believed that she would achieve A by doing B. Examples are the way I hit the piano keys when I try to play the first few bars of the Moonlight Sonata, or the way one flips the switch several times when one tries to turn the light on.

intention do to such and such. The contrast may be illustrated by looking at the difference between two possible explanations of why Samson was straining against the columns of the temple that way:

    (i) Samson intends to bring the roof of the temple down.

    (ii) Samson is trying to bring the roof of the temple down.

Explanation (i), when contrasted with (ii), implies that Samson believed his god would make sure he succeeded, whereas (ii) suggests that Samson thinks his god may have abandoned him.

When the context is one in which the explanation aims merely at describing a means–end belief of the agent, and is not expected to reveal anything about the degree of confidence involved in such beliefs, intentions may be attributed without being sensitive to the above discrimination.[28] I suggest this is why for some the two claims (i) and (ii) about Samson may not appear as contraries, and also this may be why the Strong Version of the Strong View, when discussed as a general requirement, has been so controversial.

There is a different type of case in which the Strong View seems to be violated. These are alleged instances of intending to do something in which one has no plan, no history of deliberation that resulted in a decision to do that thing. In these instances, it would be unlikely that one has a belief that one will do that thing.[29]

I say sincerely, when New Year's resolutions are being made around the table, 'I intend to lose weight.' But when I make the declaration, I have no intention of reducing my calorie intake, taking up exercising, consulting an expert, looking into weight-loss medications; I do not take myself to have undertaken a policy of turning down opportunities for second helpings or invitations to eight-course meals. I realize that at no time during the coming year will I decline an offer to have several nightcaps. It seems that I have no reason to believe that I will lose weight. And supposing that I am rational, I do not believe that I will

---

[28] Davidson (1980: 92) gives the example of the person who is writing heavily on a page, 'intending' to produce ten legible carbon copies. Here it is likely that no significant insight is going to be gained into why this person is doing what he is doing by our being informed of the degree of confidence this person has in succeeding in producing ten legible carbon copies. Hence the attribution of intention does blanket duty.

[29] Davidson (1980: 83) gives an example: 'Someone may intend to build a squirrel house without having decided to do it, deliberated about it, formed an intention to do it, or reasoned about it. And despite his intention he may never build a squirrel house, try to build a squirrel house, or do anything whatever with the intention of getting a squirrel house built.' As will be clear below, I am inclined to reject the suggestion that this person *intends* to build a squirrel house.

lose weight. Are these familiar cases not refutations of the Strong View? They are, only if we insist in allowing me the intention to lose weight. But since there is no act plan, I am committed to denying that these are cases of intending—I have to maintain that I was speaking falsely when I said 'I intend to lose weight', just as I would have said something false if I had instead said, 'I will try to lose weight'. This judgement finds support when we turn to the explanatory role of intentions. We can ask 'What information is being carried by the declaration of an intention to lose weight?' The information, whatever it might be, cannot be one that explains anything because no action is being performed nor any action projected into the future that can be targeted as an explanandum. What possibly could be explained by someone saying of me 'He intends to lose weight'? Of course, if I take myself to intend to impose certain restrictions in the way I live my life that are consistent with my alleged intention then, whenever I act in conformity with those restrictions, my action may be explained by referring to my intention to lose weight. But given the way the scenario is set up, no such constraints have been anticipated by me at the time I declare my 'intention'. The scenario I have described is one in which even the intention of imposing in the future some as yet unspecified restriction is not present. It is a scenario in which nothing can count as even a skeletal plan. So again, what information can attributing intentions to agents under such conditions carry? All I could have meant was, 'I wish I will do something (I don't know what) that will result in my losing weight'.[30] And that is a mental state distinct from what I have been calling intending. And attributing that kind of wish to an agent has no rationalizing force.

It is worth remarking on the difference between the type of case where the absence of belief that one will do A is due to the lack of a plan for doing A, and the type of case in which the linkage between the components in the plan for doing A are too weak to make it rational to believe that one will do A. In the latter type of case, illustrated by the dart-throwing example, the agent is in a psychological state of intending to execute the whole act plan. When there is such an intention, the question concerns whether attributing to the agent singular

---

[30] I should note that such misuses of 'intend to lose weight' do not lend themselves to translations into 'wish to lose weight' or 'hope to lose weight' because these latter can be (semantically) satisfied by my unintentionally contracting a debilitating disease, whereas I will not have fulfilled my 'intention' if I lose weight that way.

intentions derived from the holistic content of his intention will yield informative explanations of some actions of his. And I have been maintaining that when the belief condition is violated, intention attribution ceases to be maximally informative. In the former type of case, illustrated by the wish to lose weight, or the Davidsonian 'intention' to build a squirrel house, the agent *has* no plan, and consequently has not entered into the psychological state of intending anything. As a result, there are no singular intentions that can be derived. So, in these cases, *both* the fact that it is inappropriate to attribute to the agent the intention to do A, *and* the fact that the agent lacks the belief that he will do A are consequences of the absence of the psychological state of intending, whereas in cases like the dart-throwing example, the inappropriateness of the intention attribution is a consequence of a concern for informative explanations.[31]

Trying without Believing

In arguing for the Weak Version of the Strong View, I appealed to the rationality constraint as a constraint to which all chosen act plans must conform. Furthermore, in the discussion of the Strong Version, I suggested that the difference between trying to do something and intending to do that thing did not consist in a difference in the act plan. It would seem to follow that if one cannot be said to intend to do something that one believes one will not do, then one also cannot be said to try to do something one believes one will not do.[32] Two types of scenarios seem to present a problem.

The first type is a familiar predicament where the agent is in a bind. She believes nothing will get her out of the predicament. But all the same, she sets out to 'try'. Scotty is being chased by vicious dogs on the roof. He knows that if the dogs catch up with him, he will be torn apart limb by limb. He also believes he cannot jump over to the neighbouring roof. But he 'tries'. When his reach is short of the other roof, and he falls sixteen floors to the pavement below, how does one rationally explain his fall? Does one say that he was trying to jump to the other roof? If this is the correct explanation, is one not implying that he had some glimmer of a hope of succeeding—that he

---

[31] This difference also explains why, in the scenario described, saying, 'I will try to lose weight' would be as false as 'I intend to lose weight'.

[32] I am grateful to Sara Gavrell Ortiz for helping me to get clear on this point and for reminding me of a passage in Albritton (1985: 245) in which he, too, argues that one cannot try to do what one knows one cannot do.

was not certain that he would fail? It seems to me that the implication is there. For it seems that, if fear had not blinded him to the inevitability of failure, and he *was* certain that he would fall, then it would be false to say, 'He fell because he was trying to jump to the other roof'. If this is right, then the scenario in question does not show that one can try to do something one believes one will not do.[33] If, on the other hand, we were to explain his fall by saying he was trying to avoid being mauled to death by the dogs, then regardless of his estimate of success in jumping over to the other roof, we would be correct in our explanation. We could, without any strain, even say, 'He *intended* to avoid being mauled to death by the dogs', because either by jumping over to the other roof or by falling off he was certain to achieve the intended result.

The second type of scenario is rarer, but perhaps more interesting. In these cases, the agent intends to achieve a certain result, which she believes can only be achieved if she tries to do something *and* fails to do to it. The distinctive feature of the scenario is that, if the agent believes she will do what she intends, she must believe she will not do what she tries to do.

The Mayans are said to have had a ceremonial sport like our basketball that involved getting a ball through a stone hoop attached to a wall. The sport was a competition among individual players rather than teams. And the winner was awarded the high honour of being killed in sacrifice to the Gods—a rather dramatic way of preventing the emergence of the wage-greedy stars of our professional sports, it seems. Given the beliefs of the players, it is easy to imagine that each player was doing his best to become the winner. But we can suppose a wise and wily player, X, who believes he cannot sink that shot, which he will need to if he is to be the winner, before Y, the best player of that year, will sink his shot. However, X realizes that he will be dishonoured for life if he does not even make the attempt. So he forms the intention to try, with the desire to fail and the firm belief that he will fail. The act plan he forms has as its ultimate goal that of surviving this year's competition; it includes his doing his best in trying to sink the

---

[33] Here Davis's point about 'believing that p' being consistent with 'having some doubts that p' may be working in reverse. In some situations, one may out of desperation come up, against all evidence, with the hope that p, and hence not be certain that not-p, while it may be correct to say that one (rationally) believes that not-p. So the Weak Version, as it applies to trying to do A, should, strictly speaking, be formulated in terms of not being certain that one will not do A.

shot before Y does, and also (because he believes that his best is not good enough) failing to do so. But his luck has run out: he succeeds in sinking the shot before Y.

One reaction one may have to the example is to deny that X was trying to sink the shot before Y did. He was merely doing his best to *appear* to be trying to do so, so as to make everyone think he was trying. Even if this may the correct verdict in the particular example, it does not solve the general problem.

Ginet (1990: 9) imagines a case in which a woman is convinced that her arm is paralysed. She nevertheless *tries* to exert her arm 'just in order to see what it is like to will an exertion ineffectually'. She actually intends not to move her arm. But she is wrong in believing that she is paralysed. So she 'voluntarily but unintentionally' raises her arm. The only way this type of case can be reconciled with the Strong View is to admit that *trying to do something* may, in certain situations, describe *an action*. Until now we were focusing on the explanatory function of describing an agent as trying to do something. And we were contrasting this with the explanatory function of saying of the agent that she intended to do that thing. The present class of scenarios illustrates the fact that tryings may be component acts in an act plan. Referring to them as *tryings* does not help explain something else the agent does. It just tells us that an effort beyond what is ordinary is to be employed in bringing about something. And as Ginet's example illustrates, sometimes the ineffectualness of the effort is a necessary part of the means. If the effort ends up being successful, the end would be undermined. In this scenario what one is trying to do is a basic act. And as such, the attribution of trying to the agent cannot, by definition of basic acts, be used to explain why the agent was doing something he took to be a means to what he was trying to do. The same could be said of the Mayan player, if through years of practice sinking the shot had become a basic act for him. If all this is right, then the second class of scenarios does not present a problem for the thesis that the Weak Version of the Strong View applies to tryings in their explanatory capacity.

The Simple View

The third type of disagreement concerns the relation between intending something and doing something intentionally. There is general agreement that, once the role played by unexpected luck or deviant causal chains is bracketed, whenever one does what one intends to do, one does it intentionally. But the converse is controversial. The claim,

> *The Simple View:* If S does A intentionally, then S must have intended to do A,

has been rejected by many on the basis of two types of counter-examples.

The first type of example

Pat wants to go through a pair of swinging doors. She knows that they either open inward or outward, but not both ways. So she pulls on one while pushing on the other, with the belief that one is sure to yield.[34] By the uncontroversial Weak Version of the Strong View, she certainly cannot intend to open both because to intend both is to intend something she knows to be impossible. Hence, it is argued that she cannot intend to open either door. The argument goes as follows. (i) It is a direct consequence of the Weak Version that when the agent believes of a group of actions she is attempting that they cannot all be undertaken, she cannot intend to perform all of them. (ii) But, if she can be said to intend to open the door on the right, then because of considerations of symmetry, she can be said to intend to open the door on the left. (iii) Therefore, at the threat of abandoning agglomerativity of intending, she cannot intend either to open the door on the right or the door on the left.[35]

Leaving aside whether intentions are agglomerative, I think strong intuitions, based on the inter-intentional rationality constraint, favour the judgement that Pat does not intend to open the door on the left, nor does she intend to open the door on the right, but when she does open one she opens it intentionally.

---

[34] I borrow the example from Ginet (1990: 77). Ginet acknowledges Bratman as the original source of examples of this type. Bratman's version, involving a video game, is perhaps more entertaining, but I find Ginet's easier to describe.

[35] There seem to be good reasons to reject the agglomerativity of intentions in general. S can believe at t that some proposition, p, is true because S assigns a healthy subjective probability to that proposition. Suppose now that there are n such propositions. If the probability associated with each is less than 1, given a sufficiently large n, S may end up believing that the conjunction of all these propositions is false. If each of these propositions describes distinct actions S can perform at a given time, t, then it seems S can intend at t_0 to perform each of these actions at t, without being able to intend at t_0 to perform all of them at t. This is a straightforward application of the familiar Lottery Paradox in epistemology.

The steps of the argument seem unexceptionable. However, in order to discover the content of the intention behind this act, we should fill out the details of the act plan. Suppose, first, we change the example slightly. Given the same doors and the same beliefs, Pat decides to pull on the door on the right, and if it fails to open, she plans then to push on the door on the left. This plan is schematized in Figure 6.2.

In explaining her behaviour, we can attribute to her the intention to open one of the doors. And since she is confident that she knows how to do this, she believes she will open one of them. Does she intend to open the door on the right? The belief involved here is that pulling on it has a 50 per cent chance of succeeding. This is probably too weak to sustain a belief on Pat's part that she will open the door on the right. As a result, we should prefer to explain her pulling on the door on the right by saying that she was trying to open it. So the intention to open one of the doors and planning to do this by trying to open the door on the right provides a better rationalization of Pat's behaviour than attributing to her the intention to open the door on the right would. Of course, if the first part of the plan fails, and the door on the right resists the pull, Pat will have now no trouble in proceeding with plan B included in

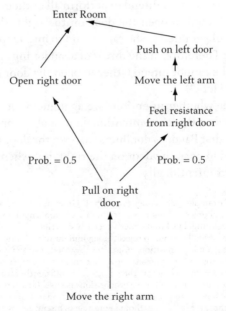

Fig. 6.2. *Fall-back plan for opening a swinging door*

the original act plan and push on the door on the left with the firm belief that it will open. Here nothing stands in the way of our attributing to her the intention to open the door on the left—with the understanding that this intention would fully explain her behaviour subsequent to the failure of plan A.

When we shift to Ginet's scenario, we get both plan A and plan B being enacted simultaneously (see Figure 6.3). Here we can still say that Pat intended to open one of the doors, also that she was *trying* to open the door on the right and that she was *trying* to open the door on the left. She certainly did not intend to open both, nor was she trying to open both. It is interesting to notice here that, although intending to do A and intending to do B may lead to intending to do A and B, there is no similar connection between trying to do A and trying to do B on the one hand, and trying to do A and B on the other. As we saw in the discussion of the Strong View, this is explained by the fact that intending to do A implies believing that one can do A, but that this belief condition does not hold in the case of trying.

The Simple View can be rescued from this type of example by noticing that the content of the psychological state of intending is the

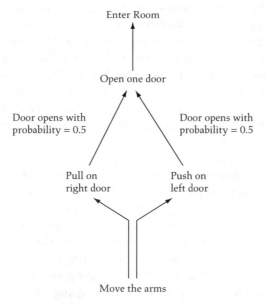

Fig. 6.3. *A better plan for opening a swinging door*

full act-tree that has been adopted as a package, with its branching nodes, fall-back plans, contemplated side-effects that have been considered in the course of the deliberation. There are no additional discrete *mental states* that are intendings that correspond to each of the contemplated properties of the actions or to each of the distinct actions in this package. We speak of the agent intending to move his finger, to flip the switch, to turn on the light, to illuminate the room, but not intending to alert the prowler, because we want to explain something about what sorts of means–end relations were considered in the process of deliberation. These are not, on the view I am defending, separate mental states. So, according to this view, in cases where two actions are included in the act plan which the agent knows cannot both be done, the content of the intention is given not only by the descriptions of these actions, but also by the causal and probabilistic relations that these actions are believed to stand in to each other and to other actions in the deliberation. Once this is accepted, the puzzle generated by these examples dissolves.

In these deliberations, since Pat does not believe that pulling on the door on the right will result in that door's opening, her pulling on the door on the right is not explained adequately by attributing to her the intention to open the door on the right. So on the explanatory front, it is appropriate to deny that she intends to open the door on the right. A better explanation for her pulling on that door is given by saying that she is trying to open it. But what she really intends is the whole package, and we have seen that discrete intentions may be attributed to her only in so far as (*a*) these intentions rationalize certain items in this package, *and* (*b*) by obeying constraints of consistency, they contain information about Pat's relevant instrumental beliefs.

It might appear that altering the subjective probabilities in Figure 6.2 may introduce problems for the view. Suppose that Pat is almost sure that the door on the right will open if she pulls. But since she is not 100 per cent certain, she decides to push on the door on the left at the same time because she *knows* that the two doors open in the same direction. Now she believes that she will open the door on the right, and hence there is no threat of inconsistency in attributing to her the intention of opening that door. Why was she then doing something which she believed could not succeed if she ended up doing what she originally intended? The new act plan, with the new probabilities substituted, will answer the question: she was taking insurance to guarantee that she got to do what she intended if she did not get to do it in the way she intended to do it. Again, if we take the whole package as the content of the mental state of intending, then it becomes easy to solve the apparent puzzles about discrete intention attributions by looking at the pragmatics of the whole situation.

In summary, in so far as attributing singular intentions, the example contributes nothing new to what was discussed in connection with the Strong View. And in order to show that the example does not defeat the Simple View (the thesis that if an act is intentional then one must have intended to do it), I need to argue that the Simple View is best understood as relating A's being intentional *not* to the singular intention to do the act type A, but rather to the psychological state of intending the whole package.

Second type of example

The question whether some action was intentional or not has the appearance of a question about a *property of the action*. But if being intentional *is* a property of the action, it is only a property derivative of something else. If it were an intrinsic property of the action, we would have to explain how one and the same token action can be intentional under one description and not intentional under another description,[36] that is, how can George's doing the tango when he tries to impress his wife be intentional and yet his doing the tango clumsily at that time not be intentional? The only graceful resolution seems to lie in our recognizing that being intentional is at best an extrinsic (relational) property of the act token.[37] And clearly the external fact, relative to which the property of being intentional is determined for an act token, is a fact about the mental states of the agent whose action the act in question is. Here it might seem that there are two types of candidates for the mental state relative to which the act acquires the extrinsic property of being intentional. The first is a mental state that involves an attitude directed towards some *property* of the action. An example would be to require that an act is intentional only if it was *desirable* to

[36] A Goldmanian principle of act individuation will not help here either. Just as on that view my answering the phone at t is a distinct act from my answering the phone loudly at t, my opening the door intentionally at t would be a distinct action from my opening the door at t. This result seems unpalatable.

[37] As I understand it, it is the recognition of this fact that prompts Davidson to prefer 'It was intentional of me that I V-ed' over 'My V-ing was an intentional act'.

the agent *in so far as* it has property F.[38] The second candidate is a mental state that involves an attitude directed at the *token act*, as it is conceived by the agent. It might appear that, following the first option, that is making what is desirable a condition for what is intentional, we might capture an intuition that some philosophers share. The intuition is that when one performs an act that has undesirable side-effects, then it is correct to say that bringing about those undesirable side-effects was not an intentional act. Sometimes this intuition is defended by endorsing the Simple View and arguing that it makes no sense to the agent that she intended to bring about those side-effects. But in other cases, the claim that undesirable aspects of acts are non-intentional is offered as a clear-cut intuition. I propose to argue that making desirable a necessary condition for intentional is a mistake that ultimately derives from conflating the explanatory role of intentions with the psychological state of intending. I shall then endorse the Simple View as it applies to the holistic state of intending and suggest that the agent performs each and everything that falls into the content of the state of intending intentionally.

Starting with an example may make the steps of the argument clearer. Suppose Sam desires a rug because it is a good specimen of a Tabriz. So the rug, under the description of being a good Tabriz (F), acquires the property of being desirable to Sam. But if, unbeknownst to Sam, the rug is also a product of intensive child labour, and if Sam does not desire the rug in so far as it is a product of intensive child labour (G), then under *that* description, the rug lacks the property of being desirable to Sam. If Sam has an aversion to things that are G, we might even say that the rug in so far as it is G is undesirable to him. So the object of Sam's desire, this very rug, has the property of being desirable to him in so far as it is F, and being undesirable to him in so far as it is G.

Suppose now that Sam buys the rug. On the thesis that what makes an act, in so far as it is F, intentional is that the act, in so far as it is F, is desirable, his act of buying a good Tabriz is an intentional act, but the same act, in so far as it is an act of buying a product of intensive child labour, an act he did not suspect he was performing, is not intentional. This is how one and the same action can be inten-

---

[38] There is arguably a sense of 'desirable' in which an object's being desirable is an intrinsic property of the object. That is not the sense intended here: in the sense intended here, object o is desirable to S in so far as it is F at t if and only if S desires an F at t.

tional in so far as it is F and unintentional in so far as it is G. So far so good.

But the proposal to identify intentional with desirable breaks down under closer scrutiny. Let us change the example into one where Sam is fully cognizant of the conditions under which these rugs are produced —that is, he knows that the rug is both F and G.

In the new scenario, again it is possible for the rug to be desirable to Sam in so far as it is F and not desirable to him in so far as it is G. Since desire is not bound by constraints of consistency, it is possible for him to desire some object in so far as it is F, and at the same time to lack a desire (or have an aversion to) the same object in so far as it is G. But when, in this new scenario, Sam buys the rug, there seems to be no unanimous agreement among philosophers as to whether his act of buying a product of intensive child labour, although an undesirable thing, was none the less an intentional act.[39] If singular intentions, which take act types as their objects, were the source of an act's being intentional, then the position, according to which Sam's acquiring a product of child labour is not intentional may be defended in the following way. Attribution of intending to do something fulfils its explanatory function only when the act is construed in so far as it has a certain property. We say, 'Sam intends to buy a good Tabriz', and when he is fully cognizant of the fact that in so doing he will be buying a product of child labour, we also say, 'Sam does not intend to buy a product of child labour', because while the first pronouncement explains why he is handing over $10,000 to the shop owner, the intention to buy a product of child labour would not have explained anything that Sam does. And an action is intentional only if it is performed in accordance with the agent's intentions. Since Sam does not intend to buy a product of child labour, his act of buying a product of child labour is not intentional (the Simple View). So being intentional *is* like being desirable.

I think the mistake involved in this defence is to attribute to the property of being intentional essentially an explanatory role. In identifying an act as intentional, we do not typically seek to explain why the agent performed some other action. We aim to describe the agent's mind-set. This is why in identifying *being intentional* as an extrinsic

---

[39] Harman and Bratman are among those who maintain that this is an unintended, but an intentional action; Moya, whose position comes closest to the one I defend, argues that such actions are both intended and intentional; Anscombe denies that it is intentional.

property of actions, I suggested that the fact relative to which an act's being intentional is determined is a fact about the agent's mental states. The mental state in terms of which the Simple View should be formulated is the actual state of intending which has as its holistic content the whole act-tree. When we look at the way that the act-tree has been arrived at, we appreciate the role of undesirable side-effects in the deliberative process. For when Sam weighs the undesirable aspects he foresees as against the desirable ones, compares the prospective course of action with other courses of action that are available under the circumstances, and chooses the one with the greatest net plus (or one with the lowest net minus), he *commits* himself to the one so chosen. *That* course of action, as displayed in the act-tree that was anticipated during the deliberation stage, is what Sam now intends. If so, on the view I am proposing, part of the content of Sam's intention would be his acquiring a product of intensive child labour. Consequently, the mental state relative to which an act is intentional is an attitude towards the *token* act, as it is conceived by the agent.

Defenders of the opposed view may not find this argument very convincing. They may deny me the claim that the role of identifying an action as intentional is *not* typically one of explanation.[40] But then they will have to face a tension in their position. In the case of Pat and the swing doors, we agreed that Pat did not have the singular intention of opening the door on the right. But we did admit that, when she opened it, she opened it intentionally. It would be hard for the defenders of the view according to which Sam's acquiring a product of child labour is not intentional to disagree with these judgements because, in order to disagree, they would have to abandon the uncontroversial version of the Strong View or give up appealing to the Simple View in their defence. And if they do agree with the judgements about the swing doors, then they have to explain why Sam does something non-intentionally when he lacks the intention to do it, whereas Pat who also lacks the intention to do something can do that thing intentionally.

So I suggest that we understand the Simple View in the following way: an act is *intentional* only if it falls within the whole package intended by the agent.

---

[40] I keep hedging by using the qualifier 'typically' because I grant that in certain usage describing an action as intentional may help explain why the agent kept tracking the *result* of that action by changing strategies as obstacles emerged. This is why the mistake is not an obvious one.

OBJECTION TO HOLISM

One might object that it seems inconsistent to deny Sam the intention to acquire a product of child labour, and at the same time, to insist that acquiring a product of child labour is part of the content of Sam's intention. Indeed this is exactly the objection Bratman (1987: 143–55) has in mind when he discusses 'the problem of the package deal'. According to Bratman, the problem arises from the joint operation of the following three theses:

(i) The choice (the decision) one reaches at the end of a deliberative process is the choice of an overall scenario.

(ii) When one chooses such a scenario, one intends to execute the whole package.

(iii) When one intends to execute the whole package, then, assuming that one is rational, one intends to execute each and every component of the package—provided that the components in question are within one's control.

These three theses yield the conclusion that Sam, assuming that he is rational, intends to acquire a product of child labour. I agree with Bratman that this is an unacceptable result.

But Bratman and I part company when we try to avoid this unacceptable result. He argues that the problem can be solved by rejecting the second principle above, that is, by rejecting the identification of what one chooses with the content of one's intention, whereas I endorse the first two principles and, following Chisholm, reject the third principle.[41] I reject the third principle simply because not every necessary concomitant of what one does in the attempt to achieve what one has decided is conceived as a *means* to one's goal. As a result, not everything one does will help explain some action.[42] For example,

---

[41] The actual wording of the principle Chisholm (1976: ch. 2) rejects is different. Its rejection is designed to block inferences of the following kind. A man 'acts with the intention of bringing about that he drive off in the car that is parked in the corner and belongs to another man. [Therefore] he acts with the intention of bringing about that he drive off in a car that belongs to another man' (Chisholm, 1970: 637). Chisholm's objective, that of 'distinguishing consequences which are intended from those which are *consented to but not intended*' only addresses half of my proposal because for Chisholm consent is not derived from a process of comparative deliberation.

[42] Bratman (1987: 146–8) in a sensitive discussion of Chisholm, accuses Chisholm of not having given an argument for rejecting the third thesis. I am hoping that my appeal to the difference between the rationalizing function of singular intention attributions and the action-guiding function of the holistic state of intending does provide such an argument. Bratman (1987: 124), quoting Sidgwick approvingly, claims that classifying an action

since there is nothing in anything that Sam does that we can explain by attributing to him the intention to acquire a product of child labour, it would be false to say of Sam that he has this intention. Bratman's argument for rejecting the second principle uses the third principle as a premise. Bratman quite rightly observes that 'what one chooses is constrained by holistic pressures…in a way in which what one intends is not' (1987: 155). So having chosen a course of action in which Sam will be acquiring a product of child labour, Bratman points out, Sam is not obliged to screen out options incompatible with acquiring a product of child labour. This is all true, and comes out as a consequence of my point that, for Sam to intend to acquire a product of child labour, this intention should be capable of explaining some action of Sam's. And given the scenario, no such explanation is forthcoming. If later, in the course of executing his choice, Sam finds a scenario in which he can avoid this act, he will have *changed his mind*, he will have replaced his intention with a different one, one that has a different holistic content. So identifying the content of intentions with the content of choices does not undermine the action-guiding and further-reasoning-promoting roles of the psychological state of intending because the act of deliberation that results in the choice is sensitive to the difference between means and side-effects: the conditionals computed in the process of deliberation are chosen because of the elements in the consequents that are the means to the projected goal, not because of the elements that are the necessary concomitant of the means.

In summary, I suggest that we have better reason for rejecting the third principle (the principle of intention division) than for rejecting the second principle (the identification of the content of choice with that of intention).

I should note in passing that the impropriety of such intention attributions is not linked to the undesirability of these consequences. Ginet (1990: 76) discusses the case of starting one's motorcycle at midnight, knowing full well that one will wake the neighbours. When one does wake them, one wakes them intentionally because, presumably, that one would be waking them was taken into account in the deliberation that led to the decision to start the motorcycle. But

---

as intentional has the function of identifying it as something for which the agent may be held responsible. In my view this is not the function of the classification, but the truth of the claim can be explained by the fact that whatever is intentional has been taken into account in the deliberative stage, and the agent may be blamed for not having given due weight to it.

even if their dog had been barking incessantly, even if the neighbours had been inconsiderate pests in the past, and even if one delighted at the prospect of waking them (so that following Austin, one can say one woke them *deliberately*), one cannot be said to have *intended* to wake them, unless some aspect of what was done could be explained by such an intention (for example, the choice of the hour for starting the motorcycle, or long revving of the engine after it was started, etc.).

INTENTIONAL ACTION

The Simple View places only a necessary condition on an act's being intentional. For there are cases where the act in question was planned, or anticipated in the act-tree that is chosen, and hence was included in what the agent intended to do, and yet the act came about 'not in the way intended' (or anticipated), but rather by chance. In these cases, due to the amount of luck (good or bad) that was involved, the judgement is that the acts in question were not intentional. Familiar examples range from the wildly ricocheting bullet that kills one's intended victim to cases in which one presses a button to explode the bomb and totally unexpectedly the ordinary connection between the button and the bomb is severed, and an improbable sequence of events occurs that makes the pressing of the button the cause of the explosion.[43] These are all cases in which the causal chain that leads to the event that is the *result* of the act in question is a deviant chain. I tend to think that the Simple View can be stated as a necessary *and* a sufficient condition if a qualifier is introduced that excludes such deviant chains. Assuming that the treatment of deviance in Chapter 4 was adequate, I will propose the following condition on intentional action:

> *Intentional Action:* A is an *intentional* (token) act of agent S's *if and only if* (i) S's intention that is reached through a process of deliberation includes (or anticipates) A in its holistic content, (ii) this intention causes the *result* of A, and (iii) S's doing A does not come about through a deviant causal chain.

---

[43] See Ch. 4 for a good selection of such cases.

Qualifications

Two qualifications to the definition of an intentional action are in order here.

(a) Habits. The process of deliberation, which I have been proposing as the standard source of intention formation, need not, of course, have taken place immediately before the act is undertaken. It could have been concluded long before the time of the performance, and kept in the back of the agent's mind. Or it could be an act that has been repeated so often in the past that it has become a habit of S's to do it when the circumstances trigger the habit. My entering the house through the back door after I park the car in the garage is intentional in spite of the fact that I do not deliberate about it any more. So an earlier deliberation that may have preceded the formation of the habit is sufficient to ensure that when one acts out of habit, one's action is guided by the intention to execute the whole plan that has been entrenched.[44] In more dramatic cases, habits can be enacted absent-mindedly *against* one's current intentions that have been momentarily 'blocked'. On a Sunday morning I decide not to shave and give my face a rest. When I get to brush my teeth in front of the sink, I start planning my daily activities. Before I know it, I find my face lathered and my left cheek already shaved. In these cases, given the thwarted current intentions, a good case can be made for denying that I shaved intentionally.[45]

(b) Simple actions. The second qualification concerns simple actions that do not involve much of a plan. Crossing one's legs, lifting one's arm to catch a flying ball, tapping one's hand to the beat of the song, answering the door when one hears a knock, or doing something just because one feels like it, are all possible examples of intentional action.[46] These are all limiting cases.[47] What makes them limiting is the fact that

[44] Ginet (1990: 88) says, 'This way of looking at absent-minded actions—as genuinely intended and intentional— becomes compelling when one considers how much deliberation and problem solving can go into absent-minded intentions.'

[45] Recall the example in which Herman absent-mindedly removes the key from the ignition right after he has decided to leave it in to allow his wife to listen to the radio. I think it is clear that he did this non-intentionally.

[46] I say 'possible' examples because one can imagine circumstances in which, for example, one taps one's hand to the music without any thought, conscious or unconscious, about the music or about one's hand. In such circumstances, the tapping may be more akin to reflexively jumping out of one's seat when one feels a wetness and, if so, the action may not be intentional.

[47] Anscombe seems to agree (1957: 34). 'This [the fact that some chain of means–end reasoning must begin] does not mean that an action cannot be called voluntary or intentional unless the agent has an end in view; it means that the concept of voluntary or

the intention to perform them has been reached as a result of a very *simple* deliberation. Presumably, the agent has, consciously or unconsciously, considered, however briefly, two alternatives—that of doing it or refraining from doing it—and has settled on one side. Since the acts in question are either basic acts, or involve *results* that are immediately accessible to the agent, the deliberation need not evaluate the different means of arriving at them. One quickly considers whether to catch the flying ball, decides to do so, and almost instantaneously the right arm shoots up. The fact that the decision is reached and executed at lightning speed is not incompatible with the thesis that an intention to catch the ball was formed, and that the formation of this intention was the result of a deliberation.[48]

Summary

I have argued that intention as a psychological state has as its content the whole act-tree that was constructed during the deliberation process, including all the expected generative relations, causal connections, and fall-back plans, and the relevant probability assignments. In explaining certain aspects of the agent's action, one may pick individual components in the act-tree, and attribute to the agent the intention to perform those component acts. In so doing, one would be rationalizing those aspects of the agent's action. Since this is a rationalization, the principles according to which individual intentions are to be assigned from the act-tree must conform to the Strong View. If an agent is said to have the intention to do A, then doing A must be consistent with the agent's beliefs—specifically, she must

---

intentional action would not exist, if the question "Why?" with the answers that give reasons for acting does not exist. Given that it does exist, the cases where the answer is, "For no particular reason", etc., can occur; but their interest is slight, and it must not be supposed that…it could be the only answer given.'

[48] Mele agrees that in these cases an intention is formed, but denies that it is the result of a decision: 'when I hear a knock at my office door, I intend to answer it; but I do not consciously decide to answer it…Nor do I think of any decisive theoretical reason to postulate the occurrence of an underlying *unconscious* mental action for such an intention' (1992*b*: 141). For Mele, intending is a mental *event*, but deciding is a mental *action*. (See also Mele 2000.) If one believed in mental acts that precede (most of) one's overt actions, and thought that deciding is one such act, then one can understand Mele's point. But the way I have been developing the causal theory of action, decision is just another event that is the consequence of the process in which different alternatives are evaluated, an event that in normal (rational) agents leads to the subsequent event of intention formation. On my view, no deliberation, no decision, and hence no intention.

not believe that she will not do A (presumably by (or in) doing B, as represented on the complete act-tree). Furthermore, attributing the intention to do A to an agent carries with it the information that she believed that she will do A by doing B. This information may be cancelled by replacing the intention attribution with the attribution of trying.

When we turn to the property of being intentional, however, that property is to be shared by all the actions (and all their aspects) that enter into the act-tree. An act, in so far as it is F is intentional if and only if that act's being F was anticipated in the deliberation and was weighed as against other anticipated properties of the intended act. So the Simple View holds between individual act-descriptions and all the components of the content of the psychological state of intending. But it fails to hold between individual act-descriptions and individual intention attributions.

MORAL RESPONSIBILITY

Some philosophers[49] are inclined to find some connection between an act's being intentional and the agent's degree of moral responsibility for that action. The view I am defending here has the virtue of showing what is wrong with that inclination and also explaining its source.

There are cases where an agent acts in ignorance of certain consequences of his action and hence what he brings about is clearly non-intentional. But if his ignorance is indefensible, then he is culpable for not having seen such an obvious side-effect: he is to be morally blamed. So being intentional is not necessary for moral praise or blame. It is also not sufficient. There are a lot of intentional actions which have no moral dimension at all. However, according to the view I have been defending, all intentional actions must be associated with a process of deliberation, which essentially includes an evaluative component. So when the values of the action in question which are considered in the deliberation are morally relevant, regardless of whether the agent did judge them to be morally relevant or not, the action does become an appropriate target for moral appraisal. And the appraisal is carried out

---

[49] e.g. Sidgwick (1907: 202).

by deciding if the agent's evaluation was morally acceptable. That is the connection between an act's being intentional and the moral responsibility of its agent.

THE PRINCIPLE OF DOUBLE EFFECT

The view I have proposed has a consequence which may seem unacceptable to some readers. The consequence is best illustrated in the context of a pair of widely discussed examples. The first involves performing hysterectomy on a pregnant woman who has cancer of the uterus and hence killing the foetus. The second involves crushing the skull of the foetus (craniotomy) that is stuck in the birth canal in order to save the life of the mother.[50] Both actions have as their final goal saving the woman's life. But it is maintained by some that, in hysterectomy, the doctor's killing the foetus is not intentional because it is a side-effect of the main, goal-directed action, whereas in craniotomy, since it is the means for the goal, it is. According to the view I have been defending, both actions are intentional because both actions are part of the content of the agent's psychological state of intending. However, individual intention attribution to the agent is not proper with respect to the action of killing the foetus in hysterectomy because, presumably, the doctor would have performed the procedure even if the foetus were not there, and hence his intention to kill it could not contribute to an explanation of any action of his. But in craniotomy, the doctor's intention to kill the foetus could explain a sequence of acts he undertakes to achieve the result of the death of the foetus. I find this result perfectly in tune with my intuitions. In terms of explanatory considerations the two cases *are* different. But the objective of making a moral distinction between the two cases by identifying one as intentional and the other as not has to fail because, in each case, the deliberation as to what to do must have included the fact that the foetus would die, and the agent's evaluation of this fact would be judged by similar moral considerations. Hence it seems to me that any view that makes

[50] The contrast between these two cases mirrors the contrast between another pair of widely discussed examples, the strategic bomber, who expects he will be killing some civilians in bombing a munitions factory, but does not 'intend' to kill them, and the terror bomber, who regards the death of the civilians in the process of bombing the munitions factory an added plus, and thus 'intends' to kill them. (See Harman 1986a.)

the act in one case a proper target for moral appraisal and in the other case acquits it from moral blame has to be wrong. But I will leave it to the reader to judge if my intuitions are being blinded by my commitment to my theory.

7
Autonomy, the Will, and Freedom

INTRODUCTION

In the foregoing chapters I developed a causal account of action. In this account I tried to avoid invoking powers unique to agency that resisted analysis in terms of event causation. Accordingly, action (behaviour done for the reasons the agent had) was analysed in a foundationalist framework as an agent's first (basic) behavioural output that is caused by the intention to bring about a network of effects. Here intentions were described as states, the onset of which occurs as a causal consequence of a deliberative computation employing the current desires, instrumental beliefs, and long-term values of the agent. Each of these elements, in turn, was assumed to be a mere non-actional event.

If the account is coherent, then it would seem that the job of the causal theorist is done.

However, there may be a nagging suspicion in the reader's mind that, if the causal theory exhausts all that there is to action, certain distinctions that are ordinarily made are hard to explain, and certain concepts that we can effortlessly apply are impossible to analyse. These commonplace distinctions and concepts seem to be best understood by reference to the will and to acts of volition. So it is imperative that a causal theorist be able to show how, given the parsimonious resources of the theory, these distinctions and concepts can be made sense of. It seems clear to me that it is mere stonewalling for a causal theorist to say of any ordinary well-entrenched concept that cannot be accommodated in the causal theory that it is bogus or vacuous. Such heroic measures usually portend ill for a theory. It was this vision that I was pursuing in the last chapter when I showed how a causal theorist could explain notions like 'doing something with the intention of doing such and such' and 'trying to do something'. And the same reason led me to try to make sense of the widespread intuition that the unintended but anticipated consequences of one's actions are intentional, and to understand why certain belief conditions might be imposed on intending, and so on.

The discussion so far has concentrated on notions that can be derived from the actual deliberative computation that was described in Chapter 5. This model utilizes only the materials (beliefs and desires) that are actually available to the agent at the time of the deliberation and decision. On the other hand, it is hard to deny that there is a range of action-related concepts that do not seem to yield themselves to an analysis using only these materials.

I propose to show briefly in this chapter that notions such as autonomy, voluntary acts, acting in accordance with one's will, acting out of one's free will, and freedom of agency do not require resources that presuppose anything about agents that is at odds with what the causal theorist admits. These notions have been well-treated in the literature, and nothing I shall say in this chapter is intended as an original contribution to the legacy of philosophical lore. I merely aim to show that treatments of these concepts exist that are fully consistent with a causal theory of action as described in the foregoing chapters.

THE WILL

Is there a place in the causal account of action for a faculty of the mind that is labelled as 'the will'? In answering this question, it is important to make sure that the causal theorist does not offer a mere stipulative definition for the 'will' that takes the reference of the term far away from the family of concepts with which the will is ordinarily associated.

Voluntary Acts

One notion that is derivative of one's ordinary understanding of the will is the notion of an action's being voluntary. Here I mean *voluntary* in the sense of being in conformity with one's will. There is clearly another sense of 'voluntary' in which it is used in contrast with involuntary as applied to basic acts.[1] 'Voluntary' in this sense merely

---

[1] It is in this sense that the patient (in Ginet's example discussed in Ch. 6), who believes falsely that her arm is paralysed and tries to raise it with the intention of finding out how it feels to make an ineffectual effort like that, raises her arm *voluntarily*, but unintentionally.

refers to movements that are caused by intentions, movements that are under the agent's control. An act which one performs against one's will is not an involuntary act. It is rather a *non-voluntary* act. Thus the notion of voluntary that is derivable from the will is one that is in contrast with non-voluntary.

A second-cousin notion is that of acting of one's own free will. It might appear that an easy way for a causal theorist to accommodate the will is to suggest that the faculty of the will is the faculty in which the decision-making apparatus, described in Chapter 5, is housed. Following this line of thought, one might say that 'the will' refers to the intention-forming powers of the mind.

But it seems intuitively clear that not all intentional acts are voluntary, or done of one's own free will. For example, a person may have his fifth drink at the bar intentionally but not voluntarily because presumably his will has been impaired by the first four. Now, given my account of an act's being intentional in the previous chapter, if the man had his fifth drink intentionally, then he must have gone through a deliberation in which he considered the pros and cons of downing that fifth drink or walking out. It is also necessary that in this deliberation his current desire for more alcohol outweighed all the undesirable consequences of having the fifth drink. (If the man was too drunk to go through any deliberation whatsoever, then I am committed to saying that he did not form the intention to have that fifth drink.) But if an act can be intentional but not voluntary due to an impairment of the will, then where in the causal network that defines the deliberative process can the causal theorist locate the source of this 'impairment'? The answer is to be found in a compatibilist account of voluntary acts, of autonomy, or acts done of one's own free will. The philosophical literature contains numerous interesting and plausible examples. I do not propose to offer a survey and a critical evaluation of the field here.[2] I will mention just two, which I find especially compelling, in order to show that capturing these notions is fully within the resources of my causal theory.

One is found in an essay by Stampe and Gibson (1992), where they identify one's will being free not just with one's actual reasoning in reaching a decision (what on my account suffices for having an intention), but also with one's disposition to make an equally reasonable

---

[2] The interested reader is referred to the excellent Introduction in Ekstrom (2001*b*).

decision in relevant alternative situations. A telling example is that of the compulsive hand-washer who decides to wash his hands because he has just handled fish. Rational as his action may be in the actual situation, his will may not be free if he is so constituted that he would be washing his hands even at the expense of missing a vitally important phone call.

So a necessary condition for acting of one's free will is that the agent's decision be rational in the actual and relevantly counterfactual situations.[3] The notion of a decision's being rational clearly goes beyond what I was calling rational in earlier chapters. Until now 'rational' was used interchangeably with 'based on the reasons the agent had', without concern for the 'reasonableness' of these reasons. Now, when we speak of a rational decision, we include the evaluative dimension to the concept. We assess the quality of the reasons on which the decision was based. The assessment is reached by making an assumption about what, objectively speaking, counts as reasonable in a given situation. Although there are clear end points to the spectrum between the rational and the irrational in this sense, the mid range is understandably hazy.[4] The difficulty in deciding where to draw the line here is not any greater for the causal theorist than it is for the volitionist.

One way of assessing whether in a particular decision the will was impaired might be to examine the weights assigned to the current desires and the higher priorities of an actual decision process, and then to ask whether the decision-making mechanism has the plasticity to alter these weights in significantly different situations. If we go back to the example of the compulsive hand-washer who has decided to wash his hands after he handled fish, we may find that his compulsion has so inalterably fixed the weights according to which he reached this decision that, even in a situation where deciding to wash his hands has significantly negative consequences, the weights will tend to remain the same, and he will still form the intention to wash his hands. If this is true of the compulsive hand-washer, then it is clear that he would be acting irrationally in the new situation. And that is sufficient for us to judge that his decision-making faculty does not have the requisite plasticity to qualify as voluntary his perfectly reasonable intentional

---

[3] I simplify the account by omitting the authors' sensitive discussion of what counts as *relevant*.

[4] Mele makes this difficulty very clear when he points out that it is very hard to judge whether individuals who answer some psychologists' characterization of compulsive personality are autonomous or not (1995*a*: 123–6).

act of washing his hands after he has handled fish. We shall say that he did not act of his own free will.

This is the judgement Stampe and Gibson reach about the case. Their metaphor is that of a weather vane that, though stuck, can sometimes show the correct direction of the wind. In the model of deliberation I have used for the causal theory, the metaphor may be captured by the requirement of plasticity in the assignment of weights. In either case, an act's being voluntary is being decided not purely on considerations of the actual decision made (as was the case with intentions), but on counterfactual considerations, too. What one looks for in either case is whether the agent's decision process may be judged to be rational on some objective grounds. All these judgements are clearly available to the causal theorist.[5]

The second impressive work (Fischer and Ravizza 1998) concentrates on the question of moral responsibility. It starts with the central thesis of Stampe and Gibson's essay and elaborates on it, making the details more precise. Using Frankfurt-style cases of counterfactual contravener, they first establish that mere ability to do otherwise is not the relevant necessary condition for voluntary action.[6] Then they offer what they call 'reasons-responsiveness' as the key to moral responsibility. Their notion of reason-responsiveness is akin to Stampe and Gibson's proposal that acting of one's own free will requires a capacity to reach a rational decision in the actual and relevant counterfactual situations. Fischer and Ravizza point out that being 'sensitive to reasons in the appropriate way' (1998: 36) is the key to moral responsibility. In developing their thesis they emphasize that it is the nature of the actual deliberative mechanism and the process whereby the mechanism chooses the action that count in judgements of moral responsibility. This point is in full conformity with the details of the causal theory of deliberation I proposed in Chapter 5.

---

[5] It might appear that in invoking a change in the assignments of weights I am presupposing the act of an inner agent. A sceptic might ask, 'who makes these assignments?' A glance at the way deliberation was depicted in Ch. 5 will show that the appearance is deceptive. Different circumstances will affect the consequents of the conditionals considered. In other words, the expected outcomes of the considered basic acts will be a function of the circumstances in which the what-if scenarios are run. As a result, the output of the comparator would be expected to recommend different basic acts in different circumstances. When this sensitivity to the circumstances is blocked, then the will loses its freedom.

[6] Although Fischer and Ravizza's main concern is moral responsibility, they would admit that in most situations, for an agent to be morally responsible for an act, the act would have to be voluntary. So any necessary condition for voluntary action would also typically be a necessary condition for moral responsibility.

In deciding whether the mechanism is reasons-responsive, Fischer and Ravizza first point out that, for the mechanism to lead to voluntary action, it is not necessary that it be 'strong reasons-responsive', that is, that it be sensitive to reasons under *all conditions*. Suppose a person chooses to go to a football game, and would have gone to that game even if it meant that she would miss an important deadline the next day. Her going to the game might be a voluntary act provided that there is *some* scenario in which some reason (such as the ticket's costing $1,000) would outweigh her desire to go to the game, that is, provided that the mechanism is 'weakly reasons-responsive'. The evaluation of what would happen in the possible scenario is made under the assumption that the deliberative mechanism is kept constant (unaltered by internal and external forces) across scenarios.[7]

Fischer and Ravizza also address the question of rationality. First, they recognize that there must be an appropriate connection between the reasons and the action. Secondly, they admit that deviant causal chains would have to be eliminated. These two issues have been addressed in earlier chapters and need not concern us here. Thirdly, and most importantly, they draw attention to the fact that there must be a coherent pattern in the array of actual and possible reasons for an action. We saw how, in the example in which the person who chooses to the football game would still go if she were to miss an important deadline, but would not go if the tickets cost $1,000, the person's action comes out to be voluntary. However, if the pattern of reasons were to be revealed to be incoherent, as it would be if it were discovered that this person would go to the game if the tickets cost either more or less than $1,000, then the judgement of moral responsibility (voluntariness) would be suspended.[8]

It is this third element, as is the notion of rationality that is employed in Stampe and Gibson's essay, that is not incorporated into the causal model of deliberation that generates intentional actions. In

---

[7] Fischer and Ravizza (1998: 44) distinguish between Strong Reasons-Responsiveness and Weak Reasons-Responsiveness in the following way: 'Under the requirement of strong reasons-responsiveness, we hold fixed the actual kind of mechanism and ask what would happen if there were a sufficient reason to do otherwise. In contrast, under weak reasons-responsiveness, we (again) hold fixed the actual kind of mechanism, and we then simply require that there exist *some* possible scenario (or possible world) in which there is a sufficient reason to do otherwise, the agent recognizes this reason, and the agent does otherwise.' It is weak reasons-responsiveness (with some refinements and modifications) that they propose as the source of moral responsibility.

[8] The authors call this requirement of rationality 'regular reasons-receptivity' (1998: 71).

addition, Fischer and Ravizza introduce several supplementary considerations that distinguish voluntary acts from actions for which the agent is morally responsible. The first consideration is the role played by reasons that are of a special kind. The authors call them 'moral reasons', reasons that respect moral claims of others (1998: 77). They point out, quite rightly, that some actions of intelligent animals and of very young children are voluntary, but these agents are not to be held morally responsible for what they do. The explanation lies in the fact that, as far as we know, such agents are not responsive to *moral* reasons. The second consideration is tied to a concept the authors call 'tracing'. Although an agent may find himself in a situation in which his will is not free—as in the case of the man who orders his fifth drink at the bar—in which his action is non-voluntary, when we *trace* the situation back in time, we might find that it was the result of an earlier voluntary action of the agent (Fischer and Ravizza 1998: 195–6). In such situations we would find the person morally responsible for the consequences of his intentional but non-voluntary actions.[9] But as I remarked in connection with Stampe and Gibson's notion of rationality, such additions as the notion of objective rationality or the considerations that yield moral responsibility are fully compatible with a causal theory of action in that they do not require the introduction of an irreducible will nor do they have to appeal to agent causation or simple acts of agency.

The third impressive work, one that deals with the related concept of autonomy, Mele 1995*a*, also recognizes that acting intentionally does not suffice for producing an autonomous act. Mele is concerned with showing how a causal theorist can distinguish actions done for what count, properly speaking, as the agent's *own* reasons (autonomous acts) from acts done for reasons that are in violation of the agent's autonomy. Although there is not a perfect match, in many respects, Mele's notion of autonomy corresponds to Stampe and Gibson's notion of the freedom of the will. Mele argues very convincingly that a compatibilist account of autonomy can be superimposed on a causal theory of action (i) by looking to the aetiology of the agent's motivational states to make sure they have not been coercively

---

[9] This type of case is one of the two exceptions to the general principle that doing something voluntarily is a necessary condition for being morally responsible for it. The second is found in scenarios of neglect due to ignorance: although the man did not know that the gun was loaded and, as a result, his killing the boy was unintentional (non-voluntary), he is morally responsible for the act because he should have known better.

induced,[10] (ii) by examining the deliberative mechanism for its reliability (its not being impaired by external manipulation), and (iii) by ascertaining that the beliefs the agent has are conducive to informed deliberation (1995a: 187).

Interestingly enough, my guess is that for Mele the compulsive hand-washer's actual rational decision to wash his hands after he has handled fish would count as an autonomous act. Mele describes the case of a scientist performing experiments on addiction using herself as a subject. At some stage of the experiment, having become fully addicted to heroin, she deliberates whether to continue the experiment or to try to stop. And based on her deliberation she forms the decision to continue. Mele says, '[She] is autonomous or self governing with respect to her use of the drug at the time, even though her addiction would not have allowed her to refrain from using it' (1995a: 192–3). This judgement points to an important difference between two different types of scenarios, but again, that difference is explicable within the framework of the causal theory of action.

In both scenarios, the inner blockage (due to an addiction or compulsion) generates an assignment of weights (desirability quotients, as I called them in Chapter 5), which dispose the agent to make irrational decisions under certain conditions. In the hand-washing scenario, the decision is partly due to the causal influence of these unusual weights, but given the circumstances, acting in conformity with these weights happily counts as a rational decision. Actions in this first type of case should be classified as non-voluntary—and, I would suggest, as non-autonomous. In a second type of case, although the same unusual weights are in place, the deliberative process is not affected by them.[11] In the example of Mele's experimenter, if she fits this second scenario, then the conditionals that decide the scientific advantages that would accrue if she continued taking the heroin, as well as those that describe the harmful consequences of doing so, would together be the

---

[10] The question of coercive induction is treated more generally by Fischer and Ravizza under the topic of what makes an agent's deliberative mechanism her *own* mechanism. Their account requires a historical perspective of the development of the agent's deliberative mechanism and her reasons (higher priorities, as I have called them). This historical perspective is what enables the authors to make sense of 'an agent's taking responsibility' in purely compatibilist terms.

[11] This is a difference to which Stampe and Gibson are also sensitive. They say of the compulsive hand-washer, 'if at the time of the act his pathological disposition to handwashing is causally quiescent, he *may*, this time, be washing his hands of his own free will' (1992: 538).

only considerations that are causally responsible for the decision. The factors that, because of the addiction, make continuing the experiment irresistibly attractive, or the conditionals that foretell the pain of trying to stop, do not enter into the calculation. This second scenario describes a case that is a better candidate for acting voluntarily.

The difference between these two scenarios echoes a distinction I tried to draw in the context of defining intentional action. There the distinction was between, on the one hand, considering doing something or refraining from doing it, and quickly, almost automatically, opting for one of the alternatives, and, on the other, being blinded by emotion (say, by fear), and finding oneself driven to one of the alternatives. I suggested a counterfactual test to see which was in effect, and I recommended that if deliberation is pre-empted, then the act is not intentional.

In a similar spirit, here we are considering two types of intentional actions. And my suggestion in these cases is that the type of act in which the deliberation is driven by factors that *dispose* the mechanism to make irrational decisions is not a voluntary act.

It is to be granted that the notion of *irrational* that is at work here is not part of the causal theory of intentional action. But it should be clear that invoking such a notion does not drag in irreducible volitional acts.

To summarize, then, a causal theorist could easily maintain that for an act to be voluntary, it is necessary, but not sufficient, that it be the causal consequence of an intention that has been formed as the result of a deliberative process. An additional necessary condition would be that the deliberation involve beliefs and desires that dispose the agent to act rationally—that is, not only must the agent's actual act be rational, but also, even if the act *is* rational under the actual circumstances, the deliberative mechanism must contain enough plasticity to enable it to reach rational decisions under relevantly similar circumstances. As I said above, what counts as a rational act is difficult to specify. But this difficulty cannot be due to some defect in the causal theory itself.

One final point in this context may be of some interest. There are cases in which decisions reached upon deliberation may be, by internal criteria, from the point of view of the agent, as rational as one would wish for, but because of the absence of some vital bit of information, the ensuing act turns out to be in violation of some fundamental long-term priority of the agent. The story of Oedipus is a perfect example. He married Jocasta intentionally; that was part of what he intended. But, in the objective sense of 'rational', one might maintain that his marrying her was disastrously irrational. And what might make it irrational is the fact that, if Oedipus possessed the crucial bit of information, he would never have considered marrying Jocasta as an option. But lack of knowledge of this kind is not itself a constraint on the freedom of the will. It would be against common sense to maintain that Oedipus did not marry Jocasta voluntarily. (He certainly did not marry his mother voluntarily, but that is an immediate consequence of the fact that his marrying his mother was not part of his intention: he did not marry his mother intentionally.) So the notion of objective rationality that is at work in generating verdicts of 'intentional but not voluntary' has to exclude the kind of irrationality we might find in Oedipus' marrying Jocasta. Distinguishing the two within the framework of the causal theory is not difficult. In examples dealing with pathological compulsions, addictions, and the like, the deliberative mechanism is frozen by the fact that the weights assigned to certain predilections are inalterably fixed. The decision that comes out is due to the lack of plasticity in the mechanism, whereas in misfortunes due to ignorance of key facts, the mechanism is functioning as it should. Thus even if we find irrationality in Oedipus' act of marrying Jocasta, the irrationality is not due to a process that renders the act non-voluntary —it is not a result of the impairment of the faculty of the will.[12]

Will Power

In Chapter 1, I briefly took up the question concerning special situations which seem to require an effort on one's part to get oneself to do what one has formed the intention to do. The familiar situation is one where some not-so-pleasant task has to be done, and one 'forces oneself' to do it. The phenomenology is usually described as 'one's making a mental effort' or, perhaps more colourfully, as 'one's using one's will power'. These expressions seem to invoke some volitional picture where there is an act of the will performed by the agent. Can such a picture be replaced by an account that confines itself only to causal connections between events?

[12] Mele (1995a) discusses cases in which the information is deliberately kept out of the agent's reach or is manipulated by other persons to misinform the agent. Mele's verdict is that the agent is not acting autonomously if his action is based on such misinformation. My inclination is to agree with Mele on autonomy, but suggest that even when there is such misinformation, the agent is acting voluntarily.

In Chapter 1, I tried to respond to the question by offering the metaphor of the heavy gate with rusty hinges. I said that, just as performing the overt act of opening such a gate requires more effort than usual, performing the unpleasant task in question may require more effort than normal. But the metaphor, as it stands, is unillumin-ating and does not explain the phenomenological difference between the two types of 'effort'.

Here is perhaps a better way in which a causal theorist may attempt to capture the phenomenon. Yesterday I formed the intention to grade the twelve undergraduate papers. The plan was to do all of them this afternoon. The details of the plan involved the usual steps—going to my study, picking up each paper one at a time, reading it through once, going back and writing comments on it in the margins, and so on. The negative side-effects that I anticipated included missing the MET Opera broadcast, not having a big lunch with wine, and the like. But on the plus side was the prospect of getting the job done before another dozen papers arrived next Monday. As I deliberated yesterday, the pluses outweighed the minuses, so the intention was formed. Today, as noon approaches, I review the whole act plan, and the negatives seem to acquire greater weight. But the original reasons for forming the intention are still there. At one point I seem to be poised to change my intention; I see myself pouring a glass of that wine my wife is drinking. But I also see myself as refraining. The weights shift around; the decision-making mechanism seems to have acquired a degree of instability. When the crucial time comes, I grab a sandwich and a glass of water and head to the study. The reasons for the original intention won over the reasons for satisfying the more immediate desires. But these frustrated desires leave a mark. It is conceivable that the mark is what gives the feel of having exerted one's will.[13] Quite clearly the causal theorist cannot invoke a homun-culus who plays the traffic cop in the decision-making mechanism. And my conjecture is designed to capture a sense of effort without the need to introduce such a homunculus.

Typically one talks of using one's will power when one chooses an act that is favoured by one's long-term priorities over a conflicting

---

[13] This attempt is borrowed from recent libertarian moves to generate freedom from indeterminacy. Kane (1996), for example, tells the story of how, in cases of internal conflict, a balance of reasons for and against an act render the outcome undetermined, and that this indeterminacy in the mind will manifest itself as an act of the will.

act that stands to satisfy one's more immediate desires. I am tempted to suggest that, when the opposite happens, and as a result of the instability, the long-term priorities are betrayed, we have a case of the 'weakness of will'. It certainly comes close to answering a widespread understanding of *akrasia* as an 'uncompelled intentional behavior that goes against the agent's best...judgement.' (Mele 1995*a*: 5) But a lot more needs to be said to flesh out this suggestion. And I do not think this is the place to do it.

FREEDOM

John Locke, in his seminal treatment of what counts as voluntary and what counts as being free, gives the well-known example of the locked room. A man finds himself in a room with someone he has long wanted to meet and decides to stay and talk to this person. Unknown to him, the room is locked. He could not have left if he had wanted to. Locke maintains that the man stays in the room voluntarily, but that the man is not free.[14]

What I maintained about voluntary acts above disagrees with Locke's claim that the will is not the sort of thing that can be free or unfree. Locke is concerned to argue that freedom is a power that belongs to a person, not to the will. He says, 'Liberty, which is but a power, belongs only to Agents, and cannot be an attribute or modification of the Will, which is also but a Power' (II. xxi. 14).

If what I said is right, then there is a way in which the will can fail to be free. Even if we think of the will as a *power* to make rational decisions in varying circumstances, certain forces can constrain or limit the exercise of this power. And in so far as they do, they diminish the freedom of the will. I suggested, following Stampe and Gibson, that this is certainly what happens when, so to speak, the locked door is placed in the mind, in the decision-making faculty. In such cases, contrary to what Locke was maintaining, the agents' acts are not voluntary, and hence the agent is not free because the *will* of the agent is unfree.

---

[14] Locke 1689: II. xxi. 10. Actually at this point Locke merely says, 'he is not at liberty not to stay; he has not freedom to be gone'.

But is there not some plausibility to what Locke says about freedom? Is it not possible, for example, that a person may act of his own free will (i.e. act voluntarily) and yet she may not be free? One needs to show some care in stating the proposition. In the locked room example, clearly the man *is* free to stay in the room. Nothing prevents his doing so. He is free to stay. It was just that he is not free to leave. And when he decides to stay in the room, nothing forces him to do so. I was suggesting above that this is exactly what constitutes an action's being voluntary. And if we want to treat being free as an attribute of actions, and use 'free' as synonymous with 'voluntary', we would say that the man's staying in the room is a free action, and that would be the end of it.

But I would like to propose a way of reading Locke that places the notion of freedom on a different plane. On this reading, the man's staying in the room would be voluntary, but the man would not be free. In thinking of freedom in this context, we need to conceive of it as something that comes in degrees, not as an all-or-nothing affair. And the degrees will be determined by the number of available alternatives. In the example, the lock on the door removes one option from the picture.

The alternatives in question here are objective facts about a given situation. If an alternative is blocked and the person knows it is blocked, that person is unfree to the same degree as a person for whom that same alternative is blocked and he does not know that it is blocked. Thus if, contrary to what Locke assumes, the man *did* know that he could not leave the room, in the sense of 'free' I am interested in developing here, he again would have his freedom limited.[15]

This way of thinking makes sense of how the intuitions can go either way in judging the action of the victim of a mugging. When the mugger says, 'your money or your life', and the victim calmly assesses the alternatives and finds the odds of keeping his money *and* his life very low, there is a strong intuition to say that he handed the money voluntarily.[16] This is certainly the judgement that would seem to be

[15] On the other hand, if an alternative is open, but the agent believes it is not, then the agent would be less free than one who has the true belief that the alternative is open.

[16] Mele (1995a: 185), who describes a similar situation with bank robbers and the manager of the bank, agrees that one possible intuition is to say of the bank manager that his act of opening the vault was an autonomous act. But he also admits that, given the coercive force, intuitions may go the opposite way and judge the act to be *unfree*.

implied by what was said above about voluntary acts: the victim's decision-making mechanism was not in any way impaired.[17] On the other hand, there is an equally strong intuition that something about the decision was forced on the victim. *Normally* when one is in a room, one has the option of staying in or going out. If one of these alternatives is blocked, one loses a degree of freedom. *Normally* one has the option of parting with one's money or keeping it without harm to oneself.[18] What the mugger does is to take away this second alternative.[19]

Specifying what counts as *normal*—beyond which the decrease of alternatives would be a restriction of one's freedom—is not an easy task. Given our physiology, it is clear that our inability to fly by flapping our arms is not a restriction of our freedom. But given our physiology, a person with severe joint disease does have his freedom curtailed. Extending this line of thinking to us as agents in what we take to be a free society, there are certain things that we cannot do (we are by law prevented from doing) which are not a threat to our freedom. That we are not allowed to take away something that rightfully belongs to someone else without that person's consent, for example, is not something that decreases our freedom by any amount, because that is not an alternative that should be available in a free society. At the other extreme, being able to keep our money without endangering our life is an alternative we naturally think we have. But in between these clear cases, the factors that define the alternatives that should be available in social contexts are interesting questions in socio-political philosophy. And the notion of a free agent is clearly dependent on the positions adopted in one's political theory. The best one might be able to do is to make comparative judgements in specific contexts: A person who can listen to pop, jazz, or classical music on the radio has a greater degree of freedom in what music he listens to than a person who can only listen to pop—even if they both voluntarily choose to listen just to pop. A person who will not be punished if he does not wear a helmet while riding a motorcycle, is freer than one who

---

[17] I am assuming that overwhelming fear was not one of the factors that caused the decision.

[18] Stampe and Gibson contrast the mugger case with one's voluntarily giving one's money to a beggar.

[19] Again, I think whether the victim knows this alternative is blocked is irrelevant. If a beggar intended to kill me if I did not give him the money, and I did not know this, it still would be true to say that my freedom was limited in that situation.

is by law required to wear a helmet—even if one would be a fool to ride a motorcycle without a helmet.[20]

It might seem that in trying to find a kernel of truth in what Locke was saying, I am endorsing here a familiar compatibilist formula that defines freedom conditionally: an agent does some action freely if and only if she could have done otherwise if she had wanted (chosen, decided) to do otherwise. This interpretation of Locke may be supported by his saying, 'In this then consists Freedom (*viz.*) in our being able to act or not to act, according as we shall chuse or *will*' (II. xxi. 27).

This is not what I intend. The compatibilist formula is designed to generate verdicts as to whether particular acts, in so far as they have a certain property, are free or not. One asks, 'was the man's staying in the locked room a free act?' Or one asks, 'did the victim hand his money to the mugger freely?' And the formula generates the verdict 'yes' to the first question and 'no' to the second. Such a conception of free action has been discussed at length in the literature, and it has been criticized on good grounds.[21]

What I am suggesting, instead, is a reading of Locke in which freedom is an attribute of *persons* in their capacity as agents in specific contexts. And I propose to add to Locke the proviso that an agent's freedom, in so far as she is contemplating a type of activity in a specific context, comes in degrees.

If upon deliberation, I choose a course of action on the merits of the case, and act in accordance with my choice, my act is voluntary. It would be voluntary in spite of the fact that I could not have acted otherwise if I were to choose to act otherwise. But if the alternative courses of action available to me were severely restricted (say by the counterfactual contravener poised to interfere if I made the 'wrong' decision), then the degree of freedom I normally enjoy in that context would accordingly be diminished.

I do not need to argue here that this is the only viable sense of freedom. I offer it as one credible explication of the notion. It should be clear that the causal theory of action does not have anything to say about such a sense of freedom. This sense of freedom is orthogonal to

---

[20] Freedom of this kind may not always be a good thing to have!

[21] Frankfurt-type counterfactual contravener cases, discussed in Ch. 4 (in which an agent is allowed to act completely on his own decision if the decision is to do some particular thing, but is forced to do that thing if the decision is going to be to do something else), seem to provide as good reasons as any for being sceptical of the formula.

the causal theory. If it has any merit, it cannot be a source of criticism of the causal theory, nor can it be used to promote it.

On the other hand, the model of the deliberative mechanism, which is an essential feature of the causal account of action, can be used to explain the notions of the will and of voluntary action. What needed to be introduced to the model were certain objective norms of rationality and some counterfactual questions. In so far as these notions (of the will and of voluntary action) could be located within the causal account, I could maintain that our ability to make judgements in ordinary situations using these notions was not a point against the credibility of the causal account. Indeed, I would like to suggest that the fact that these notions *can* be located within the causal account gives independent plausibility to it.

REFERENCES

Albritton, R. 1985. 'Freedom of the Will and the Freedom of Action', *Proceedings of the American Philosophical Association*, 59: 239–51.

Alcock, J. 1979. *Animal Behavior* (Sunderland, Mass.: Sinauer Associates, Inc.).

Anscombe, G. E. M. 1957. *Intention*. Oxford: Basil Blackwell.

Aquila, R. E. 1977. *Intentionality: A Study of Mental Acts* (University Park, Pa.: Pennsylvania State University Press).

Audi, R. 1973. 'Intending', *Journal of Philosophy*, 70: 387–403.

——1979. 'Weakness of Will and Practical Judgement', *Noûs*, 13: 173–96.

——1986. 'Acting for Reasons', *Philosophical Review*, 95: 511–46.

Bach, K. 1978. 'A Representational Theory of Action', *Philosophical Studies*, 34: 361–79.

Baier, A. 1971. 'The Search for Basic Actions', *American Philosophical Quarterly*, 8: 161–70.

Beardsley, M. 1978. 'Intending', in A. I. Goldman and J. Kim (eds.), *Values and Morals* (Dordrecht: Reidel), 163–84.

Berkeley, G. 1709. *An Essay towards a New Theory of Vision*, in *Berkeley's Philosophical Writings*, ed. D. Armstrong (New York: Collier Books, Macmillan, 1965).

——1713. *Three Dialogues between Hylas and Philonus*, in *Berkeley's Philosophical Writings*, ed. D. Armstrong (New York: Collier Books, Macmillan, 1965).

Birkinblitt, M. B., A. G. Feldman, and O. I. Fukson. 1986. 'Adaptability of Innate Motor Patterns and Motor Control Mechanisms', *Behavioral and Brain Sciences*, 9: 585–638.

Bishop, J. 1989. *Natural Agency* (Cambridge: Cambridge University Press).

Boden, M. A. 1981. *Minds and Mechanisms: Philosophical Psychology and Computational Models* (Ithaca, NY: Cornell University Press).

Brand, M. 1968. 'Danto on Basic Actions', *Noûs*, 2: 187–90.

——1984. *Intending and Acting: Toward a Naturalized Action Theory* (Cambridge, Mass.: MIT Press).

Bratman, M. 1985. 'Davidson's Theory of Intention', in E. LePore and B. McLaughlin (eds.), *Actions and Events: Perspectives on the Philosophy of Donald Davidson* (Oxford: Blackwell).

——1987. *Intention, Plans, and Practical Reason* (Cambridge, Mass.: Harvard University Press).

Bratman, M. 1997. 'Two Faces of Intention', in A. Mele (ed.), *The Philosophy of Action* (Oxford: Oxford University Press).

——1979. 'Practical Reasoning and Weakness of the Will', *Noûs*, 13: 153–71.

Breland, Keller, and Marian Breland. 1961. 'The Misbehavior of Organisms', *American Psychologist*, 16: 681–4.

Chisholm, R. M. 1966. 'Freedom and Action', in Keith Lehrer (ed.), *Freedom and Determinism* (New York: Random House; page references are to the 1976 ed. by Humanities Press).

——1970. 'The Structure of Intention', *Journal of Philosophy*, 67: 633–47.

——1976. *Person and Object* (La Salle, Ill.: Open Court).

——1978. 'Comments and Replies', *Philosophia*, 7: 597–636.

Clark, P. 1997. 'Practical Steps and Reasons for Action', *Canadian Journal of Philosophy*, 27/1: 17–45.

Clarke, R. 1993. 'Toward a Credible Agent–Causal Account of Free Will', *Noûs*, 27: 191–203.

——1996. 'Agent Causation and Event Causation in the Production of Free Action', *Philosophical Topics*, 24: 19–48.

——2000. 'Libertarianism, Action Theory and the Loci of Responsibility', *Philosophical Studies*, 98: 153–74.

Danto, A. C. 1965. 'Basic Actions', *American Philosophical Quarterly*, 2: 141–8.

——1970. 'Causation and Basic Actions', *Inquiry*, 13: 108–24.

——1973. *Analytic Philosophy of Action* (Cambridge: Cambridge University Press).

Davidson, D. 1980. *Essays on Actions and Events* (Oxford: Oxford University Press); including 'Agency' (43–61); 'Actions, Reasons, and Causes' (3–19); 'Freedom to Act' (63–82); 'Intending' (83–102).

——1985. 'Replies', in B. Vermazen and M. Hintikka (eds.), *Essays on Davidson* (Oxford: Clarendon Press), 195–254.

Davies, M. 1983. 'Function in Perception', *Australasian Journal of Philosophy*, 61: 409–26.

Davis, W. 1984. 'A Causal Theory of Intending', *American Philosophical Quarterly*, 21: 43–54; reprinted in A. R. Mele (ed.), *The Philosophy of Action* (Oxford: Oxford University Press, 1997), 131–48.

Dennett, D. 1984. *Elbow Room: The Varieties of Free Will Worth Wanting* (Cambridge, Mass.: MIT Press, Bradford Books).

Dodson, C. H. 1975. 'Coevolution of Orchids and Bees', in L. E. Gilber and P. H. Raven (eds.), *Coevolution of Animals and Plants* (Austin: University of Texas Press).

Dretske, F. 1971. 'Conclusive Reasons', *Australasian Journal of Philosophy*, 49: 1–22.

——1988. *Explaining Behavior* (Cambridge, Mass.: MIT Press, Bradford Books).

——and B. Enç. 1984. 'Causal Theories of Knowledge', in P. French, T. Uehling, and H. Wettstein (eds.), *Midwest Studies in Philosophy* (Minneapolis: University of Minnesota Press), ix. 517–28.

——and A. Snyder. 1972. 'Causal Irregularity', *Philosophy of Science*, 39: 69–71.

Dowty, D. 1979. *Word Meaning and Montague Grammar* (Dordrecht: D. Reidel).

Ekstrom, L. 2000. *Free Will: A Philosophical Study* (Boulder, Colo.: Westview Press).

——2001a. 'Indeterminist Free Action', in L. Ekstrom (ed.), *Agency and Responsibility* (Boulder, Colo.: Westview Press), 138–57.

——2001b. 'Introduction', in L. Ekstrom (ed.), *Agency and Responsibility* (Boulder, Colo.: Westview Press), 1–14.

Enç, B. 1979. 'Function Attributions and Functional Explanation', *Philosophy of Science*, 46: 343–65.

——1985. 'Redundancy, Deviance, and Degeneracy in Action', *Philosophical Studies*, 48: 353–74.

——1986. 'Essentialism without Individual Essences: Causation, Kinds, Supervenience, and Restricted Identities', in P. French, T. Uehling, and H. Wettstein (eds.), *Midwest Studies in Philosophy* (Minneapolis: University of Minnesota Press), xi. 403–26.

——1989. 'Causal Theories and Unusual Causal Pathways', *Philosophical Studies*, 55: 231–61.

——1995. 'Units of Behavior', *Philosophy of Science*, 62: 523–42.

——and F. Adams. 1992. 'Functions and Goal-Directedness', *Philosophy of Science*, 59: 635–54.

Finch, A., and T. Warfield. 1998. 'The *Mind* Argument and Libertarianism', *Mind*, 107: 515–28.

Fischer, J. M., and M. Ravizza. 1993. 'Responsibility for Consequences', in J. M. Fischer and M. Ravizza (eds.), *Perspectives on Moral Responsibility* (Ithaca, NY: Cornell University Press).

——1998. *Responsibility and Control: A Theory of Moral Responsibility* (Cambridge: Cambridge University Press).

Fodor, J. 1980. 'Methodological Solipsism Considered as a Research Strategy in Cognitive Psychology', *Behavioral and Brain Sciences*, 3; reprinted in J. Fodor, *RePresentation* (Cambridge, Mass.: Bradford/MIT Press, 1981).

——1990. 'A Theory of Content II', *A Theory of Content and Other Essays* (Cambridge, Mass.: MIT Press), ch. 4.

Frankfurt, H. 1969. 'Alternate Possibilities and Moral Responsibility', *Journal of Philosophy*, 66: 828–39.

Frankfurt, H. 1978. 'The Problem of Action', *American Philosophical Quarterly*, 15: 157–62.

Gallistel, C. R. 1980. *The Organization of Action: A New Synthesis* (Hillsdale, NJ: Lawrence Erlbaum).

——1981. Multiple book review of Gallistel 1980, *Behavioral and Brain Sciences*, 4: 609–50.

Gauthier, D. 1990. 'Deterrence, Maximization and Rationality', in *Moral Dealing* (Ithaca, NY: Cornell University Press).

Gibbons, J. 2001. 'Knowledge in Action', *Philosophy and Phenomenological Research*, 62: 579–600.

Ginet, C. 1990. *On Action* (Cambridge: Cambridge University Press).

Goldman, A. I. (1967). 'A Causal Theory of Knowing', *Journal of Philosophy*, 64: 355–72.

——1970. *A Theory of Human Action* (Princeton: Princeton University Press).

Gould, James. 1982. *Ethology: The Mechanisms and Evolution of Behavior* (New York: W.W. Norton & Co.).

Gould, S. J., and R. Lewontin. 1978. 'Spandrels of San Marco and the Panglossian Paradigm', in E. R. Sober (ed.), *Contemporary Issues in Evolutionary Biology* (Cambridge, Mass.: Bradford Books, MIT Press), 252–70.

Grice, H. P. 1962. 'The Causal Theory of Perception', *Proceedings of the Aristotelian Society, Supplementary Volume*; also in R. J. Swarz (ed.), *Perceiving, Sensing and Knowing* (Berkeley: University of California Press, 1965).

——1971. *Intention and Uncertainty* (Proceedings of the British Academy, 57; London: Oxford University Press).

Gustafson, D. F. 1985. *Intention and Agency* (Dordrecht: Reidel).

Harman, G. 1986*a*. *Change in View* (Cambridge, Mass.: MIT Press).

——1986*b*. 'Willing and Intending', in R. Grandy and R. Warner (eds.), *Philosophical Grounds of Rationality* (Oxford: Clarendon Press).

——1997. 'Practical Reasoning', in A. R. Mele (ed.), *The Philosophy of Action* (Oxford: Oxford University Press).

Harré, R., and E. H. Madden. 1975. *Causal Powers: A Theory of Natural Necessity* (Oxford: Oxford University Press).

Hendrickson, N. 2002. *The Contingency of Choice: Developing and Defending a New Method and Theory in the Philosophy of Freedom and Action* (Ann Arbor: UMI Dissertation Services).

Hineline, P. N., and H. Rachlin. 1969. 'Escape and Avoidance of Shock by Pigeons Pecking a Key', *Journal of Experimental Analysis and Behavior*, 12: 533–8.

Hobbes, T. 1840. 'Of Liberty and Necessity', *Works*, iv, ed. W. Molesworth (London), 229–78.

Hornsby, J. 1980. *Actions* (London: Routledge & Kegan Paul).

——1986. 'Physicalistic Thinking and Conceptions of Behavior', in P. Pettit and J. McDowell (eds.), *Subject, Thought, and Content* (Oxford: Clarendon Press).

Hume, D. 1740. *A Treatise of Human Nature*, ed. Selby Bigge, revised P. H. Nidditch (Oxford: Oxford University Press, 1978).

Hursthouse, R. 1991. 'Arational Actions', *Journal of Philosophy*, 88: 57–68.

Kane, R. 1996. *The Significance of Free Will* (Oxford: Oxford University Press).

Kavka, G. 1983. 'The Toxin Puzzle', *Analysis*, 43: 33–6.

——1987. 'Some Paradoxes of Deterrence', in *Moral Paradoxes of Nuclear Deterrence* (Cambridge: Cambridge University Press).

Kenny, A. 1966. 'Practical Inference', *Analysis*, 26: 65–75.

——1993. *Aquinas on Mind* (London: Routledge).

Kim, J. 1976. 'Events as Property Exemplifications', in M. Brand and D. Walton (eds.), *Action Theory* (Dordrecht: Reidel), 159–77.

——1982. 'Psychophysical Supervenience', *Philosophical Studies*, 41: 51–70.

Le Catt, B. 1982. 'Censored Vision', *Australasian Journal of Philosophy*, 60: 158–62.

Lewis, D. 1980. 'Veridical Perception and Prosthetic Vision', *Australasian Journal of Philosophy*, 58: 239–49.

——1984. 'Devil's Bargains and the Real World', in D. MacLean (ed.), *The Security Gamble* (Totowa, NJ: Rowman & Allanheld), 141–54.

Lewontin, R. 1980. 'Adaptation', in E. R. Sober (ed.), *Contemporary Issues in Evolutionary Biology* (Cambridge, Mass.: Bradford Books, MIT Press), 234–51.

Lloyd, D. 1989. *Simple Minds* (Cambridge, Mass.: MIT Press).

Locke, J. 1689. *An Essay Concerning Human Understanding*, ed. J. Nidditch (Oxford: Clarendon Press, 1975).

McCann, H. 1972. 'Is Raising One's Arm a Basic Action?', *Journal of Philosophy*, 69: 235–49.

——1974. 'Volition and Basic Action', *Philosophical Review*, 83: 451–73.

McClennen, E. 1990. *Rationality and Dynamic Choice: Foundational Explorations* (Cambridge: Cambridge University Press).

McIntyre, A. 1994. 'Compatibilist could have Done Otherwise: Responsibility and Negative Agency', *Philosophical Review*, 103: 453–88.

Margolis, J. 1970. 'Danto on Basic Actions', *Inquiry*, 13: 104–8.

Meiland, J. W. 1970. *The Nature of Intention* (London: Methuen & Co.).

Mele, A. R. 1987. 'Intentional Action and Wayward Causal Chains: The Problem of Tertiary Waywardness', *Philosophical Studies*, 51: 55–60.

——1992a. 'Intentions, Reasons, and Beliefs: Morals of the Toxin Puzzle', *Philosophical Studies*, 68: 171–94.

——1992b. *Springs of Action* (Oxford: Oxford University Press).

——1995a. *Autonomous Agents: From Self-Control to Autonomy* (Oxford: Oxford University Press).

——1995b. 'Effective Deliberation about What to Intend: Or Striking it Rich in a Toxin-Free Environment', *Philosophical Studies*, 79: 85–93.

——2000. 'Deciding to Act', *Philosophical Studies*, 64: 81–108.

——and R. K. Moser. 1994. 'Intentional Action', *Noûs*, 28: 39–68.

——and S. Sverdlik. 1996. 'Intentional Action and Moral Responsibility', *Philosophical Studies*, 82/3: 265–87.

Millikan, R. 1984. *Language, Thought, and Other Biological Categories: New Foundations for Realism* (Cambridge, Mass.: MIT Press).

——1990. 'Truth Rules, Hoverflies, and the Kripke-Wittgenstein Paradox', *Philosophical Review*, 99: 323–53.

Montefiore, A., and D. Noble. (eds.) 1989. *Goals, No-Goals, Own-Goals* (London: Unwin Hyman).

Moya, C. J. 1990. *The Philosophy of Action: An Introduction* (Cambridge: Polity Press).

Nahmias, E. 2000. 'Undesired Free Actions and the Problem of the Strength of Will', unpublished paper delivered at the APA Eastern Division Meeting on 28 Dec.

Neander, K. 1988. 'What does Natural Selection Explain? Correction to Sober', *Philosophy of Science*, 55: 422–6.

O'Connor, T. 1993. 'Indeterminism and Free Agency', *Philosophy and Phenomenological Research*, 53: 499–526.

——2000. *Reasons and Causes: The Metaphysics of Free Will* (Oxford: Oxford University Press).

O'Shaughnessy, B. 1973. 'Trying as the Mental Pineal Gland', *Journal of Philosophy*, 70: 365–6.

——1980. *The Will: A Dual Aspect Theory* (Cambridge: Cambridge University Press).

Papineau, D. 1988. *Philosophical Naturalism* (Oxford: Blackwell).

Peacocke, C. 1979. *Holistic Explanation: Action, Space, Interpretation* (Oxford: Clarendon Press).

Pears, D. 1975. 'The Appropriate Causation of Intentional Basic Actions', *Critica*, 7: 39–72.

Penfield, W. 1975. *The Mystery of the Mind: A Critical Study of Consciousness and the Human Brain* (Princeton: Princeton University Press).

Peressini, A. 1997. 'Psychological Explanation and Behavior Broadly Conceived', *Behavior and Philosophy*, 137–59.

Pfeifer, K. 1989. *Actions and Other Events: The Unifier–Multiplier Controversy* (New York: Peter Lang).

Pink, T. 1996. *The Psychology of Freedom* (Cambridge: Cambridge University Press).

Pitchard, H. A. 1976. 'Acting, Willing, Desiring', in M. Brand (ed.), *The Nature of Human Action* (Glenview, Ill.: M. Scott, Foresman & Co.).

Purton, A. C. 1978. 'Ethical Categories of Behavior and Some Consequences of their Conflation', *Animal Behavior*, 26/3: 653–70.

Reid, T. 1969. *Essays on the Active Powers of the Human Mind*, ed. B. Brody (Cambridge, Mass: MIT Press).

Robinson, H. 1994. *Perception* (New York: Routledge).

Ryle, G. 1949. *The Concept of Mind* (New York: Barnes & Noble).

Scanlon, T. M. 1998. *What we Owe to Each Other* (Cambridge, Mass.: Harvard University Press).

Schueler, G. F. 1995. *Desire* (Cambridge, Mass.: MIT Press).

Searle, J. 1983. *Intentionality: An Essay in the Philosophy of Mind* (Cambridge: Cambridge University Press).

Sherrington, C. S. 1947. *The Integrative Action of the Nervous System* (New Haven: Yale University Press; 1st edn., 1906).

Shettleworth, S. J. 1973. 'Food Reinforcement and the Organization of Behavior in Golden Hamsters', in R. S. Hinde and J. Stevenson-Hinde (eds.), *Constraints on Learning* (New York: Academic Press).

——1975. 'Reinforcement and the Organization of Behavior in Golden Hamsters: Hunger, Environment and Food Reinforcement', *Journal of Experimental Psychology: Animal Behavior Processes*, 104: 56–87.

Sidgwick, H. 1907. *The Methods of Ethics*, 7th edn. (London: Macmillan).

Skinner, B. F. 1965. *Science and Human Behavior* (New York: Macmillan, Free Press paperback edn.; (edn.; 1st edn., 1953).

Skyrms, B. 1996. *Evolution of the Social Contract* (Cambridge: Cambridge University Press).

Sober, E. (ed.) 1984*a*. *Contemporary Issues in Evolutionary Biology* (Cambridge, Mass.: Bradford Books, MIT Press).

——1984*b*. *The Nature of Selection* (Cambridge, Mass.: Bradford Books, MIT Press).

——1995. 'Natural Selection and Distributive Explanation: A Reply to Neander', *British Journal for the Philosophy of Science*, 46: 384–97.

Stampe, D. 1977. 'Toward a Causal Theory of Representation', in P. French, T. Uehling, and H. Wettstein (eds.), *Midwest Studies in Philosophy* (Minneapolis: University of Minnesota Press), ii.

Stampe, D. 1986. 'Defining Desire', in Joel Marks (ed.), *The Ways of Desire: New Essays in Philosophical Psychology on the Concept of Wanting* (Chicago: Precedent Publishing), 149–73.

——1987. 'Authority of Desire', *Philosophical Review*, 96: 335–81.

——and M. Gibson. 1992. 'Of One's Own Free Will', *Philosophy and Phenomenological Research*, 52: 529–56.

Stout, R. 1996. *Things that Happen because they Should: A Teleological Approach to Action* (Oxford: Oxford University Press).

Stoutland, F. 1968. 'Basic Actions and Causality', *Journal of Philosophy*, 65: 467–75.

——1982. 'Philosophy of Action: Davidson, von Wright, and the Debate over Causation', in G. Fløistad (ed.), *Contemporary Philosophy: A New Survey* (The Hague: Martinus Nijhoff), iii. 45–72.

Taylor, R. 1966. *Action and Purpose* (Englewood Cliffs, NJ: Prentice-Hall).

Thalberg, I. 1984. 'Do our Intentions Cause our Intentional Actions?', *American Philosophical Quarterly*, 21: 249–60.

Thompson, J. J. 1977. *Acts and Other Events* (Ithaca, NY: Cornell University Press).

Tuomela, R. 1977. *Human Action and its Explanation: A Study on the Philosophical Foundations of Psychology* (Dordrecht: Reidel).

——1982. 'Explanation of Action', in G. Fløistad (ed.), *Contemporary Philosophy: A New Survey* (The Hague: Martinus Nijhoff), iii. 15–43.

Umiltà, C. 1988. 'The Control Operations of Consciousness', in A. J. Marcel and E. Bisiach (eds.), *Consciousness in Contemporary Science* (Oxford: Oxford University Press), 334–56.

Van Inwagen, P. 1983. *An Essay on Free Will* (Oxford: Clarendon Press).

Velleman, J. D. 1989. *Practical Reflection* (Princeton: Princeton University Press).

——1992. 'What Happens When Someone Acts?', *Mind*, 101: 461–81.

von Wright, G. H. 1963. *Norm and Action* (New York: Humanities Press).

Walsh, D. M. 1998. 'The Scope of Selection: Neander on What Selection Explains', *Australasian Journal of Philosophy*, 76: 250–64.

Watson, G. 1987. 'Free Action and Free Will', *Mind*, 96: 145–72.

Weiskrantz, L. 1986. *Blindsight: A Case Study and Implications* (Oxford: Oxford University Press).

——1988. 'Neurophysiology of Vision and Memory', in A. J. Marcel and E. Bisiach (eds.), *Consciousness in Contemporary Science* (Oxford: Oxford University Press), 183–99.

Weiss, P. 1941. 'Self Differentiation of the Basic Patterns of Coordination', *Comparative Psychology Monographs*, 17: 1–96.

Wickens, D. D. 1938. 'The Transference of Conditioned Excitation and Conditioned Inhibition from one Muscle Group to the Antagonistic Group', *Journal of Experimental Psychology*, 25: 127–40.

Wilson, Donald. 1966. 'Insect Walking', *Annual Review of Entomology*, 11; repr. in G. R. Gallistel, *The Organization of Action: A New Synthesis* (Hillsdale, NJ: Lawrence Erlbaum, 1980).

Wilson, G. M. 1989. *The Intentionality of Human Action* (Stanford, Calif.: Stanford University Press).

Wright, L. 1973. 'Functions', *Philosophical Review*, 82: 139–68.

Woodfield, A. 1976. *Teleology* (Cambridge: Cambridge University Press).

INDEX